TECHNIQUES OF CHILD THERAPY
Psychodynamic Strategies

TECHNIQUES OF CHILD THERAPY
Psychodynamic Strategies

MORTON CHETHIK
Department of Psychiatry, University of Michigan

THE GUILFORD PRESS
New York   London

© 1989 The Guilford Press
A Division of Guilford Publications, Inc.
72 Spring Street, New York, NY 10012

Printed in the United States of America

Last digit is print number: 9 8 7 6 5 4 3 2 1

Library of Congress Cataloging-in-Publication Data

Chethik, Morton.
   Techniques of child therapy.

   Bibliography: p.
   Includes index.
   1. Child psychotherapy.   I. Title.
RJ504.C463   1989   618.92'8914   88-24384
ISBN 0-89862-745-1

For
Beverly, Peter, Neil, Leigh, and Jessica

Preface

This book is oriented to both students (fellows in child psychiatry, clinical psychology interns, social work students) and more advanced practitioners in these mental health disciplines who are interested in sharpening their skills in child psychotherapy.

A number of major themes are explored in the text. On one level it focuses on the specific techniques of psychotherapeutic work with children, and illustrates these techniques through the presentation of clinical cases treated by the author. The basic concepts of the process of psychotherapy (e.g., therapeutic alliance, resistance, transferences, intervention) are extremely useful in organizing any treatment, but currently they are defined primarily in adult terms. Major goals of this book are the definition, discussion, and illustration of these concepts and their reshaping as they apply to children.

A second issue is play. A fundamental aspect of work with children is through the medium of play, and its efficacy is not well understood. The author fully illustrates the use of play and explores its implications in many realms throughout the text.

A third major theme in this volume relates to differential techniques. The major psychopathologies in children present the therapist with different problems and therefore require different approaches. The central section of the book describes the treatment of several neurotic children through intensive uncovering psychotherapy, and contrasts this approach with the treatment of other major pathologies—the borderline, narcissistic, and character-disordered children. The author also focuses on the treatment of reactive disorders (e.g., reactions to divorce and death) in childhood.

No treatment of the child can be accomplished without work with the parents. The final section is devoted to describing this area of treatment, and discusses and illustrates a range of interventions with parents, stemming from parent guidance to treatment of the parent–child relationship.

The format of the book has somewhat of a workshop quality. In many of the chapters, clinical cases or sections of cases are initially presented to provide the reader with an opportunity to struggle with questions on his own. The latter part of the chapter discusses these cases and provides the author's "answers." In summary, although many basic concepts of work with children are explored here, the material also depicts and analyzes the struggles that all practitioners experience in the course of long-term child psychotherapy.

Acknowledgments

I gratefully acknowledge the contribution of my students at the University of Michigan, whose questions and enthusiastic discussions have helped shape this volume. I particularly appreciate the contribution of a "young" associate, Jonathan Falk, Ph.D., whose specific reactions to early drafts of chapters helped me to extend and explicate many basic concepts. The rigorous reactions of the Friday morning Child Psychotherapy Seminar at the Child and Adolescent Psychiatry Service (University of Michigan) provided both insights and new directions as I worked on the text.

I am also grateful to Donna Johnston and Paulette Lockwood for their typing, retyping, copying, and recopying and other duties that were instrumental in the production of the manuscript.

Contents

PART III: Work with Parents

PART I

INTRODUCTION TO CHILD THERAPY

Introduction

The purpose of this section is to introduce the reader to the child as a young patient. This means becoming familiar with the emotional and cognitive world of the child and contrasting his readiness for psychotherapy with that of the older patient (the adult). Chapters 1 and 3 focus on these differences. Some of the divergences stem from the child's "immaturity," his dependency on his parents, and the fact that he is in an ongoing developmental process. These differences alter the process of the therapy, its format, and at times the goals of the treatment itself. The material in this section illustrates and discusses the necessary revisions.

An essential modification in work with children compared to adults is the basic form of communication between patient and therapist. A primary purpose of all psychotherapy is to work with the patient's affective life. Play becomes a central medium of exchange with most children, since this is the child's major mode of expressing his emotional life. Chapter 3 introduces the reader to this medium. It focuses on how to facilitate play in the treatment as well as how to use and understand therapeutic play as it unfolds in the course of the treatment.

Whereas chapters 1 and 3 serve as a general introduction to the process of child treatment, the evaluation process in any given case alerts the therapist to the issues and problems that will emerge in a specific child's treatment. The evaluation "introduces" the therapy itself. In Chapter 2, the author describes how to conduct an evaluation, how to construct a psychodynamic formulation, and how an effective personality appraisal can be used to outline, anticipate, and enhance the therapeutic process.

1

General Characteristics of the Child Patient

Before one attempts child psychotherapy, it is imperative to become oriented to the state of childhood and to the world of the child. The purpose of this chapter is to "set the stage" and provide a general orientation to the young patient. A common, unfortunate tendency is to carry the adult world and an adult model of treatment into child therapy. In adult psychotherapy, most treatment techniques have been developed for dealing with a patient with a relatively stabilized, structured personality and ego. The hallmark of the child patient, however, is that his personality is in a state of evolution and flux, and his ego is immature. What does it mean to attempt therapy when defenses are naturally fragile, when cognitive capacity is poor, when anxiety is easily stimulated, when superego is limited, and when magic and omnipotence can prevail? In this chapter, five major issues are discussed:

1. The fluctuating state of the child's ego.
2. The child's need for action: the function of play.
3. The child's state of dependency: the role of the parents.
4. The child's developmental process: the need for growth.
5. The counterreactions to the child patient: the therapist's internal responses.

THE FLUCTUATING STATE OF THE CHILD'S EGO

The child's ego, by the nature of development, is a fluid one compared to that of the adult: it is constantly shifting and regressing and is much closer to the world of primary process. Often, a fluidity of ego boundaries exists, particularly during periods of stress. By *primary process*, we mean that there is a suspension or lack of the logical part of the mind, and the elements of the unconscious are expressed in primitive forms with no awareness of time present. With few exceptions, then, *acting out* dominates in the treatment of the child. He tends to live out his pleasures and anxieties and shows his disorders in the form of direct action and play (Olden, 1953; Freud, 1965; Anthony, 1964).

To discuss this issue, it would be helpful to consider a young child patient. Mark, a 5½-year-old youngster, in the course of his evaluation and early treatment, vividly highlights the state of childhood. His affect state was quite volatile. Although Mark is clearly a disturbed youngster, he nonetheless illustrates albeit sometimes in an exaggerated way, all of the issues in working with the child patient.

Clinical Material

Mark was referred because of his longstanding defiant fighting and his frequently out-of-control behavior. Mark was a rather short but well-built, well-proportioned child who looked "ready for action." He was pleasant looking with striking dark features and coloring, resembling his mother. He appeared extremely restless: one found Mark climbing, twisting, or hurdling rather than walking from place to place.

His parents described the fighting relationship Mark had, particularly with his mother, and they noted they were at their "wits' end" in their attempts to handle him. They felt they had exhausted all possible methods—they had talked with Mark, reasoned with him, punished and spanked, and had even given him a special half hour of "Mark time" per day, but nothing had seemed to work.

In the history, the difficulties with Mark seemed to begin during his second year, when his mother was pregnant with his brother Richard. (There were three boys in the family: Jason was 2 years older than Mark, and Richard was 2 years younger.) The summer during this pregnancy had been particularly hot and humid, and

Mrs. L. found that carrying Richard was difficult and tiring. Mark was a very active toddler. In addition, she was aware of a change within herself: she became more easily angered with him and had less patience. She had told the boys about her impending delivery the night before Richard was born, and Mark had begun climbing out of his crib.

When Mrs. L. returned home with the new baby, the difficulties began to compound. One evening she found Mark straddling the baby in his crib, and she then began to lock Mark in his room at night. Because of his vigorous protest, she recanted and opened the door. But Mark was now incessantly climbing out of his crib. She and her husband, in an effort to keep him in bed, built higher and higher barriers on his crib side. Showing incredible effort, Mark scaled all the obstacles in order to get free.

This defiant pattern carried over into all areas of the family's life. With toilet training Mark would be forced to sit on the potty but would soil right after he got off. Mother would become angered and lose her temper. Mark was "trained" at 3 years of age for bowel and bladder, although at the point of evaluation he was enuretic nightly, soiled from time to time, and wet himself occasionally during the day. The mother also described a pattern of provocative soiling—at times he would simply pull down his pants and defecate on a neighbor's lawn.

As his horizons broadened, Mark's antisocial behavior spread. He became somewhat of a "terror" in the community. He was often aggressive with street friends; he could suddenly hit and punch without provocation. He would lead little forays into neighbors' yards and might turn on a hose and have the water flow into the kitchen or basement. The mother noted sarcastically that they, as a family, had become "real popular" on the block.

Despite the history of behavior difficulty and out-of-control action, it was impossible to anticipate completely the furor of the first few months of treatment. Mark was often totally out of control after the first few minutes of each interview. His behavior seemed to evidence panic, aggression, and self-destruction. An example of an early session follows.

Mark entered the office and quickly ran to the house and block toys. Within a few moments he created a mommy bed and a daddy bed in one room; a baby bed in the other. A tremendous fight ensued between the mommy and daddy beds, with the daddy getting on top often. Frightening noises emerged from the room and the baby was scared.

Suddenly the blocks flew and the house was overturned. Quickly Mark began climbing on the furniture, heedless of anything the therapist might say; he jumped and threw himself on the couch until he hurt his arm. He cried out in pain and then rested for a few minutes. Suddenly he was off again. Now he decided to take off his shoes and socks and rip a hole in his pants. He seemed to be in a frenzy, overturning all chairs, throwing the pillows, and yelling at the therapist. He appeared terribly frightened and called out for his mother, whom Mark and the therapist then visited. He ended the interview by pulling down his pants and attempting to urinate on the floor. It seemed that any game or play that Mark turned to quickly brought forth material that had enormous anxieties attached to it. The primal-scene material above was only one example. Children typically express anxiety by motoric discharge. Thus, when Mark became anxious about the sexual material his play uncovered, he expressed his anxiety in the language of children—through yelling, throwing, and fighting.

After 2 weeks of treatment, the parents reported in an "emergency" appointment that Mark had attacked another boy so badly (dragged him by the hood of the jacket for a full block) that he had to be accompanied to and from school. The principal warned them that this incident, together with Mark's history of difficulties, might mean that Mark would be suspended from school.

It soon became clear that the therapist needed to establish firm and rigid controls. At the first sign of trouble, the therapist emptied all "throwables" from the room—chairs, pillows, papers all went into the closet, which was closed for the remainder of that hour. The climbing rules (e.g., going on the table or couch with shoes is not allowed) had to be absolutely enforced, with no second chances given. The therapist escorted Mark to the bathroom and would enter at any point if needed. Throughout this early treatment period of establishing a safe surround and structure, the therapist worked verbally and behaviorally on differentiating between control and punishment. For example, at times in the early treatment period, the therapist needed to hold Mark. Mark would, at times, look terrified, as if he expected to be hurt. The therapist then quietly explained that he held Mark so Mark would not break anything or hurt himself, and he would let him go as soon as Mark was calmer. Later, when things were calm, he would further discuss why he held him, even though Mark had the worry that the therapist would hurt him.

The openness of the therapy situation quickly brought forth in Mark internal material that was terrifying (e.g., the mommy and daddy beds), and one noted the regression, terror, and disorder. Anthony (1982) describes the young child in cognitive terms:

> The child, as Piaget was the first to point out, is dominated by egocentrism. He is not a self-conscious thinker, and he differs radically from the adolescent or the adult. His mind is essentially concrete, simplistically operational, and committed to the present. The child never thinks about what he is thinking about, has limited powers of reflection and has difficulties in making spontaneous associations between ideas and events widely separated in time and space.

This relatively undeveloped state of the child's ego has implications at the start of the treatment process.

Capacity for Motivation

Whereas the child lacks the fundamental capacity for motivation at the start of treatment (Tyson & Tyson, 1986), the potential adult patient has many different capacities. Initially the adult reviews his current emotional life and becomes aware of important failings. For example, he may acknowledge that he has repeated difficulties in making effective sexual relationships and concludes that somehow he is contributing to his own problems. Or he may recognize that he consistently falls short in his work efforts even though he is bright. He imagines a future state in which he is symptom-free and can prosper both with the opposite sex and in his work life. The new ingredient that potentially can promote this change is psychotherapy, where he can shed his inhibitions and resistances. Thus, the adult patient has a number of ego capacities, including a *self-observing capacity* to view the state of the self and a capacity to *project oneself in the future* to view an enhanced state. These capacities are not at all available to the child patient (Rees, 1978). In the early sessions described above, Mark clearly wanted to run away from this new and frightening situation. The therapeutic environment was a scary place, and he would only participate because he was forced by his family. His attitude is typical of children, and we do not see the motivation that is evident in the adult patient.

It is interesting to note, however, that Mark did express affective material in an early session, where the mommy bed and daddy bed (sexual activity) scare the baby bed. Mark did not consciously bring the material as a communication to the therapy. The underlying instinctual material emerges in the play and action of the child, and it serves as a directional force in the child's treatment. However, it would be misleading to conclude that the child "brings" this material to the therapy as a participant.

Capacity to Tolerate Pain and Anxiety

Mark, like most children, cannot sustain the idea that he has a problem at all and thus differs from the adult patient. Part of the capacity to be able to acknowledge an internal problem depends on the ability to tolerate a modicum of anxiety or discomfort. Children have an enormous tendency to *externalize* all problems and shift the blame outside (Bornstein, 1948). For example, when the therapist noted that Mark perhaps had a "fighting problem" in school, Mark immediately justified his behavior with all of his classmates. He *knew* that they were *all* angry with him, and they all wanted to beat him up. Confrontations of logic like "You mean, everybody in your class wants to beat you up?" made no inroads into his need to project blame from himself and avoid the unpleasant situation. The child patient like Mark is not an eager participant in the early stages of treatment.

The Therapist as a Frightening Object

The description of a "talking, helping person" related to Mark by his parents was seen by Mark as an attempt to lull him from dangers in this new strange surround. He reacted with terror and attacks. His clear wish was to get away from this anxiety-producing situation and flee from treatment. Children have little capacity to establish an early alliance. Many beginning child therapists feel internally that they want to be helpful and caring toward the child patient. The child's image of the therapist rarely corresponds with the therapist's image.

In summary, children rarely are motivated initially, typically seek flight from an anxiety-producing situation, and project (ascribe their own internal feelings to a person outside) aggression and attacking motivations they are encountering to the therapist. The child's ego state usually makes him an unwilling patient. Generally in child work one has to respect the vulnerability of the child's immature ego. One needs to be aware of the degree of frustration a child can tolerate and be attuned to the child's feeling state (Harley, 1986). Building an alliance and helping children become aware of their internal difficulties is a task for the therapist in the early part of the treatment.

THE CHILD'S NEED FOR ACTION:
THE FUNCTION OF PLAY

In adult psychotherapy, the basic method of transmitting the patient's affective life is through verbalization. Children, however, are in the process of developing their secondary process thinking functions as well as their capacity for symbol formation. Verbalization, therefore, is difficult, particularly for affective expression (Peller, 1954). The natural tendency for the child is bodily discharge for all discomfort and tension, as Mark portrayed above.

Children do learn the "language" of the adult world and often use it for its propaganda value. Thus, Mark told his therapist early in their encounters that he came to see him for his "fighting problems." This was not a piece of self-observation but rather a palliative thrown to the therapist to keep him at bay. Mark did not feel that his fighting was a problem at all—indeed, for him it was a necessary form of survival in a projected hostile world.

Children naturally develop their affective world and express it developmentally in active, partly verbal form—*play* (Sandler, Kennedy, & Tyson, 1980). Play emerges from the child's internal life and typically explicates major conflicts or defenses. When a 6-year-old puts on two six-shooters and a Sheriff's badge and struts through the household, he is often attempting to deal with a natural internal source of helplessness and smallness. He temporarily masters his sense of littleness in fantasy, and he makes use of this process, in varied forms, throughout his childhood. As Anthony (1986) points out, "young patients talk more freely, spontaneously and less defensively in the language of play since they seem to regard this special realm, preconsciously, as once removed from the pressures and demands of everyday life."

The child therapist needs to capitalize on this form of communication, which is "in between" primitive behavior and verbalization. In fact, the therapist's office should be a "playground" so that the child's world can be projected—an unstructured setting that has paper, crayons, scissors, blocks, dolls, etc., where the child's internal characters can come to life. The task of the therapist is to facilitate the emergence of the child's stories. The clinical material below follows the development of play in the early stages of Mark's treatment.

Clinical Material

Mark's early extreme behavior in treatment was a fusion of many fears, but slowly certain themes become discernible and therefore more easily handled. Mark was terrified of the office, terrified of the therapist, and frightened of the separation from his mother during his sessions. Through his behavior rather than words, Mark revealed that he was worried about the overhead light, the holes in the soundproofing, the closet, and its door. The therapist began an active vigorous game with Mark. This was a critical juncture. The therapist, using the fears that Mark expressed, put them into play form. The therapist announced a game called "torture chamber," verbalizing Mark's fearful appraisal of the office, and the closet became the "torture chamber." With that introduction, Mark led the action. Either he or the therapist was locked in for days. They were beaten or starved or left without any water to drink. Mark cried and wailed. Only after this game had been repeated many times did direct words make any sense. The therapist could then proclaim: "No wonder you are hitting and kicking, if you thought this could happen to you here."

Alternatively, Mark decided to play "living room." He knocked and entered the "living room," not the office. He sat down comfortably and ordered food and milk to drink, which the therapist gave in play. The office became home, the therapist became the giving mother, and Mark induced the game when worried about separation.

After about a month of treatment, Mark was using more play. The themes were often danger, attack, counterattack, and victory. For example, the pillow became a monster that suddenly leapt on him. At first he was overwhelmed, but then, as a growling monster himself, he overcame the adversary. As a growling monster, however, he might go on to stalk the furniture and the therapist. The therapist began to identify the growling out-of-control part of Mark as the "lion part." "When you become scared, you become the lion." "There, we see the lion again." "How much the wild lion part of Mark gets him into trouble." "He never knows what the lion will do—how it will suddenly come out." Mark's behavior was often impulsive. One day he smashed a favorite Etch-a-Sketch® toy he had brought to show his therapist because he was proud of his design production. The therapist could identify with Mark's own shock and surprise after the lion erupted. "What is going to happen to Mark?" the therapist wondered with him.

The lion part of Mark also did not heed the normal rules of caution and safety, and it had a daredevil quality. Mark brought a Mighty Mouse doll into the therapy, which he related he slept with. In the sessions, Mighty Mouse sat precariously at the edge of the windowsill and, with Mark's help, tottered into the chasm below. Or Mighty Mouse was perched on the top of the play table. A wind hurled him onto boulders in the valley below, but at the last moment, Mighty Mouse flew off unharmed—he was invulnerable.

A problem in Mark's general behavior was his need to flirt with danger. His mother had reported his practice of riding his two-wheeler at full speed on the streets without looking for cars. The daredevil wandered off several times, crossing heavy traffic. One day the therapist received a call that Mark had climbed out on the roof, which had a steep incline, in the rain. At first when the therapist introduced some of these incidents in a quiet and serious vein, Mark evidenced bravado. But with the roof incident, when the therapist noted that the lion part of Mark might one day take him too far and that something could happen that he could never change or make good again, Mark evinced an overpowering fear reaction. He was suddenly exhausted, lay on the couch sucking his thumb, stroking his ear, and holding onto his penis. He told the therapist that maybe he could fall off and die.

The lion part of Mark was becoming more ego-alien. In one session, after a strong tussle with his therapist, Mark became reflective. He told his therapist that it was very hard for him to be good. The therapist acknowledged that it was a problem but felt he could help Mark with it. Mark began a series of confessions, which he played out in games. He told his therapist of a boy named Gary, not Mark, who was very wild but afraid of ghosts. Mark made it "night" in the office (darkened the room) and reenacted scenes. A robber came to steal his money, and Gary was scared. Even when the robber was jailed, he repeatedly escaped to scare the boy again. When the therapist noted that Mark himself was scared every night and seemed to have bad dreams, Mark wanted to know if the therapist "could take them away."

In addition, Mark began to examine all parts of his body for sores and scratches and acknowledged worries about things being broken. The problem of soiling was played out. One day the therapist and Mark took a make-believe ride on a train (two chairs next to one another), and suddenly Mark made "doo" in his pants. He took out the pretend "doo," threw it in the therapist's face, and told him he was so ugly he couldn't look at him. When the therapist noted that it must be hard for him in school when Mark sometimes "makes doo" in his class, Mark said very sadly that his name was "underwear" in the classroom, and "You know what that means—dirty underwear."

Mark's behavior in the office, now changed dramatically. At times he could discuss some fears, show his anxieties, and yet also suck his thumb. He could also become totally absorbed in productive craftwork where he had many skills. He drew at length and constructed involved castles replete with moats, turrets, and interesting walls out of Legos® and blocks.

The therapeutic alliance began to emerge in a more mature form as Mark shifted from sheer action to some focus on inner concerns and worries.

In the above clinical case material, the therapist initially worked carefully to make a bridge between the child patient's out-of-control behavior and play. He picked up on Mark's fears and terrors by inventing a "torture chamber" game as Mark looked furtively at the closet. As this game was played out, Mark's anxiety began to take a coherent form that both therapist and patient could observe. Only then could the therapist's verbalization be integrated—"No wonder you are hitting and kicking, if you thought this could happen to you here." One of the major functions of play is to alter the raw, overwhelming affects that arise in children at times of anxiety and provide a natural vehicle for the expression of these affects.

Since play emerges from the child's internal life, it typically explicates major internal issues. After a short period of treatment, Mark introduced Mighty Mouse. Mighty Mouse faced all sorts of terrible catastrophies from which he escaped at the last moment. For example, blown off a mountain and about to smash into a deep chasm, Mighty Mouse used his magic capacity to fly just in the nick of time. Mighty Mouse was clearly a self-representation; that is, he depicted Mark. Mark himself was little and always frightened that the grown-up world would attack him—he had many fears of annihilation and castration. He, like Mighty Mouse, faced or provoked dangers, which he "fearlessly" confronted and then used magical means to escape. Should the real Mark become frightened of the cars on the street, he would "fearlessly" drive his two-wheel bicycle into the middle of traffic, defying any danger. Mighty Mouse in his play depicted Mark, who in this case had developed a counterphobic character style to deal with enormous internal anxiety. The task of the child therapist is to provide the structure to facilitate the emergence of these internal characters, so that patient and therapist can slowly think about them together.

The therapist needs not only to set the scene for play but also to become a "player" in the child's world. As Mark attacked the therapist and growled, the therapist played out roles under Mark's direction. Therapist and child played out the growling monster and the frightened man. At the same time, using words the child could understand, the therapist moved toward the goal of verbalization. The therapist sought to have Mark identify a part of himself—his "lion part." This technique promoted Mark's self-observation in a nonjudgmental manner (lions can attack and fight at times, but they are also brave). Later Mark and his therapist together could determine what triggered the lion and got him into trouble. The therapist could begin to work with Mark to determine the cause and effect of his aggression, but this interchange could only occur meaningfully through the child's play world. This theory is more fully examined in a later chapter (Chapter 3) and throughout the text.

In this period of work with Mark, one saw a change and development of his alliance with the therapist. Mark expressed genuine concern about his behavior ("It's hard for me to be a good boy") and evidenced his frightening dreams, his anxiety about scratches, his "doo" (soiling) problem. He looked to the therapist to remove these bad worries.

After a period of time in therapy, it is often possible to help the young patient give up some of his need for externalization (expelling the problem outside and denying his involvement). Several factors can foster greater internal awareness. One is the therapist's general

stance of confronting problematic behavior in an accepting, nonjudgmental way. For example, at issue was Mark's fighting difficulties.
When the therapist highlights these difficulties as Mark's "lion
feelings," they can be explored without Mark's anxiety that he is
being attacked. He was proud of his strength, though there were
times it got him into trouble. A second factor is that of identification.
As a positive attachment develops, the young patient will want to
identify with the therapist. Often the therapist will encourage secondary process thinking (the mature modes of reason, verbalization,
etc.). Thus, Mark's therapist could emphasize how well Mark was
using his "thinker" at times or convey how impressed he was when
Mark could listen to the therapist this time even though it made him
scared.

THE CHILD'S STATE OF DEPENDENCY:
THE ROLE OF THE PARENTS

Another major difference that powerfully effects the process of
therapy with the child is the marked physical and emotional dependency he has on his family. The child is exceedingly close to his
parents, and the parents provide the major source of motivation for
growth and development—the major sources of pleasures as well as
fears. The need for object love and approval and the fear of object
loss both shape the course of the development of the child's drives
(what impulses are acceptable), ego capacities (through identification), and superego formation (internalization of parental prohibitions and values), (Ackerman, 1958; Cutter & Hallowitz, 1982; Fraiberg, 1954; Kessler, 1966). Understanding the parent–child relationship must be a central part of the diagnostic process, and when
necessary, modifying the problems in the parent–child relationship
must be a part of the child treatment process.

A good working alliance with the parents is critical, since the child
will be very aware of the parental attitude toward the treatment.
Ritvo (1978) pointed out that "just as the parent invests the toy for
the young child in the interest of play, so the adult invests the
therapist for the child in the interest of the relief of discomfort and
suffering."

Unfortunately, the work with parents is often resisted or seen as
an enormous encumbrance. Several authors openly advocate little or

no contact, whereas others reluctantly shoulder the "burden" (Kohr-man, Fineberg, Gelman, & Weiss, 1971). It is the point of view of this author that parent work is an absolutely central aspect of child therapy and that most cases succeed or fail based on the quality of that aspect of the work. The following material highlights Mark's interaction with his mother.

Clinical Material

It was clear from the history that a longstanding adversarial relation-ship existed between mother and son. In the weekly meetings with the mother, Mrs. L. was extremely cooperative and consciously and quickly (on advice) established more effective limits in the home, which helped to begin to control Mark's acting out. When we came to understand that some of Mark's chaos sprang from intense excite-ments, Mrs. L. (on the home front) established privacy in the bath-room and curtailed Mark's visits to her bedroom when she dressed.

After several months of treatment, the daredevil theme became prominent in Mark's behavior. In the office, he climbed extensively; it was as if he were challenged by an obstacle and sought to master it. For instance, it became important for him to determine if he could climb to the high windowsill and sit there. But the danger was never mastered. Then he waited to see if he could move across the window-sill; and when that was accomplished, he attempted to do it in a standing position, and on and on. Slowly, it became more evident that Mark's mother played an important part in this counterphobic method of handling danger.

In a session, the mother related that Mark, a nonswimmer, had wandered off to the neighborhood pool. The family had been terribly worried for a number of hours, but as she told of the frightening event, a characteristic smile of pure pleasure illuminated her face. Mark was fantastically resourceful: he found the pool himself seven blocks from home; he persuaded the guard that he could enter, despite the rules that he needed a parent and that he was well under 48 inches, the minimum height of admission. (In his therapy at this point, Mark was preoccupied with fears of drowning.) The mother related all such events, all difficult and narrow scrapes that Mark was involved in, as high adventures and gave clear indications of an underlying intense pleasure. It was clear that a good deal of Mark's frightening chance-taking was libidinally reinforced by Mrs. L. She subtly conveyed her pleasure to him. She was aware and accepted that, although Mark's escapades frightened her, they also provided a part of her with some pleasure. These reactions became an area of mutual work.

Throughout the contacts with the mother, the therapist was impressed by the special identification she had with Mark. Although Mark might be more disturbed than his two brothers, she pointed out, he also had unique potentialities. He was brighter than they were, he had a special tenacity the others did not have, and he was the most physically attractive child. She could always get the older brother, Jason, to do what she wanted; he would dress himself without question with the clothing she laid out for him. But if Mark determined he wanted to wear something of his own choosing, she could stand on her head, and it would make no difference. As she related these incidents, her characteristic smile conveyed the obvious pleasure at the manly aggressiveness that Mark displayed.

Mrs. L.'s special tie to Mark had started early. When he was born, she had felt that he was particularly attractive partly because he was completely covered with hair. The family joke was that they would leave the hospital to go directly to the barbershop. In addition, when Mrs. L. was a child, her hairiness was a family topic for years.

Mrs. L. had been a happy child, she felt, but had always had a difficult time with her own mother. In order to maintain a sense of identity, Mrs. L. had had to fight her own mother every inch of the way. It was not that her mother had been mean, but she had always wanted to be the complete boss. Mrs. L. recalled that when she was organizing her sweet 16 party her mother had tried to take over all the arrangements. When Mrs. L. reacted, her mother had continued to interfere, and Mrs. L. moved the party to a friend's house where she could manage it completely by herself. This pattern of clear assertion continued even during Mrs. L.'s married life. Her mother would wonder whether she was keeping the dishes in the "right place"; she had new suggestions for furniture arrangements, etc. Mrs. L. would totally resist all ideas, as a result of which mother and daughter highly respected each other. This mutual esteem was in contrast to Mrs. L.'s younger sister, who acted like a child and was very dependent on her mother.

With this history, Mrs. L. could appreciate the therapist's interpretations that she cherished the feisty little Mark who would never be beaten down, since he recalled and expressed her own feisty struggles with her mother. Part of her, of course, knew that Mark needed firm and authoritative limits, but another part inside of her wanted to see Mark never knuckle down or be crushed by the authorities around him. As Mrs. L. became increasingly aware that her limit-setting would not choke the spirit out of Mark, she could effectively take command with less ambivalence. She could also, with skill, anticipate when Mark's "manly" defiance would promote her subtle pleasure, and the therapist found she went far in mastering what she conveyed to Mark. They also worked on new areas in which Mark's tenacity and activity could be appropriately expressed.

In each specific child therapy, a major diagnostic need is a review of both past and current parent–child interactions. How do they interact, and in what ways, if any, does this interaction support the child's pathology? In the above case, on a consious level, Mrs. L. was very supportive of treatment and able, with the therapist's aid, to set effective limits and control overt sexual stimulation. On an unconscious level, it became increasingly clear that the mother significantly reinforced Mark's daredevil and counterphobic tendencies. No therapeutic intervention with Mark alone could alter the pleasure he experienced in living out his mother's underlying wishes.

In this case, as in most child psychotherapies, the work with the parents was critical. The therapist helped the mother become aware of their (mother–son) mutual pleasure, helped make this source of gratification ego alien, and helped the mother understand the internal emotional origins that fostered a repetition in her new family. Dealing with the parent's role is essential in the child's case. Depending on the depth of influence, there are a hierarchy of techniques and various levels of intervention with parents available to the child therapist (Chethik, 1976). This subject is discussed in detail and illustrated particularly in the last past of the book.

THE CHILD'S DEVELOPMENTAL PROCESS: THE NEED FOR GROWTH

One of the major differences in child work is that the therapist has an additional important function that is not typically a part of adult psychotherapy. The child is in the process of development, and his presentation will often express aspects of an ongoing developmental process. The therapist must not only work with the central conflicts that have brought the child to therapy but also deal with the manifestations and stresses of normal development that emerge (Curtis, 1979). Child therapists quickly become aware that the child patient is also rapidly changing as he grows: his ego is expanding; his consciousness and self-consciousness are developing; he is tentatively establishing identities; and he develops a repertoire of defenses and coping skills (Anthony, 1982). Since new psychic structures are in the process of being formed, the therapist is in a central position to be instrumental in facilitating the child's developmental needs. Anna Freud (1965) notes that the therapist is also a "new and real object" to the child, since the child has a hunger for all new experiences and relationships. It is primarily in slowly helping the verbalization process that the therapist can help the child's ego to expand and master. The material discussed below, illustrates how the therapist helped Mark understand the typical sexual distortions all children develop as well as those specific issues unique to Mark.

Clinical Material

Toward the end of the first year of treatment, Mark brought in a series of sexual fantasies over a period of months. He announced one day that he was not afraid of snakes and spiders: they were made out of chemicals. His father had many chemicals, and he wanted the therapist to know that his father made people from these chemicals, which he could mix from a stack in the basement. His father himself had been made in the hospital by hospital men. When his father had come home, he made his mother and in turn his three children in chronological order. Since Mark could only remember things from 4 years of age, he concluded that he had been made at the age of 4.

These ideas proved a prelude to action. In the next session Mark opened his fly, and the therapist was about to restrain him. However, Mark was very involved in a fantasy and not sexually aroused (also not exposed). He claimed he had many secret pockets inside his pants legs, and each pocket held a chemical. He "took out" certain chemicals and rubbed his hands in a very deliberate and systematic way. Suddenly he thrust his hands out—an explosion and fire took place, and babies were formed. The therapist and Mark found these babies in many places; they were heard crying in different parts of the room, and Mark took them out very tenderly.

The therapist then encroached in a number of ways: "Mark finds it hard sometimes to think that you need a mommy and daddy to have a baby." "Mark has a smart idea—there *are* special daddy chemicals that help make babies. We can think about that in the Body Book we're making." "Mark would really like to make babies, like his mommy."

Several weeks later, Mark was preoccupied with birth fantasies. At first he was interested in some universal elements such as the differences between light and darkness. His thought was that the sun shone light during the day, and he concluded that the moon *shone* darkness at night (rather than perceiving that darkness was the absence of light). Thoughts of God came into the picture: was God everywhere and invisible as he was told? Could his dead grandfather be everywhere and invisible since he was with God?

He then became preoccupied with food and eating. He drew a picture of a little boy who ate Cheerios®. As he ate, his stomach grew bigger and bigger. It expanded so far that it burst, and pieces of stomach descended all over the room. He became concerned with germs: food that he brought to the therapy session could carry germs. He "accidentally" dropped his apple and rolled it on the floor picking up dirt, and he then bit into it. In his drawings, the germs entered the body and went to the stomach. The stomach changed into a fish tank, and many live things (fish) were wiggling around the body. Then, in further drawings, all sorts of "doo" (feces) in brown crayon poured out of the person's anus, completely covering the picture and the room.

The therapist and child worked together in the "Body Book," further clarifying and drawing "mixed-up" ideas that Mark had. He thought that maybe the way a mommy became pregnant was by eating food and germs; the more she ate the bigger the baby became in her tummy; and the moving baby inside was like a fish. Slowly the therapist could draw other real pictures that clarified pregnancy for Mark.

Also Mark wondered how a big baby could come out. Where was the baby hole? Did it emerge from the anus? The therapist explained that many boys had this scary idea. Again the therapist slowly drew and explained the anatomy of the mother, and how the child emerges, as he was clarifying Mark's ideas. He even kept a rubber-band in the Body Book to explain the elasticity of the birth canal. The parents reported Mark's increasing periods of excitement followed by new periods of calm.

During one period of excitement, Mark became preoccupied with matches and had strong desires to get into bed with his brothers. In his sessions he became active and agitated. He no longer wanted to draw. He brought in a long nail or a pencil and colored the tips red. He gave the therapist these instruments and wanted him to touch his (Mark's) stomach (the instruments had fire on the tip). This was very exciting—the stomach would "burst." Mark wanted to be the passive, impregnated partner, and for a period he even sang "Here Comes the Bride" as he approached the office.

Again the therapist could control the exciting play (e.g., "maybe we need to stop for a few minutes now, since this seems too exciting"). Mark was now bringing to the session his concept of intercourse (the frightening mommy bed and daddy bed noted earlier), which therapist and child could slowly discuss and draw at a pace that Mark could tolerate. The therapist could also discuss Mark's wish to be a woman. Mark sometimes had a very strong wish to be a mommy, to have babies inside and have a daddy touch him with a penis. The therapist told him that this was a wish that all boys had, at times. (Mark had identified strongly with his powerful mother.) It was a very scary idea for him, because sometimes he wanted his "dick" to fall off so he could be just like a girl. Then he became very frightened, but this was just a fantasy idea. Working through Mark's passive wishes was a critical aspect of the therapeutic work, since his castration anxiety was very intense.

The therapeutic work at this period of time was a mixture of issues related to Mark's neurotic conflicts and developmental needs. Certainly a central conflict for Mark was his intense underlying wish to be a girl and his associated passive sexual wishes. He seemed to identify with his mother and expressed this in all of his pregnancy and baby-caring wishes. These wishes, however, were highly anxiety producing because of the castration wishes they promoted. A major factor in this youngster's overt driven hypermasculinity, defiance, and toughness was the need to deny and defend against the internal feminine drive. One of the major goals of treatment was to have these underlying impulses emerge, have the youngster accept some of these wishes inside of himself (he was predominantly heterosexual), and help him understand that the fears of these internal feminine wishes drove him to prove inappropriately that he was the toughest boy in the neighborhood.

However, as therapist and child worked on these central issues, many other sexual fantasies emerged that were a normal part of childhood. Mark explicated oral (food) fantasies of impregnation, anal fantasies of childbirth, a major denial of intercourse (daddies make babies in the hospital), and a denial of sexual differences (boys can have babies). Part of the natural task of childhood is struggling with all of these sexual theories and slowly accepting the reality of the "facts of life." It is clear in the above process that the therapist had many opportunities to help Mark with these natural developmental sexual concepts as well as the central conflict that was causing him major problems. Thus, an important aspect of child psychotherapy is that the therapist comes to function as a "developmental facilitator" in which he will clarify and interpret manifestations of development directly.

THE COUNTERREACTIONS TO THE CHILD PATIENT

It has been commonly recognized that there are unusual pressures and stresses in work with children (A. Freud, 1965; Bornstein, 1948; Chethik, 1969). These pressures produce strong internal reactions within the therapist. Some authors describe these internal reactions as countertransference reactions (countertransference, as it is often understood, refers to special feelings a child might elicit in a therapist that stem from the therapist's unique childhood experiences and his own latent neurotic tendencies). In work with children, however, there are many reactions that are dramatically evoked in all therapists by the very fact of having a child patient. These common reactions often make the course of treatment difficult and impede empathy and understanding of the small patient.

One of the major feelings a child therapist must endure in his work will be *bewilderment* and *complete disorientation*. For example, in the early stages of the treatment with Mark there were sudden strong eruptions of aggression, excitement, panic, and incoherent disorder, and the therapist found himself confused and anxious. The child patient does not readily provide a context for his eruptive behavior. The therapist is flooded with questions. What does this eruptive material mean? What element is uppermost? What has caused the breakthrough? How shall it be handled? But often, with the acting-out child, the therapist has little time to think. At times he needs to act, although there may be much he does not understand. In the first period of work with Mark, the therapist quickly moved to control the chaos—setting up rules, putting toys away, holding the child.

One of the affects child therapists need to come to terms with in dealing with the "acting out" that many child patients bring is the *anger* that is induced. It is important to appreciate the intensity of the response that 6-year-old Marks can produce. Winnicott (1965) notes that in child work "objective hate" can emerge and that these feelings often have an objective basis. This recognition is significant so that the therapist will not feel a great deal of internal guilt, which can immobilize a therapist's capacity to work with the child. During Mark's eruptive and explosive periods, the therapist scheduled early morning appointments. This purpose was to get the chaotic hour out of the way so that he could have the rest of the day clear and relatively peaceful. It was certainly not unusual to anticipate the hour with Mark with a certain sense of dread.

The acting out that is produced by the child is not confined to the office alone. How the child uses the highly charged materials after the session ends is often a troubling question to the therapist. Because of the state of the child's ego, the demarcation between thought, wish, and fantasy, on the one hand, and action and behavior are not always clear to the child. How much did Mark's "lion feelings" of the hour become expressed as the bully on the playground? Would the invulnerable "Mighty Mouse" emerging in Mark's sessions induce more daredevil exploits in the neighborhood? Child therapists often work with a certain anxiety about what the treatment may evoke in the child, since reality testing as an ego function is less well developed.

At times, in work with young children, the therapist is faced with a sense of *helplessness* because the child is dependent on his parents and family. When there are changes in the family (separation, divorce, illnesses, etc.) or ongoing influences that clearly affect the child, the therapist will often experience intense frustration as he clearly witnesses the changes in the child and the treatment process. Although Mark's mother, Mrs. L. slowly became amenable to undoing her strong need to reinforce and idealize Mark's "heroic" behavior, it was extremely difficult to witness this affirmation of his pathology in the early phases of the work with Mark. The therapist came to know that his efforts with Mark would be fruitless unless the mother became emotionally able to give up the gratification she received from her son's "manly" exploits.

In our work with children, recognizing some of the contribution parents make to the pathology in the child inevitably also produces *"rescue fantasies"* within the therapist. The vulnerable little patient often evokes the wish to parent the child and protect the child from the negative influence of the "bad parent." These underlying impulses can undermine the treatment process. Will the therapist convey his indictment of the parents and disturb the alliance he has with them? Will he inappropriately seek to "make up" for the parents' deprivation in his contacts with the child and thereby distort his therapeutic posture? These are some of the potential pitfalls under the influence of the rescue fantasy.

Although the state of the child's ego, his dependence, and his hesitant motivation do cause "wear and tear" on the therapist, there are also some unique pleasures the child therapist can experience.

Mark, the stormy and trying 6-year-old, after a period of time, could begin to identify and discuss his out-of-control behavior. As noted earlier, he said during one session, "I have a lion inside me. And the wild lion gets me into a lot of trouble." One day, after a wretched hour, he commented with much sadness, "You know, it's just very hard for me to be good." Later in his treatment he discussed his terrifying dreams. He felt there was a little God inside him. This little God made bad dreams come at night when he was a bad boy during the day.

At times, in the treatment of the young child, we are involved in helping fundamental institutions necessary for growth emerge in the child. In Mark's statements one saw the beginning of new institutions. The "little God" inside him was the dawning awareness of his conscience and superego development. Seeing a lion inside himself, witnessing this wild part, all indicate a beginning ego observer and self-evaluator. As thought and verbalization grew, as his affects could be put into words, Mark's destructive behavior came under control, and new functions began to develop.

The therapist also recognizes that the child, by the very nature of being a child, has had a relatively short period of illness when we compare him with the adult. One does not have to undo a whole lifetime of entrenched and reinforced defenses or deal with an overlay of reality choices that have already been made on the basis of pathology. The changes in the child can be especially substantial and fundamental, and these changes can be the source of considerable gratification for the therapist.

The specific counterreactions identified above are not, in themselves, unique to the child practitioner. Bewilderment, anger, and helplessness are feelings that are part of everyone's practice. In addition to these internal negative feelings, the therapist often has positive affects (e.g., desires to protect the child against his helplessness) that can also form major roadblocks in the course of treatment. It is suggested that the intensity of these feelings is much stronger in work with children, that one experiences them much more frequently, and that these internal reactions come to form a very basic fact of the therapeutic work. It is important for the practitioner's own therapeutic self-esteem to distinguish these reactions from countertransference feelings. It is often reassuring, and perhaps essential, for him or her to recognize within himself or herself the naturalness of these intense reactions to his work with children.

BIBLIOGRAPHY

Ackerman, N. (1958). *Psychodynamics of Family Life*. New York: Basic Books.

Anthony, J. (1964). Communicating therapeutically with the child. *Journal of the American Academy of Child Psychiatry* 3:106–125.

Anthony, J. (1982). The comparable experiences of a child and adult analyst. *Psychoanalytic Study of the Child* 37:339–366.

Anthony, J. (1986). The contributions of child psychoanalysis to psychoanalysis. *Psychoanalytic Study of the Child* 41:61–88.

Bornstein, B. (1948). Emotional barriers in the understanding and treatment of young children. *American Journal of Orthopsychiatry* 18:691–697.

Chethik, M. (1969). The emotional "wear and tear" of child therapy. *Smith College Studies in Social Work* Feb:147–156.

Chethik, M. (1976). Work with parents: Treatment of the parent–child relationship. *Journal of the American Academy of Child Psychiatry* 15:453–463.

Curtis, H. (1979). The concept of the therapeutic alliance. Implications for the "widening scope." *Journal of the American Psychoanalytic Association (Suppl.)* 27:159–192.

Cutter, A., & Hallowitz, D. (1982). Different approaches to the treatment of the child and the parents. *American Journal of Orthopsychiatry* 22:152–159.

Fraiberg, S. (1954). Counseling for parents of the very young child. *Social Casework* 35:47-57.

Freud, A. (1965). *Normality and Pathology in Childhood*, New York: International University Press.

Harley, M. (1986). Child analysis, 1947-1984: A retrospective. *Psychoanalytic Study of the Child* 41:129-154.

Kessler, J. (1966). *Psychopathology of Childhood*. Englewood Cliffs, NJ: Prentice-Hall.

Kohrman, R., Fineberg, H., Gelman, R., & Weiss, S. (1971). Techniques of child analysis. *International Journal of Psychoanalysis* 52:487-497.

Olden, C. (1953). On adult empathy with children. *Psychoanalytic Study of the Child* VIII:111-126.

Peller, L. (1954). Libidinal phases, ego development and play. *The Psychoanalytic Study of the Child* 9:178-198.

Rees, K. (1978). The child's understanding of his past. Cognitive factors in reconstruction with children. *Psychoanalytic Study of the Child* 33:237-259.

Ritvo, S. (1978). The psychoanalytic process in childhood. *Psychoanalytic Study of the Child* 33:295-305.

Sandler, J., Kennedy, H., & Tyson, P. (1980). *The Techniques of Child Analysis*. Cambridge, Mass, Harvard University Press.

Tyson, R., and Tyson, P. (1986). The Concept of Transference in Child Psychoanalysis. *Journal of the American Academy of Child Psychiatry* 25:30-39.

Winnicott, D. W. (1965). *The Maturational Process and the Facilitating Environment*. New York: International Universities Press.

2

The Process of Assessment and Its Role in the Treatment Process

The purpose of this chapter is not merely to focus on the diagnostic process itself but also to illustrate how extensively a good assessment can orient the therapist to the specifics of an anticipated treatment. Initially, in this chapter, a full evaluation of a 6-year-old youngster is presented. A psychodynamic technical assessment of the case is then described, with specific treatment recommendations. This is followed by a discussion of how various aspects of the case may emerge and present themselves in the course of treatment. Although it is clear that no one can make absolute predictions about how a case will unfold or what new significant factors will become evident, the diagnostic context is an absolutely crucial one. The diagnostic backdrop is critical as the therapist seeks to make sense of and organize the unfolding material of the treatment hour. Therefore, this chapter is intended to serve as an example of the interweaving, the back-and-forth process of assessment and treatment.

THE EVALUATION PROCESS OF EMANUEL R. AND FAMILY

The evaluation consisted of two interviews with the mother, two sessions with Emanuel, one with the father, and reports from the pediatrician, nursery school, and first grade teacher. Emanuel was

6 years of age at the time of the evaluation, and the parents had been divorced for over 2 years. Emanuel was the youngest in a sibship of three—two older sisters (Dorothy, age 11, and Cynthia, age 9) made up the rest of the family. All lived in a single home in an upper-middle-class community with the mother, while the father lived nearby in a smaller home to which the children had easy access and visited frequently.

The Initial Phone Call

Mrs. R. noted that she wished to have her son Emanuel evaluated. She indicated she had been worried about him for a long period of time. She said she was divorced, had contacted Emanuel's father, and that he was both supportive of the evaluation and would participate. She asked about the fee. The therapist told her the fee he charged, and the mother indicated that the figure was acceptable to her. The therapist then provided directions to his office, and set up a meeting with the mother.

The function of the initial session below is partially a screening session to determine if a full evaluation should occur. Parents usually describe the behavior problems and/or symptoms in the first session, and the chronicity or transitory nature of the difficulties. There are times when a parent is actually seeking treatment for him/herself, or there is a current crisis with a child that does not necessitate a full evaluation. When a determination is made, the therapist can then outline the process that will occur.

The therapist typically meets with the parent or parents (if an intact family) alone in that first meeting. Again, this is to determine if a full evaluation should occur. Additionally, the therapist can help the parents prepare the child for the evaluation, should they decide to proceed.

First Interview: Mrs. R.

Mrs. R. was an attractive woman in her mid-30s who was markedly upset by rather chronic problems with her 6-year-old son. She felt that since the divorce (final separation occurred when Emanuel was 3½ years of age), her daughters had done extremely well in their development, but this was not true of her son. She was now completing her own undergraduate education and would shortly be looking for employment for herself.

The therapist asked the mother to describe the chronic problems she mentioned. She expressed a lot of concern about the fighting relationship she had with Emanuel. She found she was furious with him almost all of the time, and he fought back. He would not accept her authority often, e.g., about eating or dressing. He was very stubborn and ended up saying, "I won't." Since she was bigger, mother noted, she would win by subduing him with force, but they often ended up screaming and yelling, with her spanking her child. She hated what she felt she had descended to. Emanuel also embarrassed her a great deal. He had temper tantrums with the children of her friends, and he was extremely bossy and controlling of all friends. She hated to hear his voice telling others what to do. In all of the above descriptive material, the therapist asked for specific examples. The mother felt Emanuel also stood in the way of her relationships with men. Since he could be so impossible and made a fuss when she was going out, she felt impeded in her ability to get seriously involved with a man. Who would want her with this little hellion attached?

In response to the therapist's questions, the incident that made her decide to call for an evaluation occurred over the recent Christmas vacation. Emanuel was very angry and suddenly said directly that he wanted to stab his mother with a knife. To verbalize these things actually made him calm down, and they had a very good time for several days. She had ambivalent feelings about this incident—she was scared about how angry he was, but she also wondered whether the situation would improve if he could express a lot of his feelings in therapy.

The therapist asked if there were other things that worried her about her son. Mrs. R. also noted that Emanuel had been a bed wetter throughout his life (almost every night), and although he was bright, his teachers felt he was not working up to his academic potential.

At this point, the therapist felt that a full evaluation should occur, since there were indeed longstanding difficulties, apprised the mother of his assessment, and outlined the process. He needed several sessions with the mother to learn about Emanuel's developmental history, her own history, and the marriage with her former husband. He explained that how one was raised as a child often shapes how she/he is as a parent. He would also meet with Emanuel several times, and since there were some school difficulties, he would need to contact both public and nursery school teachers, if possible. He suggested that the father call him for an appointment. After he gathered this material, he would integrate it and share his impressions and recommendations with her, Emanuel, and the father.

For most of the remainder of the session, Mrs. R. discussed her marriage and the difficulties she and her husband had incurred. They had never had a good marriage, and part of the difficulty lay with her. She admired her husband but she had never loved him. He was an outstanding business executive, friendly, warm, and successful, but they had never felt close to each other. They could not talk with each other, and frankly the more competent her husband was, the less adequate she felt as a person. She felt there was greater distance between them after Emanuel was born despite the fact that they had hoped another child would bring them together. Mr. R. had always been nice and polite and had been even more effective with the handling of Emanuel during his infancy and early years than she herself. Truthfully, at times, she had felt he was showing her up.

At the end of the session, she wondered if she could ever be a competent mother at all to a son—maybe Emanuel would be better off with his father. Tears flooded her eyes when she said that maybe this evaluation should consider where custody should reside.

Second Interview: Mrs. R.

Mrs. R. spontaneously said she was very upset about the session of last week. She had felt dizzy as she left and nauseous as she had entered her car. Could she really give up Emanuel? She found that idea very difficult, and she felt very sad. She loved him and said she wanted to raise him unless the therapist found some very compelling and clear reason that they should not live together.

In terms of further history, Mrs. R. noted that she had wanted another baby more than anything in the world, and she was the most happy in her life during her pregnancies. She was, however, a perfectionist. She had taken Lamaze lessons as she had before and had not really expected the delivery to hurt her. She had been so surprised by the pain and depressed by her inability to bear it that she was initially angry with Emanuel. But it was a good first year— she had enjoyed feeding and holding him, buying his clothes, bunting, etc., and recalled that she had loved to look at him peacefully lying in his crib.

Emanuel was a very active toddler and hard to keep up with. By then her marriage was deteriorating, and she knew she was often angry and depressed and very impatient with him. As he neared 2 years of age she began toilet training him, and he was quickly successful. After a few weeks, however, he totally refused the potty, and she could not cajole him. Her use of force, however, also did not work. He soiled then for over a year, and finally when he was 3½, and she made him wash out his pants, the soiling problem disappeared forever. She has always had problems, however, with getting Emanuel to put away his toys, papers, etc. It is very clear which rooms of her house Emanuel has recently been in—the disorder is very evident.

The therapist asked about Mrs. R.'s current living situation. Mrs. R. talked more openly about her boyfriend, Larry, who had been living in the home for the past year. She was upset that Emanuel made believe that Larry did not exist and hardly spoke to him. Larry was a "natural" with children, but he felt that Emanuel was a terribly spoiled youngster. In terms of her relationship with Larry, Mrs. R. felt that he wanted to marry her, but she was terribly unsure. She was physically attracted to Larry but felt unable to really talk with him about any feelings or sensitive matters. They maintained the current arrangement partly because she hated to be lonely, but she was not sure the relationship was going anywhere.

Mrs. R. spoke of her own history. She recalled a very unhappy childhood. Her parents had separated and divorced when she was 18 but fought all the time during her early years. No one seemed to care about her—her parents were preoccupied with themselves, and she recalled "disappearing into the woodwork" so no one would notice her. Her mother told her she was an "accident," and her father's concern had been that she marry so that she would not be a potential financial burden on him. She also recalled being very competitive with her brothers, who were 2 and 4 years older than she. Mrs. R. thoughtfully speculated that her feelings of inadequacy as a child had been a central problem in her marriage. She had felt so small in contrast to her husband that she could not stand it—this was an important awareness derived from her own treatment, which she began when her marriage was precarious. Her treatment had lasted for several years through her subsequent divorce.

At the end of the session, Mrs. R. described again several incidents with Emanuel that troubled her greatly. With good intentions and a determination to have a good time, she had taken Emanuel for an afternoon to the science museum. He had taken over and had tried to determine what exhibits they would see, how long she should spend looking at fossils, etc. By the end of the trip, she had been furious. The power struggle seemed ever present.

In achieving a meaningful history of a child, the facts of a developmental history are not enough. It is the task of the evaluator to attempt to construct in his mind the emotional climate the child patient grew up within. Thus, there is a need to understand the emotional life of the parents as much as possible. Having parents describe the family atmosphere and events during the years of the child's life and learning of the childhood history of the parents themselves helps to understand the quality of parental functioning. Mrs. R. highlighted the struggle between the parents during Emanuel's early years. In other families, financial constraints, absorption in professional development, moves, or deaths of significant relatives can be important contexts to understand families, since these events can significantly encroach on the adult's available energy to parent effectively.

Emanuel R.: First Interview

Emanuel was a robust, pleasant looking youngster. He initially looked apprehensive about meeting the therapist. Since he wore a baseball cap, the therapist asked him about his interest in the Detroit Tigers. Emanuel, however, went quickly for the toys in the room, since that seemed safe and familiar. He took out all sorts of toys— trucks, soldiers, cowboys—and a chaotic mess seemed to ensue. Soldiers were killing monsters who were killing trucks who were killing other soldiers. The therapist asked questions about the fighting. Who was fighting? etc. There appeared to be no storyline, and the violence (which was very evident) seemed to have little form. As the play went on, the therapist felt there was some evidence of anxiety: questions regarding the details of the story met with little or no comment. Emanuel, however, seemed to attend when the therapist spoke about why he was coming for sessions. The therapist noted that his mommy felt that Emanuel was unhappy, and that this unhappiness came from worries. His mom felt he showed this by being angry a lot, wetting the bed, and having trouble having friends. The therapist was now trying to figure out Emanuel's worries by seeing him, his mom, and dad. After he finished seeing them a few times, he would think about Emanuel's worries and give Emanuel his ideas about them and how these ideas might help Emanuel.

Emanuel picked up on the therapist's comment about "worries," and he said he had bad dreams. He was scared when he went to sleep and sometimes stayed under the covers. He was visited in his dreams by monsters from the dead—from the underground. They sprayed in people's faces, and this killed them. He had a dream in which a monster came into a family that was eating dinner, and it sprayed into the daddy's face. Emanuel shifted from the dream and immediately began talking about his mother's boyfriend, Larry, whom he said he liked very much. Larry worked a lot on his house, fixed things, and Emanuel liked to help him. Maybe, he said, his mom and Larry would get married in the summer.

It is interesting to follow the progression of Emanuel's thoughts. His "good feelings" about Larry emerged immediately after the dream about the daddy being killed. This was a reaction formation that was noted by the therapist but not commented on directly. This kind of material would be used to understand Emanuel's conflicts (discussed later in the chapter) but would have been premature to raise with the child.

Emanuel R.: Second Interview

The therapist began the session by noting that we were still finding out about Emanuel's worries. Sometimes drawings and stories about the drawings helped to explain inside worries. Emanuel began by telling about other bad dreams. He had dreamt that his mother was a witch, and in some dreams she had been holding a dead body. He became anxious by this revelation, and he ran to check on his mother in the waiting room.

Emanuel worked on several drawings, and he told a story as he drew. A boy and his mother went to sleep together in the bedroom. When the boy was asleep the mother turned into a witch. She cast a magical spell on herself to kill herself. She did this by eating a poison apple. Bats then flew around and ate her body. The boy awakened and saw this skeleton, and it began to chase him. He was very scared and ran away and went to live with his daddy.

The therapist noted that sometimes Emanuel seemed to get very angry with his mom. He agreed he was angry with Larry and his mom.

When he went to sleep, they left him, and he was alone. A lot of times, they went walking together and did not want him there! They talked all the time, and he did not know what they are talking about. Since they only talked to themselves, he was going to get even. He would not even talk to them or listen to his mother when she told him to do anything. Emanuel expressed his anger with a good deal of affect.

At the end of the session, the therapist noted that boys can get very, very angry with their mommies. Later they often feel bad since they need them and also want things to go well. Maybe the therapist could help him and his mom get along better and be happier, if the therapist knew more about the angry feelings he and his mom had.

In the early stages of an evaluation or treatment, it is helpful to give a child some glimpse of how therapy could be helpful. Emanuel was very angry with his mother but also clearly pained by the problems between them. The therapist took this opportunity to make this issue conscious and indicate that this was an important issue that he would attempt to help Emanuel and his mother resolve. The purpose of these early comments is to foster investment in this new, strange process.

School Report: First Grade Teacher

Generally, Emanuel's teacher felt that she had learned to handle him and that he "settled down" since the start of the year. She had learned to be very firm with him, and his desk was near her. Since she provided this "structure," his learning and behavior had improved, although he was having significant difficulty with his reading progress. He was potentially one of the smartest children she had seen in a long time. His vocabulary, insight, general facts, and reasoning attested to his capabilities, but she felt he seemed to have "a lot of turmoil going on inside of him." Earlier, Emanuel had chosen to associate with a large, very aggressive youngster who was the class problem but more recently kept away from him.

Nursery School

Emanuel attended nursery school and kindergarten in this program. Overall, Emanuel was not a major "acter-outer," but he tended to associate with the more difficult children; for a period of time, he loved the use of "bad" and "bathroom" language. He did very well with firm teachers and had difficulties with lax teachers.

He had some inhibitions academically, but during the latter half of his kindergarten year, he flourished in math and science, though he had some problems in reading preparation skills.

Interview Father: Mr. R.

Mr. R. was a successful, handsome business executive in his mid-30s who enjoyed his profession. The requirements of his job demanded that he travel a good deal, and he liked moving about. He had never remarried, although he had had a number of relationships in the intervening years.

He visited with Emanuel and his sisters twice weekly (usually for a good part of the weekend) except when he was out of town. He had supported his ex-wife and family financially and was willing to support and pay for treatment. He was aware of Emanuel's difficulties with his mother, but he had not observed these directly. Emanuel was never a problem with his father. He was very well behaved, and they thoroughly enjoyed each other's company. He knew that the division of labor in raising Emanuel had not been totally fair, and he tried to take the children for weekends so that his ex-wife could have time for special things she wanted to do.

He had some concern about Emanuel's sexual interests. Mr. R. at times had had women friends over when Emanuel visited. Recently Emanuel had acted very seductively with these women, and Mr. R. was uncomfortable with the precocious quality of his remarks, gestures, etc. He expressed a desire to explore this actively in parent guidance sessions in the future.

PSYCHODYNAMIC TECHNICAL ASSESSMENT

Below is an outline of the major topics to address in a technical assessment. Following the schematic presentation, an illustration of such an assessment is presented using the case material of Emanuel and family.

I. Drive Assessment (libidinal and aggressive)
   Include psychosexual phase development, phase level, and quality object relations (mostly in regard to libido), quantity, and distribution with regard to aggression

II. Ego Assessment
   A. Defensive functions—preferred defenses, appropriateness, and efficiency
   B. Quality of object relations—extent of capacity to relate
   C. Relation to reality—capacity to adapt
   D. Nature of thinking processes—abstract versus concrete, utilization of fantasy
   E. Drive regulation and control—development of drive endowment, superego function; assessing degree of impulsivity, frustration tolerance, and attention span
   F. Autonomous functions—intelligence, memory (immediate and remote, lapses or distortions), motor function (coordination and use of body language), perception (distortions—organic or psychologic), and language
   G. Synthetic function—assessing capacity to integrate and organize experience
   H. Assessment of ego's general functioning in light of above, relative to age and developmental stage
III. Superego Assessment
   Broadly assess nature and extent of guilt versus fear of external authority
IV. Genetic-Dynamic Formulation of Child
   Discuss major sources of conflict related to:
   psychosexual phase of development
   external and internal conflicts relative to child
   major identifications and their contributions to child's adaptations
V. Treatment Recommendations

The purpose of the assessment is to shed light on specific problematic areas and explicate the underlying forces that have created the difficulties. Emanuel presented several issues. (1) The major manifest difficulty was the fighting relationship with the mother, but the problems seemed to spread into other areas of their relationship as well, and to a limited degree affected Emanuel's relationship with other authorities. He was ready to fight rules, evidenced messy behavior generally, and had temper tantrums. Emanuel's "bossy" behavior was also evident with peers. (2) In addition, he had been enuretic at night for a number of years, and the bedwetting pattern seemed related to internal conflicts (e.g., often after nightmares or bad dreams, the wetting occurred). (3) Emanuel seemed to evidence some problems at school—although he was bright, he did not work up to his potential, and he had particular difficulty with learning to read. How would we explain these symptoms and behavior problems?

As an approach to making the assessment, the outline is designed in a particular way. Sections I, II, and III focus on three major institutions of the mind (the id, ego, and superego), and these should be examined separately. Section IV (genetic dynamic formulation) is conceived as an attempt to integrate the first three sections and to describe the child's internal struggles (dynamic formulation) and trace the factors in his history that influenced these struggles (genetic formulation). After one has made this formulation, a diagnosis of the child would be more evident, and the course of treatment could be clearer.

Application of the Outline

I. Drive Assessment

There was a good deal of evidence that Emanuel had reached the phallic and oedipal levels of development. This was suggested by the dream of going into the bedroom with his mother and wishes to sleep with her. Emanuel's relationships were "triangulated," which is typical of children in the oedipal phase of development. He saw Larry, mother's boyfriend, as an intense rival, and he was jealous of the time and activities they spent together. Emanuel's sexual interests were also expressed in his seductive behavior with his father's girlfriends.

Emanuel was having major difficulty dealing with this phase of development. His phallic sexuality seemed very destructive to him. The sprayer (penis symbol in the dream described in the second hour) killed the daddy when it was squirted into his face. Emanuel expressed fear of destruction as he experienced rivalry with Daddy and Larry. Intercourse was very frightening to him. After mother and he retired into the bedroom, mother turns into a witch, and skeletons chase him. These frightening and bad dreams that Emanuel described suggested that he feared punishment for his destructive competitive strivings and his sexual wishes.

There were also problems stemming from the anal phase of development. Some of his sexuality seemed to be expressed in anal terms. The material suggested that some of his power struggles with

his mother were exciting and had aspects of sadomasochistic interplay.

Emanuel clearly had difficulty with his aggressive drives as well.
He had trouble controlling his aggression, particularly with his
mother. Some of his difficulties related to the phallic rivalry described above. He also evidenced difficulties stemming from the anal
phase, which he expressed in temper tantrums, uneasiness, and
controlling behavior.

II. Ego Assessment

Basically, Emanuel seemed well endowed, and all of his ego functions
seemed intact and well developed (intelligence, perception, memory,
etc.). In terms of object development, he certainly had reached object
constancy (basic capacity for a stable libidinal attachment to people),
although there were some problems in the resolution of ambivalence. Emanuel tended to idealize his father and devalue his mother.

Emanuel made use of several prominent defenses. When he was
frightened of the aggression of others, he utilized the mechanism of
identification with the aggressor (e.g., when he felt his mother would
attack, he became the attacker). Emanuel had considerable problems
with his aggression, and he commonly engaged in *projection*, ascrib-
ing the forbidden feelings to others around him. Another major
defensive maneuver was *regression*. Emanuel seemed to be frightened of sexual and loving oedipal feelings, and he moved from these
affects (e.g., toward mother) to earlier, preoedipal forms of relationship.

Emanuel, at times, appeared impulsive when aggressive breakthroughs seemed to emerge. This reaction served several purposes
for him. At times, his ego seemed to have difficulty regulating his
drives, and he was overwhelmed by the strength of his feelings. In
addition, the choice of his defense (identification with the aggressor)
permitted the open expression and discharge of his aggression.

III. Superego Assessment

Emanuel did not have a fully internalized superego, and he depended
somewhat on authorities (mother and teachers) for controls. He had
a growing sense of right and wrong but imagined that many sanctions would be overly harsh (stemming, in part, from the projection

of his aggression). Because of the problems he had with aggression, he anticipated (imagined) cruel and destructive punishments for his transgressions.

IV. *Genetic–Dynamic Formulation*

Emanuel was a youngster struggling to reach the oedipal phase of development, but conflicts at this stage became very problematic for him. He was very frightened both that his phallic behavior (both sexual and aggressive) was very destructive to others and that expressing these phase-appropriate feelings would have terrible consequences for him. Sprayers (penises) killed daddies, and sleeping with mother (bedroom fantasy) was associated with terrifying witches and skeletons. He was frightened that his urges were too destructive and powerful. Emanuel tended to retreat to many forms of anal functioning, where he felt safer. For example, rather than expressing the sexuality and love feelings of the oedipal phase, he maintained a fighting, controlling (anal) relationship with his mother.

Stemming from the history, there appeared to be three major factors that contributed to Emanuel's feelings that his phallic and oedipal strivings were destructive:

1. During Emanuel's anal phase of development he struggled with his mother around issues of autonomy (toilet-training history) and as a consequence built up a reservoir of anger in relation to his sexual and aggressive affects, which he carried further into his development. Affects of rage, negativism, and defiance were legacies of unresolved problems of the anal phase.

2. In addition, his fears of power were markedly exacerbated by the separation and divorce during his oedipal years. In his fantasy, he was an "oedipal victor" who had gotten rid of his father, expressed by the dream in which the monster kills the daddy with his spray. The separation had actually occurred when Emanuel was 3½ years old. Fathers, at this point in development, normally serve as a natural inhibitor for the aggressive/sexual fantasies of little boys. This loss appeared to have reinforced Emanuel's sense of omnipotent power, since little boys have a common wish to expel their fathers from the family. This event also contributed to the fear of his destructive power. The absence of the father also appeared to have exacerbated the problematic interactions between mother and son, since the father was not there to serve as a buffer in this primary

relationship. These two factors became problems internalized within Emanuel.

3. The third factor and barrier to oedipal resolution was an external factor, Mrs. R.'s feelings about Emanuel's masculine strivings. Mrs. R. was a woman who was clearly conflicted about her own relationships with men. She felt she was small and inadequate in comparison to the phallic strength of her husband (and probably earlier her father). She had competed unsuccessfully with her brothers. It appeared that Mrs. R. saw her son's activity (both autonomy and phallic strivings) as destructive and also demeaning to her. Thus, on a day-to-day current basis, Mrs. R.'s sanctions made Emanuel's oedipal strivings difficult to express.

V. Treatment Recommendations

Twice-weekly, insight-oriented psychotherapy for Emanuel was recommended to help him to deal with his internalized conflicts. In making this recommendation, it was important to assess Emanuel's potential strengths for the task. Emanuel appeared to be an intelligent youngster who showed no problems in memory, perceptions, or motor or language functions. He related well in the two evaluative sessions, and he responded to the ideas of the therapist with dreams, drawings, stories, etc. His thinking processes and his ability to imagine and fantasize were intact. Despite the disturbance evident with his mother, Emanuel was able to function elsewhere with firm limits so that part of the problematic behavior was limited to his relationship with his mother. It was also clear that this was not a youngster who had given up. Emanuel struggled to reenter the phallic arena, and this was very apparent in his visits with his father.

Weekly parent guidance was recommended for the mother. A major task would be to help the mother accept the phallic and masculine strivings in her youngster. Given the mother's history and general struggle with her own identity, this might not be easy. However, she already had some therapy, and perhaps the insights gained could be used in relation to her son. She was also strongly motivated to help her son and could potentially feel enhanced by being an effective parent.

Intermittent parent guidance for the father was recommended. The purpose of this would be to support his investment and attachment to his son.

Summary

In summary, there were now a number of hypotheses we had gathered to explain Emanuel's presenting problems. The most complex issue was his aggressive behavior (outbursts with mother, with Larry, and with other authorities). At times, Emanuel's behavior appeared to be a direct response to his mother's attacks or belittling behavior directed at her son. Emanuel's anger also seemed to have been a direct expression of reactions to the "past" mother (of the anal toilet-training period). Emanuel's fighting behavior was also defensive, since his belligerence was a more acceptable form of relating to his mother than the expression of the tenderness or sexuality of the oedipal period. In relation to men, Emanuel's angry behavior appeared to be the expression of his rivalry with an oedipal antagonist.

Similar oedipal themes seemed to explain his bed wetting. At times, the symptom appeared to reflect the expression of phallic impulses in his dreams. Emanuel used his powerful "sprayer" to annihilate men. Bed wetting also reflected his anxiety in punishment dreams. Does his penis become broken (the bed-wetting act) as an expression of his castration anxiety? The evaluation additionally suggested that since Emanuel struggled with fears regarding the expression of his power, some of his conflict may have been displaced to his intellectual power. It appeared that Emanuel needed to restrict his performance in school (associated with phallic performance), where he was expected to be competitive and rivalrous with others.

Diagnostically, using the conflict model (conflict among id, ego, and superego) described above, we can depict Emanuel's conflicts as shown in the table.

Drive	→Anxiety reation	Ego response →(defenses)	Behavior/ →symptoms
I. Aggression Anal (sadism)	→Fear of annihila- tion	→Identification with the aggressor	→Rage, temper, outbursts, messiness, etc.
Oedipal (competition)	→Castration anxiety	→Inhibition	→School restriction
II. Libido Oedipal	→Guilt/castration anxiety	→Regression (in object relations)	→Fighting inter- play with mother

TREATMENT IMPLICATIONS

Although it is taken for granted that a diagnostic assessment has many implications for the treatment of the child, it is often not specifically articulated how the assessment can be used. The most obvious area is the setting of *treatment goals*. In most situations (as with Emanuel), symptoms and/or behavior problems develop because of unacceptable internal impulses. Insight into one's internal life can substantially modify how one reacts to these "negative" or forbidden parts of the self. Therefore, the diagnostic process can specify what aspects of the instinctual life seem to be most troubling. A goal would be to have the forbidden impulses expressed, discussed, and reintegrated via the treatment into the child's psychic life. These subjects are described in greater detail below.

In addition, part of the diagnostic appraisal focuses on the ego— the special responses the patient uses to ward off, repress, and defend against the conscious emergence of unacceptable impulses. These ego responses (e.g., defenses) are the typical forms the child patient uses to take flight from these troublesome aspects of the self. These responses will emerge in the treatment hour and become the specific forms of *resistance* the child will use in treatment. The diagnostic appraisal can therefore anticipate the specific resistances that may emerge.

Another area of anticipation is the nature of the *transferences* that will emerge in the course of therapy. (Both the concepts of "resistance" and "transference" in child work are more fully elaborated in Chapters 4 and 5.) Whom will the therapist come to represent as the result of problematic object relations of the past? What major past (or present) situations will be played out in the treatment hour? Understanding, through the diagnostic appraisal, the significant relationships during each phase of development, and the significant past events in a child's life, will allow the therapist to verbalize and reconstruct them as they emerge. The therapist can anticipate his transference role and the context in which it occurs.

Treatment Goals

What can we anticipate in the case of Emanuel? In terms of treatment goals, it is apparent that aspects of his rage and aggression are unacceptable to him and cause loss of self-esteem as well as negative reactions from people in his environment. In the course of treatment, we can anticipate that a fighting, rageful representation of Emanuel will emerge—perhaps directly with the therapist or in representational form through play. A major goal would be to help Emanuel put these affects (e.g., expressed in action, in the play) into words and link them to real situations in his life. For example, Emanuel could be helped to say, "I hate my mother for such and such" as this emotion emerges in derivative play. With children, the process of verbalization modulates the raw affective drive components and helps the child order his instinctual life.

Further, Emanuel uses some "unacceptable" ways of expressing his anger. He can be enormously messy, and these aspects of his aggressive drive will emerge in the treatment hour. One could expect that at some point he would make a mess of the toys or some area of the treatment room. This would provide the opportunity for identifying Emanuel's "messy, angry feelings." A goal of the treatment might be to explicate this aspect of Emanuel's behavior and slowly give him an understanding of how he developed them (for example, how boys love to be dirty when they are little, and if there are problems at that point, these feelings remain). The purpose of this kind of reconstruction of the aggressive drive would be to give his behavior some meaningful context and historical framework. This treatment insight could be helpful in beginning to modulate the harsh internal superego reactions (I am a terrible messy boy) to these impulses.

If the fighting play in the treatment hour (e.g., between a boy and a mommy doll) appears to be defending against oedipal issues, the therapeutic goal would be to illuminate the issues. The therapist could speak to Emanuel's fears of his tender or loving feelings toward his mother so that he always has to fight with her. Again, the purpose would be to permit the expression of "forbidden" instinctual wishes so that Emanuel could move toward appropriate phase development.

This recognition of the nature of these conflicts as they emerge in the treatment hour can be enhanced enormously by an ordered diagnostic workup.

Resistance

What kind of resistances can we anticipate in the treatment hour with Emanuel? The diagnostic assessment highlights a number of typical defenses (e.g., identification with the aggressor, projection) that Emanuel utilizes, and one can expect that these forms of defense (resistance) will naturally emerge in interactions with the therapist.

For example, at some point in the course of the work, Emanuel will probably "act tough" and behave defiantly. Perhaps he will refuse to help to clean up at the end of the hour and instead dump the toys in defiance. He might throw clay pellets in the therapist's direction. The process of "identification with the aggressor" would then become apparent. With an understanding of the nature of the resistance, the therapist could interpret that "Emanuel becomes a tough guy when he imagines that the therapist will *force* him to clean up." This form of ego analysis can help Emanuel slowly become aware of his typical reactions to normal rules and expectations.

A similar process can be anticipated in relation to Emanuel's common use of projection. In the course of the work, Emanuel might become fearful of coming to his sessions. He could attribute all sorts of rage reactions to the therapist. The therapist, alerted to the defense/resistance mechanisms of projection, would have an opportunity to intervene and explain that "When Emanuel becomes angry, at times he pushes those feelings outside and onto the therapist. Now he has become scared of these angry feelings and scared the therapist will hurt him." The therapist could also draw parallels in Emanuel's life where this has happened on the playground, at home, etc. If the typical defenses are anticipated, the therapist will be able to describe the distorted reactions as they emerge in the course of treatment and help the patient become aware of a major part of his personality—his ego functions.

Transference

All patients live out their feelings and experiences in the course of treatment rather than remember them. The history of the patient provides an important roadmap in helping the therapist locate the source of current unfolding action. What would Emanuel tend to reexperience?

One could anticipate that Emanuel would become provocative, messy, defiant, and bossy in his relationship with the therapist. Whereas this would include the process of "identification with the aggressor" described above, in a larger context Emanuel would be recreating the maternal transference. He would be living out, with the therapist, some aspects of the sadomasochistic interplay he established with his mother during his early years. The therapist would become, for Emanuel, the controlling, dominating authority who would rob him of his products and freedom. This awareness would provide the therapist with an opportunity to identify the interplay verbally, reconstruct the past slowly, and to help the patient see how he tends to replay these patterns inappropriately in critical areas of his current life. (The process of dealing with transference, reconstruction, and working through is elaborated in a number of cases in Part II.)

One could also anticipate another major form of transference based on Emanuel's past. Emanuel will probably be reactive during separations. Would he be concerned that the therapist would die in a plane crash when he goes on vacation? Would he worry that the therapist would never return? These separations would touch on feelings Emanuel had experienced when he "lost" his father at age 3½. One might comment to Emanuel that when he worries that the therapist will never come back, these feelings resemble those he might have had as a little boy when his dad and mommy split up. Often in divorced families, little children feel they were the ones who really made their daddies go away. Such a transference experience would provide opportunities to explore the impact and vicissitudes of his special father loss during the early phases of Emanuel's oedipal period.

There are clearly many other possibilities of forms of resistance, transference, or reconstruction that one can anticipate as one reviews Emanuel's assessment. In the course of work with the child patient, the current material will slowly acquire specific meanings as one reassesses it in the context of the child's history and metapsychology. It is the diagnostic framework then, the history and dynamic formulations that make the ongoing material of the treatment hour intelligible.

BIBLIOGRAPHY

Freud, A. (1965). *Normality and Pathology in Childhood*. New York: International Universities Press.
Greenspan, S. (1982). *The Clinical Interview of the Child*. New York: McGraw-Hill.
Group for the Advancement of Psychiatry (1957). *The Diagnostic Process*

in Child Psychiatry. Report No. 38. New York: Group for the Advancement of Psychiatry.

McDonald, M. (1965). The psychiatric evaluation of children. *Journal of the American Academy of Child Psychiatry* 4:569–612.

Newbauer, P. (1963). Psychoanalytic contributions to the nosology of childhood psychic disorders. *Journal of the American Psychoanalytic Association* 11:595–604.

Sandler, J., & Freud, A. (1965). *The Analysis of Defense.* New York: International Universities Press.

Sandler, J., Kennedy, H., & Tyson, R. (1980). *The Techniques of Child Psychoanalysis: Discussions with Anna Freud.* Cambridge, MA: Harvard University Press.

3

The Central Role of Play

As noted in Chapter 1, a major difference between adult and child psychotherapy is the patient's *form* of bringing his/her affective material to the treatment hour. Adults use verbalization; children utilize play.

Not all child therapists have agreed that play is an effective medium. Anna Maenchen (1970) comments "that the eventual aim of child work is to have the child talk directly to the analyst and analyze with the analyst." Selma Fraiberg (1965) expresses concern that play only produces abreaction (simple discharge of feeling) and questions whether it leads to structural change (permanent changes in the ego or superego). Other authors wonder about the precise quality of play (Sandler, Kennedy, & Tyson, 1980), noting that it is neither dream material nor free association. It is the author's concern that, at times, there has been an attempt to use adult psychotherapy and psychoanalysis as a model within which the child patient must fit rather than to utilize the unique qualities of childhood. Some of the controversy around play therapy centers around this divergence in philosophy and methodology.

In many ways children are much closer to their affective life, and the medium of play provides an opportunity not only to elicit this world but also to bring it into a coherent and organized form. The child therapist has an opportunity to capture this natural form of communication. Play, in itself, will not ordinarily produce changes in the therapist's office any more than it will in the schoolyard. The therapist's interventions and utilizations of the play are critical.

This chapter has a twofold demonstration purpose. The first is to describe how the therapist "sets the stage"—induces the medium of play, facilitates its development, and works toward the *quality* of play that will be effective. Then, after the play emerges, the focus centers on utilization of the play—how to interpret the meaning of the play and how to make effective interventions. Clinicians often experience a familiar sequence in the development of play. The sequence can be described as follows:

1. *An initial period of nonengagement: setting the stage.* The child does not play, or he plays alone, or his play is unintelligible or not useful. Often the therapist is puzzled and noncomprehending. Some "talk" emerges about symptoms, "worries," and behaviors of the child.

2. *Early phase of affective engagement.* The therapist slowly becomes oriented to the play and begins to share specific meaningful metaphors that emerge in the play. A growing investment by the child becomes clear, and his tie to the therapist begins to have the quality of a strong libidinal investment.

3. *Emergence of control fantasies.* The child slowly elaborates highly invested fantasies in play that have important significance, though the therapist may only be dimly aware of their meaning. As the story-game process evolves, the parents begin to report changes (which can be symptom relief, behavior improvement, escalation of anxiety, or symptom exacerbation and behavior deterioration).

4. *Period of working through.* Often, belatedly, the therapist integrates varied meanings of the unfolding material and intervenes interpretatively, which helps either to stabilize the gain or to control the process.

It is important to note that this interactional sequence is not the only process involving the development of play, but this process does generally occur. This process is illustrated by the case of Jonathan during the first 8 months of treatment. These months traversed a period from early, unproductive play to a point when Jonathan brought significant central fantasies to his play material.

THE INITIAL PERIOD OF NONENGAGEMENT: SETTING THE STAGE

Clinical Material

Jonathan as seen when he was 8 years of age. He was a thin, pleasant-looking youngster who impressed the therapist with his emotional distance and air of remoteness. Jonathan was referred for encopresis and school problems (possible failure). After some investigation, it became clear that both problems had a common origin—Jonathan soiled his pants two to four times weekly because he invariably withheld his fecal products until it was too late; Jonathan had mounting school problems reaching critical proportions because he invariably withheld his intellectual products. He delayed, procrastinated, and finished very few school papers, and those that were finally wrested from him by coercion managed invariably to get lost and somehow never reached the teacher's desk.

Jonathan's family was an intact one—an achieving affluent upper-middle-class family. He had three siblings, all older sisters. In the history, the nature of the mother–son relationship was of paramount importance. The family was dominated by the mother who had a rather significant disturbance. She was an obsessional, hard-driving, and at times explosive woman. She had been very bitter and frustrated about what she perceived were her own limitations and lack of accomplishments (despite the fact that realistically her accomplishments had been considerable), and she clearly desired her only son to prosper, develop, and unfold along exceptional lines.

Jonathan had never lived up to his mother's expectations despite an intense investment in early training for good work habits and basic skills. For example, during Jonathan's early years (ages 2–6) the family had lived in South America because of father's business requirements. Jonathan therefore had to become proficient in a number of languages at an early age, and his mother was determined to develop these skills. She was intensely disappointed in her son's "immaturity"—Jonathan did not learn rapidly, his memory was poor, and when he began writing, he reversed letters and fought instruction. Mother was angry and critical. Another area of marked good habit training was cleanliness. The bathrooms of South America did not meet American and Mrs. K's standards; they were dirty and polluted. Jonathan was supposedly trained for bowel and bladder at

2½ years, primarily by his mother. His mother inspected him often to make sure he was clean and instructed him closely on tooth brushing since she felt it was critical to remove all plaque. Jonathan was always frightened of the bathroom, and although bowel trained, he tended to "leak" occasionally. By age 3½, the leak seemed to become a more regular "streak." At 4½, when Jonathan prematurely entered a rather demanding preprimer school, the streak became a steady stream. Jonathan had been soiling ever since.

For the first 4 months of treatment, it was exceedingly difficult to engage this youngster. His verbal elaborations were confusing and tangential. He also busied himself by obsessively building structures out of Legos® that kept him safely hidden. For example, he painstakingly built a skyscraper Lego building 20 stories high with four porches on each floor. He then proceeded to place a green clay pellet and a yellow clay pellet on every porch. These were decorative plants for each outdoor porch, so that with a total of 80 porches, we were dealing with the concentrated effort of carefully and meticulously placing 160 clay pellets. This compulsive "smokescreen" Jonathan emitted distanced the therapist. Jonathan would give cursory attention to anything the therapist said, but then dart quickly back to his safe, absorbing activities.

The therapist attempted to enter into the play so that it could become verbally elaborated. He asked many questions about the construction. Where was it located? Who lived in the skyscrapers? What was the name of the construction company? He also drove trucks filled with blocks or plants to the construction site, but Jonathan turned his back on the attempts at engagement and answered no questions. It was clear that Jonathan felt unsafe, and he was attempting to create his own isolated world.

There were a few occasions of meaningful interchange. During one session, Jonathan's Legos became people playing in a schoolyard. All of the children were clustered together, romping around, but one Lego was left out. He circled about and tried looking in from a distance. We found that this Lego was called "dumb" and "retard," and Jonathan looked very sad. The therapist noted his sadness and asked how being left out made him feel. The therapist commented though that someone who never handed in any work could get the reputation of "dumb" and "retard," even if he was smart. Later in the hour, the therapist wondered if the Lego was also called "smelly." Jonathan shook his head "no" but showed him how all the other Legos held their noses tauntingly at the boy. This interaction gave the therapist an opportunity to point out how sad and left out Jonathan's soiling problem and school problem made him feel. He explained how strong inside worries and feelings caused these problems and that a special way we have to change these inside feelings is through imagination and through play. Play, he told Jonathan, is our work. This is a condensed version of the ground rules and purposes of the work the therapist spelled out as opportunities presented themselves in this initial period.

Discussion

At this point the therapist chose to make a number of interventions directly about Jonathan. He spoke of Jonathan's sadness about his being left out because of school difficulties and soiling problems. At times, when a child is engaged in play, the therapist has a choice— his comments can be directly about the child as above, or he can comment within the play metaphor. For example, he could have talked about how the "Lego boy" felt rather than how Jonathan must feel. Interpretation within the play metaphor is a common technique in child work. If the therapist senses that his direct intervention will raise too much anxiety, he has the alternative of commenting on the characters within the play.

The therapist was also defining and outlining the special medium of communication in child psychotherapy. He explained to Jonathan how, with many children, their internal life will emerge in play and how he anticipated Jonathan would use the materials of the office and his own mind to slowly replay his internal life to both the therapist and himself. The terms the therapist used, "imagination," "stories," "books," "pictures," referred to the useful raw material that they could use to understand problems and worries. It is critical to make this explicit to the child patient and to set the expectations for their work together. Most children will passively comply with the task the therapist outlines. This is a one-sided contract, similar to the arrangement most children make at school, where they "go along" with the demands or tasks set forth by the teacher.

If the child therapist provides a variety of material and toys that can be used for projection (e.g., paper, crayons, dolls, soldiers, puppets, in contrast to structured games), most children will begin using these toys after a period of time. These activities are safe and familiar and also can provide a safe and appropriate distance from the stranger-therapist. It is generally helpful not to have board games, cards, checkers, etc. that have a built-in format. If the child uses these media extensively, he has a vehicle to avoid using his "imagination" and internal life. There are some exceptions, since there are some children who are so chaotic that they can use the structured format to feel safe and calm.

An early task in the work is to slowly help the child work toward "meaningful play" (Peller, 1954; Beres, 1957). *Meaningful play* is play in which there is a creative balance between id derivatives and ego functions, an easy back and forth between the two. In terms of the quality of their play, either young children tend to become instinctually flooded by their play or (like Jonathan) the play lacks adequate instinctual derivatives and serves the function of phobic defense. With the overinstinctualized child, the task is slowly to bring more structure (ego) into the play (for example, help the child develop a story around his chaotic play that has a beginning, a middle, and end). Mark (the child patient in Chapter 1) brought overinstinctualized play into the early phases of treatment. Any play quickly induced wild behavior and chaos. The therapist sought to make it coherent when he introduced the game of "torture chamber," and the direction changed somewhat. Mark played out his terror, but in the game the therapist and Mark assigned words to the intense game. Once there was a mixture of the raw play (id derivatives) as well as verbalization (ego functions), Mark's play became more meaningful and useful in the treatment process. The therapist could comment on Mark's early fears, and since Mark's affects were somewhat held at bay, he could better listen and integrate the therapist's words.

Jonathan's early play represented the other end of the spectrum. His tedious, complex Lego structures represented his obsessional rituals and comprised part of a frozen mode of behavior that he was compelled to construct over and over again. When the therapist commented to Jonathan about "inside feelings" and that "play, *imagination* is our work," he anticipated with his patient the need for greater freedom to emerge eventually in the quality of Jonathan's play. The eventual goal of treatment with Jonathan was to have his forbidden instinctual life (e.g., his anal sadism) emerge in play and for him to become more tolerant of these aspects of his personality.

There are some important technical differences in child and adult work at times, particularly in dealing with resistance. One could clarify with an adult patient how he brings material. For example, with an adult obsessional patient who might bring his verbal material in great and exquisite detail, the therapist might call to his attention that through an elaborate overlay of detail, he seems to be avoiding feelings. Ordinarily, because of the nature of the alliance, most adult patients will make conscious efforts to bring their affects or work on why this is so difficult. However Jonathan, if confronted, like many child patients, would tend to continue to build his tedious skyscrapers, perhaps adding more floors, porches, and outdoor clay pellets until he had constructed an entire city. Children do not share the same alliance as adults and fear the anxiety of moving away from something familiar. If the play does not get sufficiently "animated," the therapist should point out that this play does not help the work and directly limit the resistance. The therapist commented to Jonathan that since he likes building, he could build his structures for a period of time (e.g., 10 minutes of the hour), but then it would be important to do things that were more helpful.

In terms of the nature of the alliance, children tend to externalize their inner conflicts, making *sustained* motivation for work more difficult (A. Freud, 1965). An ongoing task in child treatment is to restimulate the awareness of the internal nature of the difficulties. The child patient is made aware that the rejected "Lego® boy" in the playground is called "retarded" and "smelly" because he has a school problem and a soiling problem. The therapist also points out that this special play can help many boys with problems such as these. Thus, the therapist highlights the internal concerns so that therapist and patient can come to share similar goals. The purpose is to specifically make the "play-work" a contributory process in conjunction with the therapist. The child contributes through his stories and play. The child therapist slowly erects the standards for the *quality* of the material to emerge and defines and redefines the purpose for the work in ways the child can understand.

EARLY PHASE OF AFFECTIVE ENGAGEMENT

Clinical Material

As Jonathan searched for a new medium to use, he came upon the clay in the office and began to use it each hour. The therapist offered Jonathan whatever help he needed with the clay. Under Jonathan's direction, they mixed all the colors to get a dirty gray. The therapist's function was to kneed and soften the hard clay so that they could develop flat writing tablets. They sent messages to each other invented by Jonathan—usually simply rhyming words. Jonathan then developed an interesting game. A tiny Lego person stood in the middle of our large play table, and a huge clay bomb was tossed high in the air to see if it could destroy the victim. The pleasure in the game, however, became the special sound effects that emerged as the clay hit the Formica® top, the "smack" and "whomp" sounds. The white Formica top was also often smeared and streaked by the time they finished, with the therapist following Jonathan's lead. The sessions began to develop an anal ambience with hard and soft clay bombs, streaks, and smears on the white table top and the "whomp" sounds of flatulence.

Jonathan, now with some greater freedom, began to rummage in the wastepaper basket searching for "junk" (his word) such as used light bulbs, spent ink cartridges, empty Kleenex boxes. He tried to steal those items that interested him most. The therapist interceded and suggested that they create a special "junk drawer" where all the discards could be collected. Jonathan was very interested and added frequently to his collection. In fact, the therapist began, between their appointments, to keep items from going directly into the trash so that Jonathan could determine what would be sorted into his drawer and what would be totally dispensable. The parents noted that Jonathan's attitude toward therapy had improved. Instead of his typical noncommittal stance, Jonathan was eager to come and hurried his mother so no time could be lost. At times he looked at his collection in the drawer fondly and added some items he had brought into the office from outside. The therapist began to make some comments: "Jonathan was showing me that his junk was very special and very precious. He was showing me that he didn't want any of his junk to ever be thrown out or lost."

Discussion

Jonathan, like many latency-aged children, at first found it difficult to express the forbidden instinctual derivatives in his material. How do we help the child patient bring these aspects of his internal life into the hour? How do we foster the necessary "regression in the service of the ego" in child work? This is a term used in adult psychotherapy to describe how the adult patient slowly relaxes the normal taboos and barriers in his thinking and verbalizes these thoughts so that he and the therapist can examine his internal emotional life. The adult psychotherapist "permits" this regression through his nonjudgmental attitude and through encouraging free association.

With many patients in child work, the therapist has a critical role in fostering a similar "regression in the service of the ego." Since the child uses play as a central medium, the therapist's involvement also has a reciprocal action component. It is often very helpful for the therapist to become a *player*. For example, in the above material, when Jonathan left behind his obsessional Lego structures and turned to the clay, the therapist joined in. Under the child's direction, the therapist also squeezed and shaped the mess of clay. When they removed the clay from the white table, smear marks were left. The therapist was aware that the clay activity was an instinctual expression of Jonathan's anal, messy, forbidden feelings. Thus, by the therapist's actions and as a player, he permitted a regression (display of these early childhood feelings) so that they both could explore this further. This shared play (always under the direction of the child) further developed. The clay bomb game emerged, with the loud flatulence sounds. The junk drawer developed where all special discards were saved. Thus, anal affects of smearing, squeezing, and hoarding became expressed in the office under the aegis of the therapist. The play becomes a shared affective experience, and a special language and metaphor developed between the two ("junk," "junk drawer," etc.). London (1981) notes that in an effective psychotherapy, the patient develops a growing tolerance of id derivatives through an identification with the therapist. The anxious child patient, like Jonathan, is not left by himself with this material since the therapist (by his active participation) sanctioned this expression.

Within the play, the environment must be secure enough so that the child can risk this forbidden expression. The therapist needs to create boundaries within the sessions, so that an effective "holding environment" (Winnicott, 1953) will emerge. Although Jonathan and his therapist entered the anal world of pleasure, each session had an ending "clean-up" time when the office was repaired to its former state. When Jonathan sought to "borrow" the items he found from the office, he learned the rule that all "junk" had to remain within the playroom. These special boundaries became defined in action, and they slowly began to have an internalizing function for the child patient. He can become aware that the regressive experience within the hour is separate from ordinary life, limited by time and space. He becomes aware that the pleasures he experiences in the hour stand outside of his immediate real wants and appetites (he cannot steal the junk to take home). The therapist, within the structure of the play, acts as an auxiliary ego to create the necessary boundaries. In addition, the dual function of the therapist as *player* and *observer* also has a binding and limiting effect. The therapist (as the observer) comments to Jonathan that "Jonathan treats his junk as very precious and special and is afraid to lose any of his junk." As the observer, the therapist implicitly imparts that the play is not for pleasure alone but has a serious important purpose to be looked at and understood.

Again, the early processes in work with the child patient, using the medium of play, parallel the early stages of adult treatment. The unstructured quality within the therapeutic hour, the accepting attitudes of the therapist toward forbidden instinctual material, and the boundaries of the session itself foster the early "regression in the service of the ego" in both adult and child work.

As meaningful play intensifies, we often note that the child patient develops a sense of absorption, enjoyment, and intensity. What is the nature of this positive affective response to treatment? There is clearly some direct pleasure in the expression of the instinctual derivatives. In addition, the child experiences some mastery over the anxiety that would normally emerge as forbidden material is expressed (Waelder, 1933). Within the play, he learns to titrate and dose the accompanying anxiety so that it will be in manageable levels. But most important, within the sessions, children often experience a new sense of freedom. Because of the absence of the demands of reality and the absence of superego restraints, the child allows himself, at times, to experience feelings that have been stifled in the service of defense for years. Jonathan now plays openly and directly with his junk in full view of his therapist. It is this sense of freedom that promotes the pleasure investment.

EMERGENCE OF CENTRAL FANTASIES

Clinical Material

When Jonathan announced that he had a "great idea," the therapist was rather stunned, since spontaneity was not one of his virtues.

With great enthusiasm, Jonathan announced that he was going to build a racetrack with all the junk they had collected. He also rounded up extra junk that was not evident, everywhere in the office (bits of crayons, pencil stubs, strings as well as clay). In that first session in this sequence, the therapist watched Jonathan build a complicated racetrack that had jumps, traps, slalom obstacles, etc. Jonathan worked with extreme diligence. Jonathan directed that the therapist become a rich owner who had hired a special construction engineer (Jonathan) to develop this racetrack. The owner was instructed to be very impressed with this intriguing structure that emerged totally out of junk. This scenario was followed out in play. However, with about 10 minutes left in the hour, Jonathan became very anxious, and the therapist verbalized his worry. What will happen to the track when the hour ends, will it get lost? Since it covered the work table of general use it would have to be dismantled. After a few minutes of intense anxiety, Jonathan had another "great idea." He meticulously drew a precise pattern of the track so that it would not be lost, and he could then recreate it at will in the future. When he had dismantled the track, he took it apart in the exact reverse order that he had built it—the last item of the track was the first deposited in the drawer, etc., until the track had been totally taken apart.

Over the next few weeks Jonathan built replicas of his first track and then elaborated, creating new and more complex racetracks with more items from the office. They featured greater and greater obstacles and more involved twists and turns for the drivers. (Races were, by the way, never held.) The sessions ended with the familiar blueprint recording and the reverse dismantling process. The therapist was, as the audience in the play, very interested and impressed with his work and would tell other potential racetrack owners of his unique construction skills. As the observer, he had repeated opportunities to comment on a number of themes: "sometimes when boys are little, they are very scared their precious junk will be lost and flushed away, so they hold it in as hard as they can. When it comes out, they want someone to appreciate it and enjoy the special present. As they grow up, they sometimes worry about all the things that come out of them—not only their BMs but later even the *ideas* that come out of their brain. They have downstairs worries that their BMs will get lost, and later upstairs worries that their mind ideas will get lost." The parents began to report some major changes in

Jonathan. Jonathan's soiling was markedly decreasing, and his schoolwork began to improve. He began handing in assignments in a number of areas in school.

Discussion

Jonathan began to bring some central and important fantasies into his play that emerged because of the "compulsion to repeat." Freud (1914) initially introduced this concept when he noted that past traumatic experience gets repeated in the patient's life in action over and over again, but it is also kept from consciousness by the patient. The child's play is characterized by the "compulsion to repeat." Ritvo (1978) describes this process fully. He notes that in play, ideation is connected with wishes and conflicts return from repression (are lived out where they were formally hidden), and these ideas receive representation in the play characters. He maintains that there is a quality of persistence and continuity in the treatment sessions, though the child (like the adult patient) will have little conscious awareness of the process. What impells this need to repeat? Again, Freud and others (e.g., Plaut, 1974) note that, on an unconscious basis, individuals attempt to master past anxiety and pain by reexperiencing the events in an active rather than passive way. The repetition is also a way of achieving some gratification.

These concepts can be applied to the racetrack play episodes that Jonathan brought repeatedly into the treatment hour. A central problem in Jonathan's life was production: he refused to produce his bowel productions or his mind products in school. Because of early traumatic experiences (involving toilet training and learning) with his mother, he anticipated that his products would be disgusting and despised by the person who demanded his productions. He was both frightened of producing and angry, so he passively withheld. When he introduced a "great idea" (the racetrack), Jonathan unconsciously began to reproduce the past. He set up the play to live out producing (it is interesting that he used the waste products of the office). This time he created a character in the rich owner (parent substitute) who admired his products enormously. Jonathan thus reproduced the past. He produced his waste. Rather than being greeted by an important libidinal object who found his products contemptible, the rich owner-therapist was conceived to express delight in his creativity. In his new repetitive play, he attempted to deal actively with the past overpowering situation. He defecated symbolically and received love and admiration from the object, a reversal of the past. In this new format, he tried to master the past by changing and controlling the outcome.

Freud (1914) went on to describe the enormous potential therapeutic value of the "compulsion to repeat." "Past experience can be rendered harmless by virtue of its admission into the transference as a playground in which it is allowed to expand in almost complete freedom, and in which it is expected to display to us everything in the way of pathogenic instincts that is hidden in the patient's mind." Two elements are important in this statement. One is the concept of the transference. The therapist (the transference figure) will often become the representative of an important person of the past. Secondly, Freud refers to the display of pathogenic instincts that is hidden in the patient's mind. What does Jonathan display in his repeated play? On one level, he played out his childhood fear that when something (his feces) is produced, it can be separated and lost from his body. Therefore, he desperately attempted to retain so that he would avoid body damage. This was an unconscious idea but an extremely powerful one in his life. This was visibly enacted in treatment when he produced the racetrack and the treatment hour was about to end. Would his creation be lost and flushed away again? He turned white with fear. Thus, a powerful pathogenic ingredient in Jonathan's life was the maintenance and persistence of his unconscious fantasy. He could not let go of his bowels or his cerebral productions because of the internal childhood fear that he was losing his body. This fear controlled his current functioning and made him symptomatic.

How does change take place, and how can we trace the elements that allowed Jonathan to decrease his soiling and begin to hand in his work at school? Many authors have described the change process in psychotherapy. Essentially in the new transference (replayed) situation there is a special opportunity. The therapist has an opportunity to make interpretations, to help the patient understand the unconscious idea and anxieties that control him. The rational (ego) part of the patient can potentially grasp the meaning of the fear that controls him as it is put into words by the therapist, and this understanding (insight) will begin to defuse the power of that fear.

When Jonathan repeatedly showed in his play the terror that his (racetrack) waste product would be lost, the therapist interpreted the worry over and over again for the child patient. "Jonathan was frightened his product would be lost forever. He confused the racetrack with parts of his body. This idea came from feelings many boys have when they are little: they are afraid when they have a BM that it is like a part of them; so they cry when the BM is flushed, and they fight going to the bathroom. Now Jonathan is afraid to let go of his BMs, just like the racetrack and all of his papers in school." In his sessions, Jonathan grapples with these interpretations, not in words, but in his actions. He developed the blueprint idea. He built, dismantled, and rebuilt his structures using his new blueprints, and he slowly developed a new way of representational retention. He learned that even though he "flushed away" his racetrack, it was not lost forever. This appeared to be an important developmental step that Jonathan could not traverse earlier because of childhood trauma. The repetitious play, the comments of the player–observer, and his own new solution helped him assimilate a past overpowering experience. He made a new accommodation: he learned that all is not *really* lost if it is separated from his body.

In the above situation, Jonathan's functioning changed because he had gained "insight." He came to understand aspects of his functioning (soiling) that were driven by an unconscious fantasy (body loss), and he altered his functioning because of his new understanding. Producing insight through interpretation is the cornerstone of uncovering psychotherapy. Insights have two components—an affective component and a cognitive component—and they need to work in unison. In the above material both were present. Jonathan affectively experienced the anxiety of body loss as his racetrack was to be dismantled, and he cognitively assimilated the knowledge that this feeling was an irrational fear as the therapist interpreted his worry.

In some ways, however, insight in child work differs from insight in adult work. Effective insight with children is often limited to the "here and now" experience, whereas the adult patient (with more fully developed ego resources) can often explore more derivatives of the past using free association. The therapist limited his interpretations with Jonathan to the "here and now" body anxiety feelings and their implications for producing ideas and feces. There were aspects the therapist left untouched. In the transference play with the therapist, Jonathan created a new "parent," the rich owner, who was the opposite of the old depreciating mother. A possible direction of interpretive work could have been to highlight the defense (e.g., "Jonathan is having the rich owner praise his work so that he doesn't need to remember his old mother who didn't like what came out"). The defenses of denial or reversal of affect were in use. The therapist chose not to develop this line because he felt that the ego resources were limited in dealing with memories of the past "toilet-training" mother. In child work, the ability of the child to reconstruct the past is generally limited.

Despite the fact that in the process of play, children repeat the past in action, there is very often a major resistance to understanding the material that is unfolding. The child is often driven to bring out this material of the past (e.g., the struggle with production, in Jonathan's case) because the instinctual life seeks expression. This does not necessarily mean that the child patient expresses these fantasies as part of an alliance. Many children will simultaneously play out an important struggle but react very strongly when the therapist attempts to put meaning to the play. "I'm just playing . . . shut up" is an extremely frequent reaction. Children often use the mechanism of "splitting of the ego" in the service of defense. They play out the past problems symbolically to discharge anxiety but resist learning of their meaning consciously, since this would induce anxiety. This does not mean the therapist should not continue to make the play intelligible to the child patient. Often the therapist gets upset and angry about the child's ability to dismiss his or her interventions. Since the function of self-awareness is less developed in children, it is often helpful to stimulate this function. One might comment, when the child avoids the therapist's verbal intervention, "It is hard to let your 'thinker' work today," or "your 'thinker' seems to be running away." In the clinical material with Jonathan, there was no verbal acknowledgment of the therapist's comments about body loss, but Jonathan seemed to respond in his play. By constructing the blueprints, he clearly demonstrated that he was finding a new solution to potential loss because he was able to use the therapist's interpretations.

PERIOD OF WORKING THROUGH

Clinical Material

After the racetrack sessions, Jonathan began meticulously to draw a series of "inventions" that went into a special inventions folder. A dirty-looking penny contained (when opened up) the tiniest solar-powered telephone or a unique battery-powered watch. A simple-looking pen-knife on the outside opened with 15 incredible interior "blades." If he looked closely, he would find each blade had special functions—one blade was a color TV set; next to it was a blade with a magnifying glass so that one could view the set more closely; another blade supported a small digital clock; a fourth held a hi-fi set with an adjacent "blade" that contained tiny cassettes for the amplifier. These drawings were blown up in size and contained the details of all the knobs and buttons necessary to use the complicated machines. Again, the therapist as the rich owner in play was directed to be interested not only in racetracks but also in the inventions. The therapist noted that behind what might look like junk on the outside existed a very complicated machine, full of wonderful ideas and inventions. He thought even other rich owners would be interested in the patents. In a difference voice, as the therapist–observer, he began to deal with Jonathan's sense of omnipotence. He noted that sometimes boys held on to their ideas because they wanted to believe forever that they were superincredible. They were afraid to find out that they were really just like other people and not really so super-special. Jonathan smiled and told the therapist that his work in school was really very boring.

In the years after this material emerged, Jonathan's academic growth was solid and sustained. This was not the case with the soiling symptom, which came and went, related to subsequent issues in the treatment. For example, there was a major period in the treatment when Jonathan tauntingly withheld and produced only barren, constipated stories. He pleasurably and sadistically deprived the therapist of the products they needed for their work. Jonathan loved to rouse desire and expectation and then provide his therapist with small and insignificant satisfaction. They spent much time on his powerful, negative "Mr. Opposite" feelings, which were intended to get back at the therapist in much the same way he wanted to get back at his mother. This phase was accompanied by much soiling and streaking. Eventually, Jonathan became symptom-free.

Discussion

The invention material, following the racetrack play, illustrates two important concepts in psychotherapy: the concepts of "multiple determination" and "working through." It often becomes clear, as one works with a patient, that specific symptoms or behaviors are complex and carry more than one meaning. Often several conflicts will come together to form a specific symptom, and therefore practitioners often note that a clinical problem is multiply determined. In Jonathan's withholding symptom, he expressed several conflicts that had coalesced in his mind. On one level this symptom was fostered by his unconscious fear that he would lose a part of his body as his products emerged from him. When Jonathan brought his invention play, he expressed another motivation for his withholding. He had another unconscious fantasy that his products were incredibly brilliant (omnipotent), and he wanted to keep this idea hidden. If he exposed this idea (his inventions), he might learn that it was not true, and a motivation for his withholding was to maintain the self-enhancing illusion. Therefore, in Jonathan's play, he evidenced multiple aspects of his withholding problem.

In psychotherapy, when we speak of the concept of "working through," we refer to a series and variety of interpretations that are necessary to effect change in a symptom. Changes do not occur with one interpretation, but various elements that are part of the symptom's formation need to be addressed repeatedly, in different contexts, until the varied levels of unconscious meaning are worked out (worked through). In addressing the symptom that Jonathan presented, the therapist made a variety of interpretations over a period of several months aimed at various aspects of Jonathan's conflicts that went into the withholding problem. As noted before, he interpreted Jonathan's unconscious fear that his waste (junk, BM) was a part of his body. Second, he made the connection explicit that Jonathan linked his anal products with his brain products. In the later work on the inventions, he also made a series of interpretations. He made conscious for Jonathan his secret idea that he was very brilliant and "superspecial." In addition, the therapist interpreted that Jonathan was frightened that this idea would not be true and that he withheld (e.g., in school) so that he would not risk learning the reality. In order to effect change in Jonathan, various aspects of his conflicts needed to be "worked through," or brought to his consciousness repeatedly, and the multiple meanings of his symptoms had to be dealt with.

Earlier in this volume, it was suggested there might be problems with using methodology from the adult process of psychotherapy when doing therapeutic work with children. Nonetheless, it is implict that there are both parallels and divergences in the treatment process with adults and children. In adult and child psychotherapy there are clear similarities as we observe the therapeutic process: an assessment of how the patient produces material and the nature of defense/resistance during the treatment hour; the process of producing a "regression in the service of the ego," which is enhanced by both the empathic capacity of the therapist and his ability to establish boundaries of the treatment hour; the growing libidinal attachment to the therapist, which permits the safe emergence of the "compulsion to repeat" past traumatic events within the transference. Essentially, then, there are specific and clear parallels in the unfolding treatment process in child and adult patients.

The major divergence is the form of communication. The language of the child is more concrete, and the dialogue between patient and therapist is often in action and behavior, the language of play. Because of the need for action, the therapist becomes, in part, a *player* under the direction of the child patient. The therapist, as player, represents the transference aspect of the treatment relationship, and the therapist as *observer* represents the therapeutic alliance aspects of the relationship. In work with children, some parameters can more easily emerge. Since play by the child patient lends itself to greater ambiguity and does not have the immediate "confirmatory" quality of verbalization, there are added risks to understanding the treatment communication. It is clear, however, as we more fully understand the play language of the child, that these ambiguities do eventually become decipherable.

BIBLIOGRAPHY

Anthony, E. J. (1986). The contribution of child psychoanalysis. *Psychoanalytic Study of the Child* 41:61–87.
Beres, D. (1957). Communication in psychoanalysis and in the creative process. *Journal of the American Psychoanalytic Association* 5:408–489.
Fraiberg, S. (1965). A comparison of the analytic method in two stages of a child analysis. *Journal of the American Academy of Child Psychiatry* 4:387–400.
Freud, A. (1965). *Normality and Pathology in Childhood*. New York: International University Press.

Freud, S. (1914). *Remembering, Repeating and Working Through* (standard ed.), Vol. 12 (pp. 147–156). London: Hogarth Press, 1958.

Freud, S. (1920). *Beyond the Pleasure Principle* (standard ed.), Vol. 18 (pp. 3–64). London: Hogarth Press, 1958.

Greenacre, P. (1971). Play in relation to creative imagination. In: *Emotional growth*, Vol. II. New York: International University Press.

London, N. (1981). The play element of regression in the psychoanalytic process. *Psychoanalytic Inquiry* 1(1):7–27.

Maenchen, A. (1970). On the technique of child analysis in relation to the stress of development. *Psychoanalytic Study of the Child* XXV:175–208.

Nagera, H. (1981). The problem of insight: A comparison between children and adults. In: *The Developmental Approach to Childhood Psychopathology*. New York: Aronson. pp. 129–154.

Peller, L. (1954). Libidinal phases, ego development and play. *Psychoanalytic Study of the Child* IX:178–198.

Plaut, E. (1979). Play and adaptation. *Psychoanalytic Study of the Child* 34:217–232.

Ritvo, S. (1978). The psychoanalytic process in childhood. *Psychoanalytic Study of the Child* 33:295–305.

Sandler, J., Kennedy, H., & Tyson, P. (1980). *The Technique of Child Psychoanalysis*. Cambridge, MA: Harvard University Press.

Waelder, R. (1933). The psychoanalytic theory of play. *Psychoanalytic Quarterly* 2:208–224.

Winnicott, D. W. (1953). Transitional objects and transitional phenomena. *International Journal of Psychoanalysis* 34:89–97.

PART II

THE PROCESS OF TREATMENT

Introduction

This part introduces the reader to both the major psychopathologies of childhood as well as to the specific treatment process for each of these pathologies. There are several chapters on the neurotic child (Chapters 4 and 5) as well as chapters on children with character pathology (Chapter 6) and borderline and narcissistic disturbances (Chapters 7 and 8). This part concludes with a chapter (Chapter 9) on reactive disorders in children, illustrated by the treatment of divorce and bereavement cases in childhood.

Throughout these chapters the general natures of these different pathologies are discussed. From this material, for example, the reader can come to understand what is meant by childhood neurosis and how it differs from character pathology in children. In each chapter there is not only a general discussion of the pathology but a full case illustration that is descriptive and discusses the underlying psychodynamics.

Each disturbance presents the therapist with different treatment problems and calls for different techniques and interventions. The major focus of each chapter highlights these issues. The author describes the process of insight-oriented psychotherapy with neurotic children, the process of defense analysis with children with character pathology, the supportive techniques with severely disturbed borderline youngsters, etc.

There is an additional theme that weaves through this section as well. In the literature there are a number of basic concepts of psychotherapy that help the practitioner to organize and evaluate the ongoing process of treatment. The concepts of "therapeutic alliance," "resistance," "transference," "countertransference," etc. are used to assess the treatment process. Throughout these chapters these concepts are defined and discussed as they emerge in the clinical material. For example, one can follow the nature of the therapeutic alliance in children and see how it differs in neurotic, character-disordered, and borderline youngsters. Many of these concepts have been discussed primarily with respect to adult work, and therefore the author attempts at points to define and reshape them in terms of child patients.

4

*Treatment of the Neurotic Child**

This chapter has a twofold purpose. A major focus is on the process of treating neurotic children—that is, specific techniques highlighting the use of uncovering interpretations and the utilization of transference are presented. Another major purpose is the introduction and definition of the important psychotherapeutic concepts that help to provide a framework for and assess the treatment process. These concepts have been derived primarily from adult psychodynamic psychotherapy. Both the focus on the concepts themselves and the techniques with the neurotic child are discussed in conjunction with a clinical presentation.

The case of Fred, an 11-year-old obsessional male in residential placement is presented and a technical assessment follows the evaluative material. Fred presents somewhat like an adult patient for two reasons. First, he is an obsessional patient. Obsessional youngsters often precociously develop many ego functions (e.g., memory, intelligence, secondary thought processes) and are therefore able to develop highly structured and enduring defenses that have an adult-like form (there is a stabilization of their egos, and they tend to use verbalization extensively). Secondly, Fred is moving out of childhood into early adolescence, and we see the natural development of many ego functions. Thus, when psychotherapeutic concepts are discussed

*A version of this chapter, "The Therapy of an Obsessive Compulsive," by M. Chethik, was published in *Journal of the American Academy of Child Psychiatry*, July 1969, Vol. 8, No. 3, pp. 465–484.

71

and illustrated in this chapter, there is something of an adult quality to the definitions. In Chapter 5, a second neurotic case (Amy) is reviewed that is much more childlike in character. The psychotherapeutic concepts are reworked in the next chapter in an attempt to integrate more of the features of childhood. There is also an opportunity to discuss the dimension of age (older and younger child) and its implications for treatment as we compare these cases.

FRED: BACKGROUND, HISTORY, AND THE PRESENTING PICTURE IN TREATMENT

Fred had been in treatment for a 3-year period, between the ages of 11 and 14. During his treatment he lived at Sagebrook, a residential treatment center for emotionally disturbed children.

Fred had initially been referred because of growing problems during his latency years. His school performance had caused his parents increasing concern. Although he was well-behaved and intelligent, he evidenced many severe symptoms that made it hard for him to function on a daily basis.

Within his home there had always been a great deal of tension. There was much constant conflict between the parents. The mother complained of her husband's violence and uncontrollable rage with the children, his social bluntness and inappropriateness, and his "obsession" with dirt in the house (particularly in the bathroom). In turn, the husband felt that his wife was stubborn and insensitive to his needs and feelings. Both were aware of their marital difficulties.

The father was a driving, aggressive, successful businessman who tyrannized the household. In contrast, the mother was quiet and ineffective with her children. She lacked any self-assurance, and her constant self-questioning and self-effacing made it difficult for her to act decisively and set limits for her four children. The home was characterized by uproar during the day with mother at the helm and severe repression during the evening when father returned from work.

An evident fighting and sadistic interplay existed between father and son. Conflict between them had begun during Fred's earliest years. A pattern of stubborn refusal and resistance by Fred was met by overwhelming force and suppression by his father. During Fred's second year, he developed what his parents perceived to be some eating difficulties. He refused many foods, and the mother's anxiety and helplessness mounted. His father resolved to "make" Fred eat, and he was tied to the highchair for all evening meals. Similarly, it was the father who struggled with Fred about bowel training. Fred was often hit for his infractions, as this symptom particularly disturbed his father. Furthermore, the father handled Fred's insistence on climbing out of the crib by locking him in his room. During Fred's later childhood years, many little attempts at assertion were often similarly interpreted as "defiance." Coming in late for supper, climbing trees, and wading in a nearby brook were all events that were met with harsh and unrealistic punishments.

It is important to note that behind the father's "tough" appearance, there were glimpses of softness and fearfulness. As he described moments when his rage made him beat Fred, he became tearfully guilty and frightened by his own aggression. There were many occasions he sought to undo the damage, and there were short-lived periods when father and son enjoyed each other.

Fred's own temper, however, became a dominant theme during his preschool and early elementary school years. The excessive roughness he exhibited with other children in nursery school at age 3 and 4 had precipitated the initial contact with a guidance clinic. The clinic's impression was that Fred was a very tense and frightened child, as well as an enraged one. When Fred was 5½, his mother returned to the clinic because of Fred's continued impulsive aggression toward schoolmates and her management difficulties with him at home. The mother also noted that although they did not get along well when they were together, Fred had many fears of separation from her, particularly in accepting babysitters.

During Fred's eighth year, the parents noted some important changes. Fred appeared much more polite and well-behaved outside the home, but his academic problems and difficulties in going to sleep became acute. He was unable to concentrate, follow directions, or complete assignments. He developed fears of dirt, touching the walls, and going outside into the street. These fears could become extensive and incapacitating. An extensive evaluation indicated there were many internalized problems, and since there were multiple pressures within the home as well, placement was recommended. It took several years and increasing symptom intensity before placement was actually effected.

During Fred's initial year at Sagebrook, the effective outer controls that were developing were maintained. He still appeared to be a manageable youngster who was cooperative, conforming, and thoughtful.

From his first session, Fred seemed to take his treatment seriously. When he entered the room, he carefully laid down his jacket, seated himself at the edge of the chair facing the therapist, and stiffly proceeded to talk. Fred impressed the therapist as a "little intellectual." He was small and dark with a thin frame. His glasses appeared very prominent on his face, and his use of words and phrases indicated he was well-read and knowledgeable. Fred totally related to the treatment in this studious manner. He was intent on talking, and in the first year, with no exception, he never left the chair that faced the therapist for any reason (to use play equipment, go to the bathroom, or even stretch).

In the first session Fred outlined many difficulties and "deep worries" in abundant and precise detail, and although he spoke quietly and carefully, it was evident that he was quite pained and troubled about his symptoms.

He was worried about his schoolwork. He felt that he was slower in math than the other children. In the time that they were able to do four to five pages of a long division assignment, he would linger over one page. This was because he was concerned about errors, and he laboriously checked and rechecked his work. He felt that reading was a problem too. For some reason he needed to read very quickly. He read almost continuously and devoured many books weekly, but he was troubled because by rushing through the pages, he often did not have time to understand the content. He was interested in reading *sets* of books and was now working his way through a 25-volume series by the same publisher. (These books also had similar bindings.)

Fred mentioned some of his fears during that first hour, primarily animal fears, and he elaborated on them during the first few weeks of treatment. He was concerned about bee stings and about the cats that came onto the campus. At night his imagination would sometimes control his thoughts, and the alley cats would turn into "bobcats" hiding behind the shade in his room. Mosquitoes became troubling, particularly because they extract blood; he described a fantasy of swallowing a mosquito while he was asleep. He feared the mosquito would find its way into his heart and pierce the wall with its stinger. He commented on the fantasy's irrationality, yet he noted he could not stop the growth of such worries. Sometimes in the morning he was convinced there was a bull under his bed. Afraid to put his feet on the floor because it would attract the animal, he would gather his clothing very quickly and dress in the bathroom. At times he would decide to lie quietly, but the elaboration and escalation of his fears would continue. The thought would come that as he lay still, the horns of the bull would soon pierce the mattress. Often one could sense in Fred the new underlying wishes and impulses breaking through, followed by the new elaborate fear-defense.

He was concerned about his eating habits. At times he ate little. Smells disturbed him, and the milk seemed to have a trace of ketchup. Pudding often had lumps in it; liver and tomatoes gave him a choking feeling; hamburgers had grease on them, and on and on. He often felt great disgust in the dining room. As with his animal fears, his food aversion would dramatically spread. Some days, only the long-established dislikes were avoided, but on other days, Fred might eat absolutely nothing at mealtimes. He vacillated. At times this was an external problem because of the horrible food standards at Sagebrook. At other times, however, he recognized that his eating difficulties had existed at home and in restaurants as well. On one occasion during that early period he said, "If I didn't have to eat in order to live, I would give up food entirely."

There was also one plaguing memory. Fred wanted to confess that about a year prior to his placement he threw a large rock and killed a baby mouse near his home. It left a red stain on the driveway. He had tried twice to wash the spot away, but for a month he had to walk by and see it every day. As he described his memory (which he repeatedly referred to), he could not contain the smile of pleasure that broke through. At the start of treatment, this last memory was the only direct allusion to some problem with his inner aggression.

The therapist was somewhat surprised with these initial interviews, surprised because they seemed so clearly to fit the well-defined structure of the obsessive–compulsive: the compulsive systems themselves, the doubting, the escalation and spread of fears, the intact, cold, sadistic memories, etc.

Psychodynamic Technical Assessment

The purpose of the assessment was to understand and give meaning to the problematic behavior and/or symptoms that Fred evidenced. Fred appeared quite paralyzed in school, checking and rechecking his work. He was controlled by rituals or systems he had to live by. He *had* to read the books in order, or something terrible would happen. He was often frightened of going into the street, fearing attacks of animals. He showed a number of phobias. At times, he had problems eating because he was disgusted by the smells and the "lumps" in the food. There was also generalized guilt, as he thought about the plaguing memory of killing the baby mouse, or feared the attacks of the bobcats from the woods (form of punishment).

I. Drive Assessment

The clinical material highlighted that the major ongoing problem that Fred had was a struggle with his *aggressive drive*, focusing particularly on the *anal components* of that drive. History indicated that during Fred's early years (second and third years of life) he had been treated very severely by his father. Battles occurred around eating, toilet training, and issues of anatomy. This interplay appeared to have stimulated counteractive rage within Fred (preoedipal rage, since this occurred during that phase of development). In Fred's history we saw evidence of his impulsivity as a child, but during latency and early adolescence, his aggression was highly defended against. Actually, we saw a youngster with an absence of aggression but one who was highly symptomatic.

The anal form of the aggressive drive is expressed in cruel and sadistic wishes, in desires to be messy and dirty. These components were not directly evident at all but intensely warded off (defended against). Evidence of dirty, messy wishes were expressed in the opposite—Fred was disgusted by the "smells," the "lumpiness," and the textures of the food. Although Fred gave no evidence of his own sadism or cruelty, he feared the attacks of vicious, cruel animals in the environment (these specific defenses are discussed in the section on Ego Assessment). This sadism and messiness (anal forms of aggression) were salient issues for Fred, although in his perception they came from outside and not within.

There were also some problems of *aggression* that seemed derived from the *phallic-oedipal period of development*. Normally, the aggressive drive in this phase of development is expressed in competition. Boys seek to be powerful men, and pit themselves against other children and father. Again in the history, the father had treated Fred very harshly when he had expressed his early manliness and prowess (climbing trees, exploring, etc.). Fred's difficulties in school appeared to be related to his problems in competition. The sense of power that youngsters express physically in early childhood is typically also expressed intellectually when they enter school. They compete by seeing who is the smartest and the quickest. Despite the fact that Fred was endowed with considerable intellectual gifts, he was unable to use them competitively and achievement was considerably impaired.

With respect to the *libidinal* nature of Fred's drives, the evaluation process provided relatively little material. One theme appeared to be Fred's penetration worries. He feared the piercing of the bull's horn and the mosquito sting. There had been a strong sadomasochistic interplay between father and son, and this kind of early interaction can promote a sense of passivity and excitement (anticipating attack) as well as the fears and rage already discussed. This suggests that one libidinal legacy could be translated into some homosexual wishes, where Fred would fear/wish to be the penetrated female partner.

II. Ego Assessment

Generally, Fred's major ego functions appeared to be intact, and he seemed well endowed. He was highly intelligent, his memory functioned well, and his speech and vocabulary were extremely well developed. He was able to abstract well and had no problems with reality testing (distinguishing between an internal thought and an external reality). For example, when he became fearful of the "bobcats" in the Sagebrook woods, he was aware that this fear was a product of his imagination and not a current reality.

Fred's ego was under a great deal of strain, and there were breakthroughs of anxiety (the indirect fears) when his defenses did not work adequately. This experience of anxiety was the basis for the subjective pain that Fred described during his first few sessions. His defenses were used primarily to ward off his experiencing his aggressive impulses consciously. The following are the defenses he used prominently:

1. *Isolation/Intellectualization.* This process involves separating appropriate affects from actual events. Fred had a meticulous and detailed way of explaining all sorts of experiences, but he would not let himself experience the feeling components attached to these experiences. This was a method of warding off aggressive feelings.

2. *Undoing.* Undoing involves a need to perform some particular act to avoid a feeling of anxiety. Often the act is the opposite, or an "undoing," of a previous act. There is often a compulsive need to "undo." Fred evidenced many problems in school, and the mechanism of "undoing" was involved in his paralysis with his work. For example, he described being unable to do his math, and he needed to erase and recheck, erase and recheck his answer. Internally (unconsciously), Fred was frightened that any actions (in this case, answering a question) were a sign of his aggression. He was frightened that any action could be a "mistake" (which in his mind was equated with a sadistic act), and he "undid" it by erasing and rechecking his work over and over again.

3. *Reaction Formation.* With reaction formation, impulses are changed into their opposite; this mechanism is often associated with undoing. Fred was *repelled* and disgusted by the "smell" and the "lumpiness" of his food. Internally the anal child finds enormous pleasure in dirt, and these impulses appeared to be intensely defended against by Fred. In addition, his sense of fairness and concern for others in his early period at Sagebrook seemed to be excessive and pushed away his internal wishes to hurt others. In general, this internally angry youngster was consciously good and compliant, orderly, and well-mannered.

4. *Projection.* In this mechanism, the ego alters the source of the dangerous impulse from within and attributes it to someone else. The animals at Sagebrook carried the dangerous hurting impulses that were originally within Fred. They, rather than Fred, expressed the biting, attacking feelings.

5. *Displacement.* This mechanism also involves a shifting of the source of frightening perceptions but does not involve impulses from within. Fred was terrified of the rage of his father, but kept himself unaware of this idea. The source of the terrifying feelings instead became the bull under his bed, and he "displaced" this affect state (rage) from father to the bull.

The constellation of reaction formation, undoing, and isolation is frequently seen together and often provides the ingredients of obsessive-compulsive neurotic mechanisms (Kessler, 1966). The formation of these mechanisms was clearly developed in Fred. Similarly, the mechanisms of projection and displacement are often seen in conjunction, and they form the basis for phobias, which were also a part of Fred's pathology.

III. Superego Assessment

From the above clinical material, Fred presented as a youngster "weighted down" by his superego. There was a very clear struggle with his aggressive drives for which Fred used a variety of defenses. These impulses activated his superego responses. He appeared to have a harsh and hypercritical superego as well as a demanding one (he lived up to very high standards of nonaggressive behavior).

There were a number of powerful sources that fueled his superego development. His strong aggressive and anal drives had contributed to building the severe nature of his superego. Fred also appeared to have identified with his strict, obsessional father. He additionally needed to deny these drives, since (as a child) his father had reacted so strongly when he had expressed them.

Fred's troubling superego appeared in a number of ways. He was beset by his "worries" and bad thoughts. He expressed a good deal of guilt, for example, the spot of blood on the driveway, and he feared punishment (the animals of the Sagebrook woods would attack him).

IV. Genetic-Dynamic Formulation

The central problem that Fred exhibited was conflict with his aggressive drives. He appeared to have reached the phallic level of development (competition theme) but primarily regressed to an anal structure. At the point of evaluation we saw the defenses and character traits associated with anal conflicts—reaction formation (he was compliant, good, etc.) and orderliness (he was attempting to control his internal aggression).

There had been a number of significant factors that had contributed to Fred's preoedipal struggles with his aggression. The major factor had been the father's sadism and uncontrollable rage expressed against Fred. The father's defensive style (his obsession, preoccupation with dirt) had also contributed to Fred's choice of defenses through an identification with his father. His mother had also influenced his development. She appeared to have had difficulty handling Fred's early aggression and had allowed too much expression of his early rage. There was also a question of whether the mother had been depressed during Fred's early years. Perhaps she had been unable to provide for him in other ways as well.

In Fred's history, he appeared to express his early rage directly and impulsively with his siblings and in nursery school. His behavior problems were also accompanied by anxieties, especially separation anxiety (early fears of abandonment as a punishment). In early latency, he became well-behaved but severely symptomatic. When his superego was fully formed and his ego became strengthened by maturation, he became able to contain his impulses. However, he spent an inordinate amount of psychic energy defending against the awareness of his internal aggressive life. This was a youngster dominated by his neurosis at the time of his evaluation.

Diagnostically, Fred illustrated problems of a youngster who had developed an obsessional neurosis. How could we distinguish between an obsessional neurosis and pathologies such as borderlines or psychotics who also manifest obsessional symptoms? On one level, it is important to examine the quality of the child's ego functioning. Neurotic youngsters, like Fred, are well endowed, and their ego functions operate on a high level (this can be compared to Matthew, Chapter 7, who used obsessional mechanisms within a borderline personality). More primitive youngsters make use of more primitive defenses, such as introjection and projection. Although Fred used projection, his prominent defenses were isolation, undoing, reaction formation, etc. Fred also evidenced a number of phobias as well as his obsessional symptoms. The phobias related to conflicts on a phallic-oedipal level and provided an indication that Fred had reached higher levels of development (thus suggesting less primitive conflicts) (Nagera, 1976).

V. Treatment Recommendations

Residential treatment was recommended because of the ongoing severe problems at home, particularly the pathology of the father. Earlier outpatient attempts had not proved fruitful. In addition, uncovering psychotherapy was recommended to help Fred deal with his "intolerable" underlying aggressive impulses.

PSYCHOTHERAPEUTIC CONCEPTS

These components of psychodynamic psychotherapy are used by both child and adult therapists to follow the process of their work.

Therapists, in the course of their clinical experience, will be attempting to assess the quality of the alliance, the nature of the transference, the readiness of the patient for an interpretation, etc. In this chapter, these concepts are initially defined and examined as they emerge in the course of treatment with Fred. Throughout the rest of the book, they are refined further as we deal with a variety of patients.

   I. Therapeutic alliance
  II. Production of material
     A. Direct: verbalization, play, etc.
     B. Resistance
     C. Transference
 III. Interventions (particularly used in uncovering psychotherapy)
     A. Confrontation
     B. Clarification
     C. Interpretation
     D. Working through

CONCEPT OF THE THERAPEUTIC ALLIANCE

The *therapeutic alliance* is defined as the nontransference part of the relationship between patient and therapist. It is the reasonable rapport that the patient has with the therapist that enables him to work purposefully in the treatment and share the goals of the treatment. An earlier example of an emerging therapeutic alliance was described in Chapter 3. It occurred with the patient Jonathan when the therapist outlined early that the Lego boy (Jonathan, in displacement) seemed to have a problem being called "smelly" and "retard." Jonathan, in the process of self-observing, indicated that the other Lego children held their noses away from the smelly Lego boy. The therapist and child were together defining the current problems that Jonathan was experiencing and together reinforcing that the goals of the treatment were to deal with the soiling and learning problems. The therapeutic alliance is the observing part of the relationship rather than the experiencing part (Greenson, 1967; Sandler, Holder, & Dare, 1973). Contributions to the alliance are made by the patient, therapist, and the structure of the treatment.

Patient Contributions

The patient implicitly makes many contributions in order to produce an effective alliance. He needs to be willing to produce material, to regress through fantasy or play, and to convey the nature of the regression to the therapist. An alliance implies some ability to use and mull over what the therapist observes. It also implies some motivation of the patient to overcome his/her illness. For an effective alliance, the patient needs to have some capacity to tolerate the frustration of treatment (e.g., when the therapist comments on painful issues or points out problematic behaviors).

These capacities are based, in part, on the quality of earlier object relationships, particularly the capacity for "basic trust" (Erickson, 1963). They are also based on the development of particular ego functions including memory, intelligence, verbal capacity, and the ability for self-observation.

Fred, in the above clinical material, evidenced an unusually highly developed therapeutic alliance for an 11-year-old. He immediately shared goals with the therapist in a detailed and elaborate way, produced abundant material, and had a major capacity to observe himself. In fact, it was clear that he had a powerful motivation for an alliance *before* he had met the therapist, because he was experiencing a great deal of pain and wished to be rid of his emotional burdens. They were clearly interfering in school and also made it difficult for him to be comfortable or at ease in his surroundings. This adult-like alliance is not typical with children. As discussed earlier, children tend to externalize, avoid pain, and struggle against self-observation. Much of Jonathan's alliance (Chapter 3) in treatment had an "immature" quality (A. Freud, 1980, discusses the "immature therapeutic alliance" in children). Children often become attached to treatment because they become attached to the therapist. In fact, the nature of this attachment has some similarities to the young child's attachment to the teacher. The child wants to learn and do his work because he wants to please the teacher rather than being motivated by a vision to learn as part of his own educational goal.

One further note on the nature of Fred's alliance. Although it was productive and served the treatment process early in the work, the "studious" quality of his alliance was also an expression of Fred's compliance (to an adult authority) and fear. Later in the treatment,

Fred's method of producing material became a resistance, a way of avoiding any rebellious, angry, nonconforming feelings and was discussed with Fred from that point of view when it was appropriate in the treatment.

Therapist's Contributions

The therapist contributes to the alliance in a number of ways. Above all, he/she implicitly conveys that he/she wants to help the patient become well. He does this through his persistent pursuit of uncomfortable material, his capacity to produce insight, and his continuous work with the resistances. In Chapter 3, when Jonathan continued his tedious Lego building in never-ending, nonproductive play, the therapist "worked with the defensive resistance" by limiting the amount of the session that could be used for the building. Within the context of the alliance aspect of the relationship, he underscored that this play would not help Jonathan with the "inside" problems they needed to work out together. Another important aspect of the therapist's contribution is his/her relative nonobtrusiveness and his need not to impose his own standards and values. For example, the child patient can say anything, draw or describe anything obscure, perverse, etc. without any sanction from the therapist.

Contribution of the Structure

The fact that there is a fixed quality to the session, that there are regular and orderly working routines, that the therapist conveys that the hour is important (through rarely missing, making changes, or allowing interruptions), all contribute to a sense of security and enhance the alliance. The therapist strives to create a work environment that supports the unfolding of the child's inner world. In work with children, the fixed quality of the hour is more commonly interfered with than in adult work. For example, the accompanying parent, at times, may seek to talk with the therapist before he sees the child, therefore encroaching on the treatment hour of the child. Although one cannot always reject this request out of hand, exploring if it can wait until after the patient's hour conveys the importance with which the therapist holds the child patient's working time.

CONCEPTS OF "RESISTANCE" AND "INTERVENTIONS"

These concepts are discussed after we follow some of the early work with Fred in his treatment at Sagebrook.

Clinical Material

The impact of Fred's neurosis on his total personality became clearer in the first year of treatment. One could follow the debilitating effects of the primitive defense mechanisms Fred needed to employ: isolation, undoing, and magical thinking. We could also witness the widespread suffering induced by his severely demanding superego.

After 4 months of treatment, the problem of aggression began to show itself directly, although not at first in the sessions. Fred took a sudden acute interest in war games in the cottage and became a subtle negative leader. Accidents began to crop up; there were a host of small injuries to younger peers. Attempts by staff to point out his behavior were met by protest. Fred insisted everybody was just picking on him.

Fred began to report some very alien thoughts in the treatment hour. He had the impulse to throw the basketball at one of his cottage mates; he wanted to stab little Jeff with a knife. He was embarrassed bringing these thoughts, but it might help to tell, he said, and he did have them. Simultaneously, rat fears began to appear. He began seeing them around Sagebrook, particularly in the bushes. Some of them had strange shapes and seemed to be a hybrid of several small animals.

Some sadistic memories came into the hour. He described how he and a friend found the severed head of a deer in the woods. They hid it and returned daily to see all the white things crawling around. His already difficult reality behavior appeared aggravated by these recollections. His aggression toward his younger peers in the cottage mounted, and staff became concerned about their safety. Glen, an 8-year-old, was pushed off a swing; little Jeff, climbing at Whips Ledges, almost had a dangerous fall; David, recently returned from eye surgery, was hit by a ball that narrowly missed the operation site. Fred's aggression was at times out of control, and the cottage staff took many direct steps to isolate and supervise Fred.

At first Fred was totally unable to hear anything the therapist said about his behavior: for example, that these driven, angry feelings must come from something from his past. At the time of the David incident, Fred began complaining about his own eyes. He was sure the doctor had made an error in his recent glasses prescription, and he said, "A little mistake can cause a lot of damage to the eyes." The therapist pointed out that perhaps he was saying that his little mistake could have caused severe damage to David's eyes. Sudden strong guilt and anxiety came out in a rush; he was frightened that he was really going to hurt someone; he had even tried other times to injure David, but he could not help it; it was so hard to stop. Confessing to many instances when he had had impulses to hurt others, he cried that he only wanted some control.

With direct cottage management, Fred brought more material to the hour. Little Jeff, he reported, fools everybody in the cottage, and he gets away with everything because all the staff feel he is cute. If Jeff talks out or even interrupts the prayer during supper (a major cottage offense), the counselors just giggle. He had seen Jeff steal cookies and put soap on toothbrushes. We could see, the therapist noted, that all of Fred's recent angry feelings must be connected to very strong jealous feelings. As jealousy was discussed, Fred's rat fears spread dramatically, and he worried at night. Did he hear rats in the basement? Would they gnaw through the kitchen door and enter the cottage proper? When he began to doze off, he would awake with a start; he imagined they were nibbling on his cheek. Those notions caused an immediate outbreak of anxiety, and Fred wanted my reality assurance; did rats actually thrive at Sagebrook or not? I began to interpret and connect these worries with punishment thoughts that Fred was erecting against himself. I noted that the conscience part of Fred devised fears because he felt he was so terrible.

Fred's jealousy had its roots at home. Fred felt that he had lost his place in the family. He described how his room had been given to his sister, and his furniture was now in the attic. He had a runaway dream: he reached home, and when he looked through a window, he saw Brad, his youngest brother, and his mother alone on the couch. He expressed an unusual amount of sadness, the first major affect of his treatment. He felt so outside, so left out and alone, and the therapist wondered if little Jeff and Glen in the cottage had not come to represent the brother from home. The ability, at this point, to link the cottage situation affectively with his feelings about home and family and to understand some of the meaning of his aggression was

a source of relief. There was a marked abatement of his animal fears
and general anxiety as well as a marked decrease in his rage toward
his peers.

Touching on Fred's aggressiveness gave both Fred and the therapist some awareness of the amount of sadism within him. Fred,
himself, quickly was becoming aware of how profoundly his "inside
feelings" and "inside thoughts" (as we came to call them) were
affecting his life. His rational ego witnessed to what lengths he could
be driven and to what degrees he could conceive thoughts that
punished himself. He was becoming more interested in what the
therapist could do ultimately to restore order and provide relief, and
there seemed to be a growing strength in the working alliance.

At times during the first year it was striking to see the quick
escalation of anxiety and the sudden elaboration of symptoms. Fred's
use of and belief in magic and omnipotence were impressive, especially at holiday time.

"Holiday time" was a cultural phenomenon at Sagebrook, beginning in November and lasting through Christmas. During this
highly charged period all of the anticipation and anxieties about
contact with family often become focalized and acted out.

We noticed early in November that Fred was making special long-
distance calls to his home, pleading with his parents to make some
extra weekend visits. If money or expenses were a problem, he
suggested they use *his* bank account at home. He had to see them.
During sessions, when the therapist noted his recent desperation, he
expressed great anxiety. He had been increasingly concerned that his
parents did not want to visit him at all. He was suspicious about the
last postponed visit. Yes, he had received a postcard from his father
in Oklahoma (where his father had to conduct some business that
month), but he felt that despite the evidence of the postmark, the
card had somehow really been mailed from home in Iowa. His
parents just did not want to come. On the other monthly visits he
had kept track of the time they spent with him, and it seemed to be
growing shorter. There had been many signs, he felt, that they did
not want to stay. The therapist slowly began to wonder if the reverse
might not be true: perhaps there was a part within Fred that did not
want to see his parents.

How does a therapist make a judgment that the manifest content a
patient presents (e.g., Fred's concern that his parents were rejecting)
serves an important defensive function? The therapist was not aware

of any real change in parental attitude. Fred's concern seemed increasingly irrational (e.g., he had received a card from his father from Oklahoma, but he felt it really had come from home in Iowa). We were then led to try to work out what could be internally producing this concern in Fred. A plausible hypothesis was that Fred was defending against his own aggressive, rejecting impulses toward his parents and using the mechanism of projection by attributing his impulses to them.

After some initial denial, Fred became much more conscious of his aggressive feelings. For several days he became preoccupied with knives, long kitchen knives that he had seen both at home and at Sagebrook. He could not help some of the thoughts he had, he protested. He thought of stabbing the therapist, of plunging the knife into him; he just could not stop his killing thoughts. Since Fred was so frightened by these thoughts, the therapist conveyed acceptance of these ideas and encouraged him to elaborate. (The direct retaliatory fears came quickly. He became afraid to leave the therapist's office, fearing that he would be stabbed in the hallway.) About a week before the November parent visit, Fred began making unusual mistakes at school. He was beside himself with his error. He had a perfect spelling paper, with one exception. He had substituted the work "bury" for the word "berry." His associations were to a tool set his parents had given him. One day he buried it in the Sagebrook woods, and when he had returned to get it, it had been taken. Maybe he had wanted to get rid of it. The following day he left the "d" out of the word "hundred," and with much anxiety he had the thought that "d" stood for "dead"—"bury the dead." He then confessed some of his preoccupations: he feared his parents would never make it to Sagebrook and would have an accident on the road. He himself commented (intellectually) that this could be an aggressive thought on his part, but it was also (feelingly) a dreaded fear. Fred worried each day that he would make other spelling mistakes as the week wore on, and the therapist interpreted that he feared thought mistakes. Perhaps a lethal killing thought would mistakenly slip out.

In this period of time, a new level of participation emerged from Fred. The reason for this was that Fred was again experiencing intense anxiety and dread, and that he already had experienced relief when he had conveyed his thoughts in his therapy. Although this was a productive period, it is important to understand that the pace of therapy generally ebbs and flows. There were often significant periods of time (weeks) where little was learned or understood.

When the therapist prepared Fred for the fact that he would be gone Thanksgiving Day, Fred had an interesting reaction. Even though he had known the therapist would take the day off, he could not really believe this would happen. Further, if the therapist really missed a session, Fred knew he could not avoid killing thoughts toward him. Fantasies spilled out. The therapist was caught in a snowbank or consumed by lung cancer. During this period, when Fred fearfully asked whether the therapist thought he could be a real "murderer," we began to work on the magic omnipotent quality of thoughts. He had many killing thoughts and killing wishes, the therapist explained, and he acted as though these thoughts could really hurt. Just as when he was little, he now mixed up his thoughts and deeds. If he angrily thought the therapist would die of cancer, he feared that the idea would happen. This was an old idea that had been strong when he was little and that he still kept. But everyone has a whole variety of thoughts and feelings all the time. (Many rat fears and eating inhibitions were plaguing Fred during this period. He was down to drinking only milk at one point.)

Several weeks before his parents visited in December, Fred began counting. At a children's concert at the Music Hall he counted the leaves in the decoration on the ceiling, somehow, to keep the roof from falling in. He counted the colored glass panes in the chapel at Sagebrook, again to keep the roof intact. And each day he counted and recounted the number of days left before his parents would come. Yes, it was magic! If he stopped, and he could not, his parents might die on the trip. He then quietly discussed all the plans he had ruminated about, should the event occur. He would live with his grandparents in Florida, or with his aunt in Chicago, or with another aunt in South Bend. As visiting day approached, he had many "nervous" feelings, and his neck became stiff. The stiff neck, we finally understood, was the result of a struggle. He fought his desire to look out of the window at the passing cars. Would he have a lethal look? He kept his parents safe by stiffly looking forward at the therapist. With this awareness, Fred fought his fears and allowed himself to look out the window. His parents arrived safe and sound.

As we anticipated the Christmas holidays, new material appeared in the transference. Fred's killing thoughts toward the therapist were active and prominent. The therapist made him feel helpless every day when he was kept waiting before his hour started. Slowly, memories came about home, and they stirred up an enormous feeling of helplessness: the helpless feeling he had when he tried to get his mother's attention, but she only had time to play cards with Brad; the helpless feeling when his father started yelling or when his father threw his sister's shoes or silverware across the living room; the total helplessness when his father stood over him with a face red with anger. The therapist spoke with Fred about the only means a little helpless boy *could have* in coping with such situations and attempted some reconstruction: a little boy overpowered could get back only by magic. He would make many killing, hurting, getting-even ideas, and they were these "inside" getting-back thoughts that came out now. He had never had help, and this old kind of anger never grew up.

Not only during "holiday time" but throughout the treatment, there was a significant problem with Fred's loyalty feelings. The many contrasts that Fred saw between Sagebrook and home provoked constant guilt, for Sagebrook often did so much better. The more he liked his therapist, the more he responded to the staff's interest and concern, the more he witnessed their efforts to erect effective controls, the greater became his outrage and disappointment in his years at home.

This clinical material highlights several aspects of Fred's treatment that will be discussed; the nature of his early *resistance* and the *interventions* by the therapist dealing with his presenting conflicts.

Concept of Resistance

Generally, resistance is defined as those forces that perpetuate the status quo of the neurosis (illness). Resistance operates against the reasonable ego and wish to change. It interferes with the ability to remember, gain, and assimilate insight (Greenson, 1967; Langs, 1973; Sandler, Holder, & Dare, 1973). Resistance can be conscious, preconscious, and/or unconscious.

A major part of every treatment is dealing with the phenomenon of resistance, which accompanies the course of treatment each step of the way. Therefore, the most cooperative patient will simultaneously evidence resistance, since it is natural for all human beings to repress painful, shameful memories, experiences, and affects. For example, even when a patient is bringing a dream, the therapist meets resistance since the dream material is a disguised version of some unconscious idea.

However, in a colloquial sense, therapists often comment about the "resistant patient," thinking of someone who is very overtly noncooperative, misses sessions, etc. This use of the term "resistance" is often also applied to children more generally, since they tend more to take flight from treatment and evidence a wish at times to deny the whole treatment process. Technically, however, this is only a form of conscious (or more crass) resistance, and all patients will manifest many forms of resistance.

In the outline of psychotherapeutic concepts above, the term "resistance" was placed under the heading "Production of Material." The reason is that the process by which a patient "resists" illuminates how that patient's ego is working. It is the ego of the patient that has developed many mechanisms to keep painful and intolerable issues of the past hidden from consciousness. Thus, in helping a patient understand and verbalize his resistances, the therapist helps the patient to gain insight into how a major part of his personality operates. At times, understanding the defenses a patient employs may be the crucial part of the treatment. For example, after a period of work in the case of Mark (Chapter 1), Mark became self-observant about his "lion feelings" and how they emerged when he was scared. The therapist had done a good deal of work on his defense/resistance of passive into active. Although he did not know exactly what frightened him, Mark gradually became sensitive to and contained these "lion feelings" (his acting out) as they emerged.

A number of authors enumerate a large variety of classes of resistances (Sandler et al., 1973). It is helpful to conceptualize three major categories of resistance: (1) *ego resistances*—the prevalent defensive processes of the patient as they emerge in the treatment; (2) *id resistances*—particular instinctual activities that are used to ward off insight; for example, a patient who fears underlying homosexual wishes acts continuously to prove his heterosexual prowess, denying his homosexuality; (3) *superego resistances*—resistances linked to unconscious guilt and a need for punishment. The conscience of the patient works against the treatment, since progress with one's illness would be experienced as too great a reward. Generally, *id* and *superego resistances* are more formidable to work through than the *ego resistances*.

How were the resistances evident in this case? Fred, in his first year of treatment, evidenced a number of ego resistances in his sessions. Early in treatment, as Fred had begun to show some of his aggressive problems with peers in the cottages, he brought "alien thoughts" about his cottage mates into the sessions. These had included the thought of "throwing a basketball" at a peer and "stabbing little Jeff." These observations had been made in great detail, and as though observed from a distance. The therapist became aware of the defenses (ego resistances) of *intellectualization* and *isolation of affect* that Fred used prominently. He pointed out that when Fred brought the ideas of hurting others, he discussed them in a very detailed but detached and intellectual way. The therapist suggested that perhaps Fred was afraid of allowing himself to feel angry, and he therefore needed to push these feelings away by his special way of describing things. Since the therapist understood the purpose of this ego resistance, he interpreted its function to Fred. The major initial goal was to slowly help Fred come closer to his internal aggressive life, which he actively pushed away. The defense interpretations would help to erode the repressive barrier that Fred created against his affects.

Somewhat later in this period of work, the therapist focused on other ego resistances. At holiday time, Fred was worried that his parents would not want to visit. The therapist understood the mechanism of "projection," putting one's forbidden impulses outside and attributing them to another person. When the therapist made the defense interpretation, "Perhaps the reverse was true, and there was a part in Fred that did not want to see his parents," the therapist helped Fred to focus on his own aggressive impulses. This allowed Fred to experience subsequent aggressive thoughts of kitchen knives and death preoccupations about his parents.

During this intense holiday time, Fred was driven to count the leaves in the ceiling decoration at the Music Hall in order to keep the ceiling from falling in. The therapist was aware of the mechanism of "undoing," which Fred used prominently. Fred was compelled to act (count the leaves correctly) to magically keep a disaster from happening (the roof from falling). The therapist described this driven, repeated act. The therapist spoke to several aspects of Fred's driven behavior. He seemed very concerned about making a mistake and tried to correct it by counting. But what could the mistake be? Fred worried about the ceiling falling in, but did he have to "undo" some other disaster that he feared? Perhaps it was the fear that his thoughts could hurt his parents. Again, in the early work with Fred, the therapist helped him to understand how his ego worked, how he used a variety of defenses to ward off affects.

Concept of "Intervention"

Interventions are techniques (usually verbal) used by the therapist to ameliorate the problems of the patient. In psychodynamic psychotherapy with neurotic patients, these techniques are typically uncovering processes (to "uncover" the warded-off internal life) whose purpose is to provide insight to the patient (Langs, 1973). The process is often conceived in four steps:

1. *Confrontation* wherein the phenomenon in question is made evident and explicit to the patient's ego.
2. *Clarification* during which the phenomenon is sharpened and further clarified (blends with the process of confrontation).
3. *Interpretation* is the process of making the unconscious meaning of the phenomenon conscious to the patient. This can include simply providing the meaning of the phenomenon, but also the source, history, and past events connected to the meaning.
4. *Working through* refers to processes and procedures after an insight is gained. This can include repetitions and elaborated explorations of the meaning of the insight, assessing the resistances or symptoms connected with it, and seeing its effect on daily living and current relationships.

The confrontation and clarification aspects are critical parts of the intervention process, since the patient must slowly become prepared for an interpretation. Only when a patient accepts and self-observes some aspect of his functioning, and to some degree finds it ego-alien, can an interpretation become useful. The interpretation is clearly the heart of the intervention process—the process of making some unconscious aspect of the patient conscious—and provides both the insight and a potential ingredient for change.

There is no formula for the effective timing of an interpretation or the effective presentation of the ideas interpreted. Intuitively, one learns about the patient's capacity to hear, and this capacity provides clues about what and how to interpret. The internal state of the therapist will affect his sense of timing. Often new therapists want to share their insights and discoveries immediately (though the patient may not be ready) because they seek affirmation of their effectiveness. New therapists can also be frightened about providing pain and disturbing the young patient, and therefore withhold the necessary confrontations and interpretations. They may fear that the intervention will make the child flee from treatment.

In the above clinical material with Fred, we can follow the above sequence in the intervention process. An example of this occurs early in the treatment with Fred, as his good behavior changes in the cottage, and he "accidently" roughs up some of his peers. The initial *confrontation* is brought by the cottage staff. They make explicit to Fred's ego that he is acting aggressively with his peers and trying to hurt them. This is brought clearly to his attention, although Fred did not overtly acknowledge his "accidents" to his peers. Fred did bring the aggressive feelings into his treatment hour and described a number of his destructive impulses (toward David, Glen, etc.). As Fred describes these incidents, the therapist was able to *clarify* (to bring the phenomenon into sharper focus). This aggressive behavior was not aimed at peers in general but specifically at the younger children. The aggressive impulses thus had greater specificity. When the focus became the little children, and particularly the youngster Jeff whom Fred described as loved by the cottage for his cuteness, there was an opportunity to make an *interpretation*.

The function of an *interpretation* is to give meaning to behavior, which is controlled by unconscious processes. The therapist noted that "Fred was so angry because he felt very jealous." Although this interpretation was rather simple, Fred had no idea why he felt the rage. The motive for his anger was unconscious and repressed, and becoming aware of this dynamic brought back material about his family in the next few weeks.

Fred's rage/jealous feelings were painful to him, since they centered on his younger siblings at home, who he felt were loved by his parents, whereas he had been rejected. The motive for repression was to avoid this painful awareness. When the interpretation was made, these memories could become available to his consciousness. In the treatment he described that he currently felt displaced by his sister and brother, recalled his furniture being sent to the attic, dreamt that his mother and youngest brother Brad were close on the couch. As this material emerged, Fred experienced the affects of loss, rejection, rage, and killing wishes toward his young siblings.

The therapist then had an opportunity to *work through* the initial insight, to examine further meanings of the jealousy interpretation. For example, he noted with Fred that jealous feelings experienced toward siblings at a very young age very often contain intense rage and killing ideas (e.g., "put the baby in the garbage"). These ideas can often be maintained when one grows up. Additionally, there can be many new, similar situations that will trigger these early feelings. They now emerged in the "new family" with new "siblings" in the cottage at Sagebrook.

If we look at the above sequence, it is important to underscore the fact that the "jealousy" interpretation to Fred was a simple one. Often new therapists feel that an interpretation must be profound for it to be effective and bring many complex ideas to the child patient. In reality, simple ideas are usually most effective and more easily integrated by the child.

How do people change? Does the above *insight* have any effect on Fred, and can we credit the therapist with a *"mutative interpretation"* (an interpretation that produces a change in symptoms)? This process did provide beginning relief for Fred (some fears and troubling dreams abated), and it can be understood in the following way. Although Fred repressed his rage and sadistic feelings, it was clear he was experiencing unconscious guilt, and he lived with many fears of punishment from his surround. During the above treatment process, he became more consciously and affectively aware of his "killing feelings" and great rage toward his peers. As he and the therapist attempted to understand his rage, insight provided a new perspective. These current sadistic feelings were manifestations of the old repressed feelings of his childhood when he had felt displaced by new siblings. These were typical "little boy" feelings, which he had to totally push away, and they returned currently in unmodified form with the same intensity he had experienced as a younger child. The effect of this period of psychotherapy was to give these current and troubling feelings a new context for Fred. Rather than serving as evidence that he was a murderous monster (his own harsh superego reaction) to himself, these feelings now had an understandable history and context that could ameliorate Fred's severe internal superego reaction. There was evidence for this change, since Fred could slowly allow more natural aggression in his daily behavior with peers (he was no longer always fair and good, with sudden "accidental" outbreaks), and his fears and terrors disappeared for a period of time.

His aggressive feelings became increasingly more tolerable to him, and he did not need to have his conscience torture him for these feelings.

CONCEPTS OF "TRANSFERENCE" AND "INTERVENTIONS": ELABORATION

The concepts are further discussed after we follow some of the clinical work with Fred in the latter stages of psychotherapy.

Clinical Material

Whereas the early part of Fred's treatment dealt primarily with his problems of aggression, it was not until well into the second year of treatment that sexual conflicts emerged clearly. Phallic urges and masturbation feelings appeared in a way that could be used in treatment.

At first Fred became preoccupied with the therapist's pipe smoking. He hoped the therapist would not be angry with him for his comment, he noted in preface, but he did feel it was rather a dirty habit. Did he know he could make himself sick? Hadn't the therapist read the medical reports about smoking? His father had stopped. It was mentioned that often boys thought about the therapist's habits when they were concerned about their own. When we came to *his* habits, we discovered a "bad one": Fred picked his nails. While it gave him pleasure, he would continue until his fingers became sore and painful. He could not stop even though his mother had told him to. He picked whenever he was bored, such as during his social study lecture each afternoon at school. With boredom came a restlessness. Several days later, he solved the school dilemma. The restless, bored feeling completely vanished when he took notes and kept his hands busy. I had to wonder what he thought idle hands might do.

The hand theme continued. He was having a daily debate now about washing his hands. Should he go and wash or not? He confessed to strange solutions. Sometimes he would eat a meal with several days' dirt on his hands (he would make believe he washed), and other times he found himself rewashing already clean hands just to make himself feel better. This habit had started about a year before he came to Sagebrook. He stuck himself with a pencil and it had left a lead mark on his palm. He had become concerned about blood poisoning and had tried to wash the spot out. Since then, there had been many times when the hand-washing idea became strong. Recently, at night, as he lay in bed he got the bored, restless feeling, and then got up and washed his hands, experiencing relief. He was interested in my comments. The therapist suggested that some "inside" struggle must be going on at night. Did he need to wash away something dirty?

He was plagued with many disgusting thoughts. He was troubled by smashing animals and had a recurring memory of a squirrel hit by a bus. He could not forget a science film at school. The heart of a dog was removed during an operation. Fred found it hard to look at the dissected rabbit in his biology class, and he also worried about how frequently he had been getting colds during the winter. The therapist noted with him his preoccupation with injury and his concerns about his body, tentatively suggesting that boys worried sometimes about their "habits." The worry that "habits" could hurt them physically was a very common concern. For several days Fred brought a recurring dream: he was climbing high on a roof (sometimes at home, sometimes in the cottage at Sagebrook), and suddenly a shingle broke and he fell. Through his association it emerged that the high climbing was really being alive and manly (he always wanted to climb, even mountains), but something in him made it all feel very dangerous. (Look at what happened when you tried!)

A very strong avoidance set in, the first major avoidance. Fred became quiet and sullen. His treatment hour was the gloomiest hour of the day, and he could not wait until it was over. Each hour he waited for the time to go by, and for the first time, he came late to his sessions. The therapist began to interpret the reversal and suggested Fred was really expecting him to stop treatment. He feared the therapist would just get disgusted with his disgusting thoughts and disgusting habits and throw him out. These seemed to be his "outcast feelings."

With great shame, he finally told me of his wetting symptoms. He had long since stopped wetting his bed, but under certain circumstances during the day, several drops came out, and he could not control this. Most people, he felt, controlled themselves at age 3 or 4. No one else had a problem like it. Slowly he described the following situations that produced the wetting: just before being tested in the gym (racing or rope-climbing); writing on the blackboard in front of the class; acting in a community night play at Sagebrook. He was really frightened of his forthcoming confirmation. What would happen if he completely wet his pants during his service? He could begin to feel that performing in some way made him very anxious. The therapist noted that just when he was to show some ability or his intelligence or physical strength, another part of him suddenly became broken or defective.

The therapist then drew a number of things together: Fred's worry about bad habits he could not stop, his need to clean his hands, his fear of bodily injury, and his sense of danger when he felt manly. It was noted that with boys his age, these feelings were often brought up when boys had a struggle with their sexual feelings and fought the strong urges to touch and play with their penis.

He began to tell me that recently he had been masturbating a great deal. Fred related that he had always been worried that something was wrong with his penis, since he had wet for years. His penis and groin area hurt him a lot recently, and sometimes he had stabbing pains. He had heard that boys had growing pains, and he wondered openly if his bad "habits" could hurt the body in some way. We came to understand much more that his compulsive need to touch himself was to find out repeatedly if he was still all right.

A torrent of sexual questions came out, questions about body structure, about his new external and internal physical changes. He thought about the differences between men and women, about pregnancy, and he had concerns about his semen, ejaculation, and his short stature. There seemed to be much relief in this expression. For a while there was relief from the compulsive need to masturbate and the disturbing wetting symptom. The therapist felt that Fred had taken an important step; he could look directly at phallic material.

In his last year of treatment, another aspect of phallic threat was explored. When masculine urges were associated with achievement in schoolwork, Fred reacted with an inhibition of activity and competition.

During Fred's final year at Sagebrook, he began to look much more like an adolescent. He was changing physically, developed an interest in girls, and participated actively in all sports. He began, however, to have some major trouble in junior high school, but the source was not the earlier ritualistic checking and rechecking of his work. He just "neglected" work that he could do; he did not fail but did less than he was capable of. This inhibition was rooted in his competitive feelings toward father. Slowly we could come to understand more about the effect of his early sadomasochistic interplay with father.

Fred now openly deprecated his father. His father was successful in business, he felt, without even working for it. He took 3 hours for lunch, gabbed all the time with people, and his grandfather had really set him up in the business anyway. He knew his father's pretentions; he brought his portfolio home but never worked from it. His father called himself President, but it was really a one-man company. Besides, Fred himself would be different. He was going to have a profession and help people. When news came from home that his father had been elected Chairman of the United Fund or appointed to the executive council of the local Republican Party, Fred always felt they could have found someone more suitable.

Fred's relationship with his therapist changed markedly, as did his overall adjustment at Sagebrook. He began to wonder about the author's competence as a therapist. He felt he was being helped much more by the cottage staff, just by talking with them for 10 minutes each day. Words like "stupid" and "ignoramus" began to come into his vocabulary, and he became much more direct and brave. Slowly the hours became an enormous and immensely plea-surable flight. Yes, he certainly had thoughts, but he definitely was not going to share them with the therapist. He became sarcastic. If, for instance, using his material, the therapist discussed some anxiety about his health, Fred might say he had a great new solution. He was going to take Carter's one-a-day vitamin pills. He came late for an appointment and entered with a pleased smile. He got up and left abruptly just when the therapist would begin some "profound" interpretation. He would outargue and outfox every move and now reported that he was going to be a famous trial lawyer. And this was so pleasurable and wonderful he felt he would never stop.

In the cottage he talked with peers about how much of a "clod" Chethik (the therapist) was, and he had the boys laughing at the clumsiness of the therapeutic staff, questioning the logic of every rule and regulation imposed. Slowly, the therapist began working with Fred to show him how he was fighting his father in the guise of other people. He seemed to be reliving a past relationship with his father, with one difference. Before, when he was little, he could not fight back or stand up to his father's anger. Now he seemed to be fighting and expressing a long-withheld rebellion that had been within him for many years.

Fred, in his retaliation, found many victims. He began to take advantage of the weaker boys in the cottage; he rented his baseball glove for 25 cents per hour to a very passive boy. He made bets with another helpless child, bets that he had to win. All of this was justified, he claimed, since he had always been made a victim. He described how the cottage staff resorted to physical punishment when they were frustrated. He resolved that "if I get it, I am going to give it back." He recalled how humiliated he had been on a recent home visit when his uncle had switched off his program to watch a football game. He had had no resources; he had been helpless. Here the therapist noted with Fred that these feelings were emerging so strongly because he had once felt so helpless and little with his father. Now, however, instead of being in the frightened role, he had become the tormenter. Even though he felt terribly guilty about his behavior, somehow it was safer for him not to be the victim. This was his way of warding off his memories, and it kept him from reexperiencing the old humiliations he had felt.

He was just overcoming some of his past humiliations, Fred said. He had always been short, and as a youngster he used to play baseball with a group of older boys. They had called him stupid and shrimp, and while he was batting they used to make him swing at balls over his head. Now he was becoming a good ballplayer, and he was determined to become a professional. One day, those same boys who had attacked him would be shocked when he became a star. Yet he was still very concerned that he would never grow adequately. If at age 18 he was too small to reach the gas pedals of a car and so unable to drive, he would be so angry that his anger would never end!

He came in hopelessly and terribly beaten one day because his wetting had started again. The therapist wondered with Fred how much, no matter what he did in reality, he still felt like the "little drip." Inside, from his memories, he always compared himself to his father. His father was the big gun, but he remained the little leaky one. Until he could know more of the past, a part inside of him would find a way to humiliate him.

Slowly memories came of his beatings, and with much affect. His father had chased him, and he had run because he was terrified. His father had used a doubled-up belt, and he would hit him sometimes without stopping. Often before the beating started, his father just stared at him, his face red all over, and his eyes seeming to bulge. He used to have a compelling wish during a beating that he would be dead, and only come to life after the beating because he so dreaded the pain. He used to become numb and paralyzed; he wanted to say something, but his vocal chords would not work. He remembered the scene of the dog in *Call of the Wild*, the one that was beaten with a club until his master was exhausted. How the dog tried to think of something else! Many times he felt his parents were like the Romans, throwing him to the lions and getting great pleasure from it and cheering wildly. Again and again, Fred came back to his reaction: the numbness, paralysis, dreamlike feelings he experienced. He said on several occasions that when he remembered what happened to him when he was little, he could now see why he was so angry with the world. When he was young, he never stopped getting into trouble, always provoking his mother and brothers and thus invoking further beatings.

Fred's descriptions of his beating experiences helped us understand a number of patterns in Fred's behavior. One aspect was how he constantly seemed to invite force. Often in his present reality, Fred described parallels. He tended at times to neglect his homework until the cottage staff was looking over his shoulder. On several occasions he let his schoolwork lie undone until the teacher insisted that he do his work in after-school special help classes. At times, as we worked on this material, Fred stayed away from his sessions. He seemed intent on getting the therapist to act, to have him escorted from the cottage, or to threaten the treatment in some way. The therapist could now begin to work with Fred to show him how his wish for the beatings was as strong as ever, and that in many ways he continued to lead the life of a young child with a dominating father. He tried to provoke me to take action in the treatment situation, as he did in other facets of his life. He repeatedly became humiliated, but part of him wanted to get to the point where people overpowered him again. He seemed to have very mixed feelings about the beatings, as if part of him had come to enjoy them.

Another important element of the beatings was how frightening it became for Fred to be active. We saw evidence of this in Fred's problems with his schoolwork. Sometimes he was unable to do his homework, especially when he had a large load. He was afraid to study too hard, since it brought on headaches. His fantasies were that the stress of the work would affect his brain, would ruin his brain and make it deteriorate. He was often ambivalent about his exams; there was a desire to fail them and do poorly so that in life he could be a failure. If worse came to worse, he could always work for his father. In school he would take copious notes, usually more than the other students, but often he would completely neglect reviewing them before an exam. He could not hand in an insect collection for his science project. The most repugnant part of the assignment was that he would have to mount the insects, and he did not feel he could "stick the pins in." In summary, Fred was very frightened of his ambition and drive, and part of him needed to keep himself impotent. The therapist worked with Fred to show him how a similar "paralysis" (similar to the paralysis associated with his beatings) seemed to develop when he needed to perform. Now he seemed to become paralyzed in his learning situation. He became terrified whenever he needed to show what he could do. Where could this come from? Slowly we came to understand that he had interpreted much of his father's wrath as an attack on his activity. We knew, for example, that he had been beaten for his house climbing, and this was his young masculine pursuit. He had also been beaten for his wetting, and he had come to feel that this was for his genital and exciting manly thoughts. Now, in every current manly and achieving area, he became "paralyzed" since he thought he would be attacked. And, of course, his ambition was strongly linked with the killing revenge on his father. Neglect kept his father safe. This was the major area of work before termination.

Concept of Transference

A very important aspect of the psychotherapy experience is the phenomenon of transference. Transference is defined as the patient's experience of feelings, drives, attitudes, fantasies, and defenses toward a person in the present that do not befit that person but are a repetition of reactions originating in regard to significant persons of early childhood, unconsciously displaced onto figures of the present (Greenson, 1967). These present figures can be anyone significant in the patient's current life. Thus, Fred was clearly experiencing "transference" earlier when he transferred the killing feelings toward his siblings onto his current cottage mates. With the regressive pull in the process of psychotherapy, the therapist himself will often take on various transference roles.

When this occurs within the therapy, understanding and working out the distorted transference can be either of irreplaceable value or a major threat to the treatment. The patient is living out and reenacting the past, with the immediate and intense feelings of the past. On the one hand, this can be the key to many insights, and because of the quality of the affective experience, it can often provide the patient with a sense of major conviction regarding the origin of the events. However, when the patient begins to experience these affects toward the therapist, this can stir up powerful resistances that can become major obstacles to any further work.

In the above clinical material, Fred began to experience a significant transference reaction. The earlier conforming youngster was now angry and belittling of his therapist. Chethik was a "clod" and "ignoramus" and the object of scorn and humiliation. One could certainly say that the quality of the relationship with the therapist had changed, and Fred was experiencing affects toward the therapist that did not befit the relationship.

When the therapist understood that this change in the relationship was a manifestation of transference, he felt he could slowly bring this to Fred's awareness (see below) because this would be beneficial to him. Despite the new anger with the therapist, Fred had a good therapeutic alliance with the therapist and a history of meaningful work together where changes had occurred. The attachment that was developed within the alliance would help Fred gain some distance as patient and therapist explored the current anger in the transference.

What was being transferred? What was being repeated in regard to significant persons of the past, displaced onto the present? Fred had had a significant sadomasochistic relationship with his father that was a very significant factor in his pathology and that reemerged in the present in action but not in awareness. Fred sought to justify his demeaning of the therapist—he felt the therapist had wasted Fred's time, and he was therefore a major ignoramus. One can see some of the dangers to the therapy as the transference emerges, particularly the danger of gratification. As a little boy, Fred felt helpless and suffered much humiliation at the hands of the powerful father-bull. In demeaning the present authority, there was intense gratification in living out a revenge opportunity to undo the past. Now, at last, he could put down and humiliate a major authority. Insight brought by the therapist would destroy the immediate opportunity—therefore, Fred noted with pleasure that he could out-argue and outfox the therapist, and he would never stop. Other dangers were Fred's fears and discomfort as his rage emerged. He naturally feared that the therapist would retaliate and react to his provocations, and the danger would feel immense since the fears stemmed from the childhood situation with his father. For a significant period, Fred did not listen or take in any of the therapist's comments.

When a therapist is under attack, there are natural internal counterreactions he often needs to handle. Is the patient justified in his assessment? Am I really a "clod" and an "ignoramus"? There can often be a blow to one's therapeutic narcissism and self-esteem. There is often significant counterrage and frustration. How can this patient do this when I have invested so much, etc.? These are some of the natural internal thoughts and struggles until the therapist can understand why the material arises. These counterreactions are typically more intense in the new and inexperienced therapist whose professional self-assurance is naturally fragile, but they remain the internal response of experienced therapists as well.

Concept of "Intervention"

Over a period of time, the therapist's *interventions* became effective, and we can follow the process of the uncovering interventions. Initially the therapist *confronted* the patient—he noted that the relationship had changed since Fred was fighting and angry all the time in the hour, and questioned whether this behavior was justified or coming from somewhere else. As Fred continued to berate the therapist, further *clarification* was made explicit to Fred's ego. The therapist brought into greater focus the interplay between himself and Fred. Fred seemed to need to humiliate the therapist, as though he was taking revenge for some major experience of the past. Fred commented that this might be true, but that the situation would continue forever. Timing of an interpretation is important. The quality of the transference should be established and lived out some (since gratification needs to be experienced, as well as its inappropriateness more fully established).

The therapist then slowly made the transference *interpretation*, giving unconscious meaning to this fighting behavior with the therapist. Fred seemed to be engaged in a fighting relationship with the therapist (and other "authorities"), and it had the same form of his old relationship with his father, where he felt humiliated and helpless. These past memories always made him feel uncomfortable, and he smoldered inside. Now they were reemerging, but with one important change. Earlier he was a child and could not fight back, but currently he had reversed the process, and he now was the aggressor and humiliator. At first, there was little overt acknowledgment, but Fred did describe tormenting his peers. He subsequently discussed the humiliation by his uncle, and there was a temporary return of a humiliating daytime wetting symptom he had had as a child, which brought back more of the past. Slowly he gained access to many memories of the beatings of the past by his father he described above, with the affects of terror, paralysis, and helpless rage.

In the process of *working through* (the elaborated process of examining the implications of an insight), Fred and his therapist sorted out how this early, intense conflict with his father had shaped significant aspects of his personality and how he was currently affected by this history. Three themes were discovered. (1) They focused on how this past trauma had established a reservoir of rage/ hatred within Fred that could easily be provoked by current authorities. (2) They also identified the patterns of current provocation. The clinical material illustrated the pervasiveness of Fred's current need to invite force. In treatment, he missed sessions and provoked the cottage staff to bring him; in the cottage, his aggressive actions brought sanctions; in school, the teachers reacted to him for his lack of preparation. In an unconscious way, Fred "set up" authorities to "come down" on him, and he thereby relived the provocation-humiliation pattern with the "fathers" of today. (3) Similarly, Fred was terrified of his active–assertive behavior. He feared using his mind and intellectual skills, because this meant competition even though he was currently encouraged to achieve. The past wrath of his father for assertive behavior continued to instill fear and inhibition. These themes and further insights (the process of working through) developed from the original uncovering of the early struggle between father and son. The working-through process took a 6-month period.

Fred was discharged from Sagebrook, and he continued to live away from home. He attended a coeducational boarding school with high academic standards. In follow-up contacts, we learned he was performing well academically, was free of any obsessional symptoms, and he seemed to be making a rather typical heterosexual adjustment. He was quite assertive with teachers and peers and internally felt relatively untroubled.

The concepts of the psychotherapy process discussed in this chapter are further explained with respect to a variety of cases in subsequent chapters.

SUMMARY

In this chapter, we have introduced the neurotic child. The aspect of an emotional disturbance that makes it a neurosis is that it is based on internalized conflict, conflict between different parts of the personality within. A major struggle evident with Fred was the conflict between his aggressive impulses (id) and his conscience (superego). This internal conflict led to repression/defenses and an outbreak of symptoms in latency.

The neurosis is generally felt to be a benign emotional disturbance (Kessler, 1966) because it responds most favorably to psychotherapy. In this case presentation, a variety of insight-oriented techniques were described. For the neurotic child, the past is unconscious (repressed), yet it lives on as though it were real in situations akin to the past. The "uncovering" process of psychotherapy allows the child patient to see how his past distorts his current reality. Since neurotic patients are generally intact in areas that are conflict-free, the insights they gain about "distorting" the current situation help them alter their behavior. When Fred gained the "insight" that his rage toward his younger cottagemates reflected his feelings about his family as a child, the intensity of his current aggression abated.

Another neurotic youngster is described in the next chapter.

BIBLIOGRAPHY

Erikson, E. (1963). *Childhood and Society*. New York: W. W. Norton.

Greenson, R. (1967). *The Technique and Practice of Psychoanalysis*. New York: International Universities Press.

Kessler, J. (1966). *Psychopathology of Childhood*. Engelwood Cliffs, NJ: Prentice Hall.

Langs, R. (1973). *The Technique of Psychoanalytic Psychotherapy*, Vol. I. New York: Jason Aronson.

Nagera, H. (1976). *Obsessional Neurosis.* New York: Jason Aronson.

Sandler, J., Holder, A., & Dare, C. (1973). *The Patient and the Analyst.* New York: International Universities Press.

Sander, J., Kennedy, H., & Tyson, R. (1980). *The Technique of Child Psychoanalysis: Discussion with Anna Freud.* Cambridge, MA: Harvard University Press.

5

Treatment of the Neurotic Child: The Younger Patient*

The discussion of the treatment of Fred (neurotic youngster, Chapter 4) provided an opportunity to discuss the major psychotherapy concepts. In this chapter, which highlights the treatment process of a younger child, these concepts are elaborated and refined in relation to a patient in early childhood. We also compare these two cases, discussing the differences in treatment in work with an older and younger child.

The case of Amy, a 6½-year-old elective mute youngster, is presented. A diagnostic workup is included. Although there is an elaboration of the discussion of the therapeutic alliance, resistance, and transference, this case also provides a further opportunity to look at the critical role of the parents in child treatment.

AMY: THE PATIENT, HER HISTORY, THE EVALUATION SESSIONS

Amy was 6½ years old when she began treatment, and she had had her "talking problem" thoughout her life. In her kindergarten school experience, she had not spoken to her teachers or the other children

*A version of this chapter, "Intensive Treatment of an Elective Mute," by M. Chethik, was published in *Journal of the American Academy of Child Psychiatry*, July 1973, Vol. 12, No. 3, pp. 482-498.

for the entire year. At home she whispered occasionally to her parents and siblings but never communicated verbally to street friends, adults, or relatives. The most general characteristic that Amy evidenced was a stubborn, passive, withdrawing quality that not only was evident in her speech difficulty but permeated many areas of her life. She ignored or passively refused to comply with the normal demands in the house (dressing, washing, chores, etc.) and, therefore, was difficult to manage at home.

In addition, there were a number of prominent fears. Amy evidenced strong anxiety about dogs, and at times she avoided going out in the street because she was terrified of being bitten. There were also many bedtime fears. Amy was very frightened of being alone, and she established many rituals and procedures before she could allow herself to remain in bed. Enuresis was a sympton that reappeared during stress, and there were some occasional periods of soiling.

Amy's parents also expressed concern about the vividness of her fantasy life, which they felt had persisted beyond an appropriate age. Amy would become nonverbally involved with younger children, usually playing games, and there was often a very intense excitement and aggression accompanying this play.

Amy was a member of a large family, the fifth child in a sibship of six. Her father was a prominent social scientist who had an absentminded quality. He was externally preoccupied, highly intellectualized, lost in work and theory building. Her mother was an obese, unkempt woman, overwhelmed by the reality demands of her household and children, and filled with rage that was primarily self-directed.

As the mother described Amy's history, for the first half year of her life she had seemed to be a very contented baby. Mrs. B. noted that when Amy was about 6 months old she had begun to "scowl," and this seemed to coincide with the beginning of mother's next pregnancy. It seemed harder to get Amy to smile, and this "scowling" characteristic was maintained throughout Amy's childhood. The birth of Bobby (male), the next child, came when Amy was 16 months old, and it was, in general, a difficult time for the family. There was much illness, and the mother had been depressed. Amy developed many reactions during this period. She became a severe feeding problem. She fought with her mother, refusing to feed herself, and her mother angrily left the food for her to take. Amy's "will" seemed strong, her mother noted, and she went for many days eating almost nothing.

In addition, Amy became overtly hostile toward the new baby, and Bobby had to be protected from her physical assaults. Amy also could not bear to be separated from her mother—she screamed and could not be comforted even with the father present. She refused to stay in her crib and consistently fought sleep and naptime.

Toilet training was begun at 2 years of age, and the pattern of fighting and stubborn refusal (as with the food) continued. Mrs. B. had a "potty time" that Amy avoided; she hid from her mother and would only place her BMs outside of the potty chair. The mother had been severe with Amy: she had used spankings and had forced her to remain on the chair for long periods. Slowly Amy had seemed to yield, although there had been "accidents" between ages 2 and 3. The toilet-training struggle spread to other areas. Amy had then dawdled a great deal, refused or had been slow to dress, etc., and had messed with and shredded papers for the mother to clean up.

During Amy's third year her mother had become concerned about her aggression to herself. She scratched herself endlessly; for instance, chicken pox scabs were made into sores and became sources of skin infections which had lasted for months. In a similar way, she had picked on all bites and scratches so they were unable to heal. During this period of self-injury, a dangerous and frightening accident had occurred. Amy had fallen into a pool, had been unconscious for several minutes, and had been revived by resuscitation.

Amy's difficulties seemed continually to compound as she grew. When she was 3 she became acutely ill with a lung infection (a legacy of her pool accident) that did not respond to any mediation. Amy was hospitalized for about a 6-week period during which there was a time when the doctors did not think she would survive. There were extensive medical procedures that Amy endured—intravenous feeding, a drainage tube in her back from the lung, a need for extensive use of oxygen, etc. In addition, she was physically immobilized for long periods of time. Amy was described as "submitting herself" to this experience. She never uttered a word or a cry. Throughout her hospitalization she had never spoken, and she had also refused to eat (to the point where there had been great concern). Amy had regressed in her partially completed bowel training, and on her return from the hospital she did not speak with anyone (including the family). The mother noted that Amy had never really recovered from the hospital experience; her eating had since remained poor and her talking markedly restricted, as described above. The growing concern of parents and school had finally led to the referral for treatment.

When the therapist first met Amy for the evaluation, she was an appealing little blond-haired, blue-eyed girl. Although she had pleasant features, her face was like a mask. It was very strained, and her body was quite stiff. Amy appeared to separate easily from her mother and surprisingly took the therapist's hand to walk down the corridor. The door was purposely left ajar, indicating that if, at any point, she wanted to, she could go back to visit mother.

Once in the office, Amy kept to one corner of the room. She looked furtively at the toys but did not touch them. Knowing of her difficulty with speech, the therapist commented that often children had trouble talking and suggested that Amy could use some of the toys in the office. He added that he knew she had some worries, and sometimes play would help explain a little bit about some of these worries. A few moments after this comment, Amy lost control of her bladder. She wet herself and the chair completely and looked terribly uncomfortable. Her mother was called in and helped Amy clean up; the mother then remained for the rest of the session. The therapist commented that it was all right for her mother to stay until Amy felt more comfortable and knew the therapist better.

Amy, for the rest of the session, continued to sit in her corner of the room and play with the clay. She rolled long, even strands of yellow clay and also made neat little tiny red pellets. This seemed to be a very safe, absorbing activity, which completely denied the therapist's existence. Any comment made was completely ignored.

In the second evaluation session, Amy was able to separate from her mother, and after a few minutes Amy began to use the toys. For the major part of the hour, she played with a doll family. The children drove off in a car leaving the parents behind, and the adults waved good-bye. The children settled in one house while the parents were busy in another house. Each separation, however, was followed by a loving reunion. The children suddenly returned, and the mother picked up the children and hugged and kissed and comforted them. The therapist commented to Amy that it must be scary to be away from Mommy, and felt she would be so glad to get back to her. He wondered if she felt scared about coming to see him in this office. Maybe she worried that he was like a mean doctor or some kind of hurting person. During these comments Amy did not look in the direction of the therapist.

Psychodynamic Technical Assessment

How can we understand the major symptoms and behavior difficulties Amy presented? The paramount difficulty was her elective mutism. She was also generally withdrawn and withholding. She evidenced separation fears and fears of being bitten by dogs that inhibited her comfort in going out into the street. She was shy, retiring, and rigid in her movements and gait. Amy also continued to bedwet.

I. Drive Assessment

The major conflicts that were evident appeared to be in relation to Amy's struggles with her aggressive drives. Preoedipal components of the aggressive drive were significantly involved. "Preoedipal" refers to the early development of the instinctual drives before the oedipal phase of development, which begins at about 3½ or 4 years of age. The history pinpointed problems in Amy's eating function and her relationship with her mother in the oral phase of development. At the point of evaluation, Amy was preoccupied with issues involving the mouth. This was evident in her speech inhibition (mutism), her continued difficulties in eating directly, and her fears of biting dogs. These behaviors suggested she was defending against forbidden oral rage impulses—the sadistic biting impulses that children experience at this phase of development (defenses are described in the Ego Assessment section). This seemed to be a central component in Amy's Pathology.

Some of Amy's oral fears (dog threat) also seemed to relate to fears of attack, which stemmed from early childhood. There was a time in Amy's life history when she had seemed assaulted. She had faced a very enraged mother as well as the overwhelming hospitalization experience. Both experiences seemed to form the possible basis for a traumatized youngster.

The aggressive components in the anal phase of development also seemed to be heavily involved in creating difficulty. There had been significant problems in toilet training and struggles with mother over will and autonomy. Cruelty and messy-dirty impulses express the aggressive components of the anal drive. The above material suggested that Amy had warded off these intense impulses by a variety of defenses (this is discussed in the Ego Assessment section), which made her excessively compliant and inhibited. Nonetheless, she had appeared to express some of her messy impulses through bed wetting and a significant amount of the aggression in the passive forms of withholding (speech) and defiance (dawdling).

Aspects of these preoedipal issues appeared in the quality of her object relations particularly in relation to her mother. We saw oral forms of the object tie in her problems of separation, needs to stay at home, and her whiny, demanding behavior. At other times the anal components were prominent in her relationship to mother, and she became stubborn, withholding, and provocative with her mother and others.

The material also suggested some more basic concern about self-regard and self-esteem. She had a history of hurting herself, scratching herself, and self-injury. With the significant early mother–child problems, the evaluative material suggested there was a possibility of some primary deficit in a narcissistic sense of self. If a child is not adequately loved and cared for as an infant, she/he can develop a major fundamental problem in valuation of the self and the body. The evaluation material raised this issue in Amy's development.

II. Ego Assessment

Despite the intense fears and some primitiveness in her play (with younger children), Amy did well in school (written achievement) and on IQ tests (superior range). This suggested that many of her ego functions were intact. The evaluative material also indicated that there could be some problems in reality testing (the profound fear reactions to the therapist in the evaluation) and perhaps some difficulties in the synthetic function (the ability to bring together past and present experiences). Could the early problems and the traumatic hospitalization have disrupted Amy's ability to integrate experience? Further assessment of these functions would be necessary and would occur in the course of treatment.

Amy was quite symptomatic, and she used a variety of defenses against the oral and anal aggressive drives. In terms of the oral components (the biting, devouring wishes), a major mechanism she used was *projection* (expelling the impulses from the self to an object outside). She became frightened of attacking and biting dogs. Another prominent defense was involved in her elective mutism. Amy *inhibited* the use of her mouth so that no destructive biting impulses could emerge (the defense of *inhibition*).

The mutism appeared to be involved in her anal comflicts as well, where she struggled to contain cruel and dirty/messy forms of rage. Amy seemed to see her speech as her products and productions, and attitudes about her speech represented her feelings about her feces (and autonomy). In a general way, she displaced the anal products to her speech products. This form of *displacement* is not uncommon in development, since speech development is rapidly expanding precisely at the same time of the anal phase of development. Thus, it appeared that Amy retained and withheld her words instead of retaining and withholding her feces.

In addition, Amy appeared to attempt to handle her destructive impulses by deflecting the drive through *turning of the aggression on the self.* We saw evidence of this mechanism in her scratching and self-injury. Amy also appeared overly neat and fastidious, very concerned about being dirty. She used the mechanism of *reaction formation* (turning the impulse into its opposite) to ward off her powerfully dirty/messy impulses.

III. Superego Assessment

Amy's superego appeared to be fully intact and autonomous (she did not depend on regulation of her behavior by outside authorities). She seemed to have a severe and demanding superego. This was evident in her general overcompliance. In fact, her defenses against her impulses were so extensive that she functioned in a restricted, rigid manner. She was extremely frightened of any impulse expression. The experience of the hospitalization seemed to be interpreted by Amy as a form of punishment for her badness, and we noted the severe restriction of her impulses (eating, speech) after her protracted illness. Amy seemed to identify with her mother's highly critical and attacking attitudes toward herself. Later this became her own attitude toward herself and her impulses.

Amy's dog fears also provided evidence of her severe superego.

The dog fears (biting) not only expressed her projected wishes but additionally indicated that the "Talion principle" seemed to be operating within Amy. She feared that she would be hurt in the same way she would want to hurt others.

IV. Genetic-Dynamic Formulation

The predominant picture that Amy presented was that of a youngster evidencing a great deal of preoedipal psychopathology. There was little evidence of conflicts on a phallic-oedipal basis, and the degree of fixation seemed prominent.

It is often helpful to make a distinction between the concepts of "fixation" and "regression" in the assessment process, since the treatment course with patients who have reached higher levels of development is less protracted. "Fixation" indicates that there is a certain amount of arrested development, whereas "regression" indicates that development has gone beyond the apparent levels of functioning but conflict at the higher stages forces the developmental process to retreat. For example, Fred (Chapter 4) evidenced competitive (phallic) strivings, but the castration anxiety he faced fostered a regression to the anal constellation he then developed.

In the evaluation with Amy, we saw little evidence of oedipal conflicts. What factors in the history could have provoked the quality of fixation that emerged? Amy appeared to have had very extensive conflicts with her mother during the preoedipal years, which promoted an absorption in these stages of development. In addition, the overwhelming experience of her hospitalization further appeared to solidify her arrest. This experience (as already alluded to) was interpreted by Amy as a punishment for having her destructive impulses, and it reinforced the idea that Amy could face death. Therefore, she appeared to redouble her efforts to control these impulses: since they could be expressed through eating-biting, or through speech-verbal destruction, these functions were further restricted. This frightening event reinforced the powerful defensive retention (a major anal mode) and further enhanced her inhibitions and rigid controls. Her energies appeared to be totally absorbed in containing the feared instinctual components of the preoedipal years, fostering the fixation.

The major diagnostic impression at the time of the evaluation was that Amy was a youngster with a severe neurosis, since there was evidence of major internalized conflict.

V. Recommendations

The recommendation was for uncovering psychotherapy (three times per week) while the parents were seen weekly in parent guidance. The fundamental goal was to help Amy become less frightened of her instinctual life which had created such pressing conflicts. The major symptom, the elective mutism, appeared to have a number of meanings, particularly at an anal and oral level.

THE CONCEPTS OF THE "THERAPEUTIC ALLIANCE" AND "RESISTANCE"

Clinical Material

Despite the fact that Amy was totally silent throughout the 2-year period of treatment, there were many forms of vivid communication that slowly developed—drawing, writing, intense play, body gestures, and finally sounds. The following material focuses on the first 6 months of work.

For the first few weeks in her sessions, Amy remained very involved in compulsive play in *her* corner of the room. She continued to roll long, even, successive strands until she had used up all the red clay, as well as to make the little neat piles of tiny pellets out of the yellow clay. At times, in these early meetings, she showed evident distress about some minor messiness. She might smear herself with some of the clay or wipe her nose on her dress and then become quite concerned about the spot. She accepted a tissue from the therapist and seemed to listen when he explained where the washroom was. This was the first accepted communication.

Amy seemed to go to great lengths to maintain this early control. One day another child screamed loudly near the office window. Although the therapist was startled, Amy remained absorbed in her clay work. The therapist used this incident to point out how Amy needed to keep from seeing or hearing anything. It seemed safer for her not to allow anything to affect her. Perhaps she had seen or heard some very scary things before, when she was younger.

Slowly there were signs of gradual relaxation. There was a fleeting but pleasant smile when Amy entered. She assumed a certain possessiveness over her toys in the office (they were so foreign at first). She wrote her name and grade on the crayon box and arranged her toys carefully when she left. She also wanted some drawings hung on the bulletin board, and she somewhat resisted leaving when her sessions were finished.

She began to use the scissors in the office, and her scissors work absorbed most of the time. At first she cut out all sorts of drawings, mostly animals. Then she began to trace the scissors itself on sheets of paper, and she constantly cut out scissors replicas. She began a game that she at first hid from the therapist; she put the scissors near her mouth and simultaneously opened and closed both scissors and mouth. At times, she slid from the chair and she became a fearsome four-legged animal with a mouth–scissors. (The therapist also learned that at this time she was using scissors inappropriately at home, cutting up her sister's doll clothing and making attempts to cut her own hair.) He began to point out to Amy that she was showing him that she felt sometimes that her mouth was like a cutting or biting thing. Maybe this was one reason why she was so afraid to talk. Did she get mixed up that when she would talk, it would be like biting or hurting someone? Was this why she kept her mouth closed? Amy's only response was to intensify the animal game.

Shortly thereafter she developed trouble reentering the office; she delayed getting into the car at home and resisted leaving the waiting room at the start of the sessions. She went back to her isolated games, doing schoolwork and making believe she was in class rather than in the office. In her doll play, again Mother comforted and hugged the children. She was anxious and frightened, and the therapist began to note with her that she seemed scared of him. At this point she began to draw pumpkins. In her series of pumpkins, all of which were very large, the mouth and teeth were very prominent. The therapist said that sometimes children made pretend games; children pretended people were all sorts of things. He wondered if Amy was making believe that he was something else than a Mr. Chethik—maybe someone like a pumpkin with a big scary mouth. Maybe Amy worried sometimes that he could get angry? Would he have a big mouth and bite? Could this be why she was scared of coming?

Although Amy rarely looked in the therapist's direction when he made an interpretation, her work now stopped. In response to the mouth interpretation, she drew a series of pictures of dogs, all of them with blood spots on them, and the therapist commented that maybe Amy was showing him that she had so many biting worries. It seemed as though her original fear of her own oral aggression in the sessions had become projected. Her own mouth–scissors feelings become less acceptable. She expelled them onto the therapist. She became worried that he, as the therapist, might retaliate by biting, and thus she feared the treatment for a period of time. The effect of this work was to begin to restore her comfort in the treatment sessions, and Amy seemed to be freer to talk outside of treatment.

During these first few months, the parents remained quite ambivalent about the treatment, despite some immediate gains. The mother reported that Amy was talking much more elsewhere. The implication was "Why go on?" One day, when Amy asked her mother why she had to come to see me, the mother replied, "You just have to." It seemed like a dreaded obligation. The mother seemed to fight and control any progress that Amy made. For instance, Amy began to express a desire to use the telephone for the first time, and she actually made her first calls to relatives. Rather than showing pleasure and delight, the mother immediately curtailed the number and length of calls Amy could make, not wanting to impose, she said, on the relatives' time.

Payments for the treatment were in arrears, and a pattern of lateness to hours continued. When these matters were discussed with the mother, she felt the therapist was "just creating" an issue and that Amy would only react because the therapist made it so important. When the therapist underscored the fact that she seemed to have a great deal of questions and doubt about the treatment, grievances emerged. Their friends felt they were silly and were wasting so much money. The mother's practical problems were enormous with six children, and there was reality to this complaint.

Slowly, however, Mrs. B. brought out her *enormous* fury with Amy, how this little girl was so capable of getting under her skin. She described how she could not stand her daughter's deliberate dawdling whenever there was someplace to go, which happened every day. She reacted with rage to her daughter's deliberate whining and baby talk, and she also felt very guilty about her punishments and slappings. There was evident intense relief as the mother described her tremendous fury with her child. Material also emerged about her strong anxiety that Amy would follow in her (Mrs. B.'s) sister's footsteps. Amy physically closely resembled Mrs. B.'s sister, who had been hospitalized several times for mental breakdowns. The therapist communicated to Mrs. B. how excessively upset she must become when she saw any "danger signs" or problems with Amy, with the specter of her sister in the background.

The therapist, in work with the parents throughout the treatment, found that when they were confronted with their interference and ambivalence, they would come to understand and work out the immediate impeding forces. But there remained a strong tendency for them to act out their resistance—usually through bringing their child late for sessions—and this became an index and barometer of underlying feelings.

Elaborations on the Concept of the "Therapeutic Alliance"

In the early stages of work with Amy, we saw a shift in her presentation of material. She became comfortable, less frightened, and elaborated her play (e.g., the scissors play) with the encouragement of the therapist. Amy did not bring this material (the mouth play) because she shared the goals of the treatment. She was unconcerned about her "talking problem" or her general withholding patterns and inhibitions. The material emerged in play because of an internal unconscious pressure (similar to dream expression) and not as a communication in the therapy. Yet once it emerged, Amy wanted to further the play and please her therapist. Amy had begun to develop an *immature therapeutic alliance*, which characterizes the treatment of many young child patients.

The *immature alliance* is based on a positive relationship with the adult therapist. The adult becomes trusted as a helping person, a person whose lead is followed, and the child therefore becomes more willing to work. After a period of fear of the therapist as the dreaded doctor, we saw the signs of a growing positive attachment. Amy began to accept tissues from the therapist, smiled when she entered the sessions, and showed a possessiveness over the toys and crayons. Therefore when the scissors play emerged, she elaborated it more fully because of the therapist's interest.

There are typically two aspects to this positive *immature alliance* (Sandler, Kennedy, & Tyson, 1983). Some of it is based on a libidinal component—a love relationship founded on earlier aspects of positive relationship in the child's life (positive transference). Perhaps this stemmed from Amy's attachment to her father. In addition, there are nonlibidinal elements. Often the child finds that the therapist is helpful. When the therapist puts into words and clarifies matters that have troubled the child, it often arouses positive feelings. In the early sessions with Amy, when the therapist clarified verbally that she was worried about being separated from her mother, or that she "mixed up" the therapist with the doctors who had operated on her, the statements seemed to provide some relief for her. She recognized that she only had a worry and that the therapist would not perform operations. She could begin to turn to the therapist as a source of comfort.

In child work, an alliance with the child is not enough. One of the functions of the child therapist is to develop an effective therapeutic alliance with the family (Sandler, Dare, & Holder, 1973). Just as a parent approves a playmate, toy, or activity for the child, the child must come to feel that the parent approves of the psychotherapist and the process.

Amy's mother was often angry and frightened about the course of treatment. It was clear to the therapist that the work with Amy was in jeopardy unless the mother could become more comfortable with her feelings about the therapy. Two issues were clarified with the mother. She unconsciously feared that the fact that Amy was in therapy "confirmed" that Amy was like her disturbed sister. Her resentment was also a vehicle for the expression of her general resentment of being abandoned by her husband to totally raise, handle, and educate her large family. When these issues were discussed, clarified, and acted on (the father became more involved with transportation), the mother's positive investment in her child's psychotherapy was restored. The need to monitor the nature of the parental alliance, then, is a critical aspect of child work.

Elaboration on the Concept of "Resistance"

At the start of the treatment, Amy evidenced a form of early resistance that the young patient typically expresses. She dreaded coming at first (wet her pants) and longed for the reunion with her mother. She would have nothing to do with the therapist during the first session. Mark (Chapter 1) threw missiles at his therapist to express his fear and anxiety. These are forms of crass resistance discussed earlier. Whereas the adult patient can indicate verbally "I didn't feel like coming today" to express his discomfort, he often works with the therapist to understand the felt resistance. The young child patient's intolerance for discomfort often leads to total dramatic flight and avoidance. For the new child therapist, this open rejection of the therapist and the process is often discouraging and disheartening. It is often felt to be an attack on competence rather than the expression of the child's limited ability to tolerate frustration. Crass resistances are often manifested in child work.

In addition, in the above clinical material, the therapist worked with Amy on a prominent form of *ego resistance* (the understanding and interpretation of a common defense that Amy used). After expressing many of her biting impulses through her scissors play, there was a shift, and Amy became frightened of the therapist and the office. How did the therapist come to understand what this shift meant? During the evaluation, the therapist inferred that Amy defended against her oral rage (biting impulses) by the defense mechanism of *projection*: the expelling of her impulses outside to another object. Thus, she came to fear the biting dogs. The therapist felt that Amy was using this mechanism in her current sessions—the scissors—biting feelings had become too frightening to continue to own, and she had "projected" them onto the therapist. When he interpreted this mechanism (maybe Amy saw Mr. Chethik as a mean biting man), she "confirmed" this idea by her frightening drawings of pumpkins and dogs. The interpretation of this defense (ego resistance) helped Amy, since she could understand that this was only a scary idea (internal idea) and not real (Mr. Chethik was not really a biter). Understanding the familiar defenses the child used allowed the therapist to act quickly in this treatment period.

THE CONCEPT OF "TRANSFERENCE"

Clinical Material

After about 6 months of work, Amy continued to be very busy with her schoolwork during her sessions. She practiced the alphabet and numbers, but there was a very different quality to her affect. This seemed no longer to serve as a safe flight from the dreaded therapist but instead, a very stong teasing quality. The teasing became more apparent around her use of speech; she spoke loudly to her mother in the waiting room, practically shouted to her mother upon her return, but was mute the moment she crossed the threshold into the office.

The therapist began to tell Amy the story of "Little Miss Opposite," which she enjoyed immensely. The little girl always does the opposite of what she is asked: her mother tells her to dress, and she takes her shoes off; the father tells her to eat, and she leaves everything on the plate; Amy is supposed to spend the hour with her therapist, and she makes believe he is not here; she is supposed to talk, and she does not let a single peep come out of her mouth. Following this kind of discussion, the therapist would comment how sad it was that Amy had to make such a fight about the talking, and he would describe the painful and difficult events of Amy's week that had been told to him by Amy's mother (dog fears, night worries, or loneliness), all worries that Amy did not herself get help with.

After some of these early confrontations about her withholding (which was a repeated theme in the treatment), for a period of time, Amy became much less of an adversary. She began to write on her pictures, to inscribe, for example, "this is a picture of Bobby and Amy" in an effort to tell the therapist more. She indicated she wanted to play tic-tac-toe and also began to play some silent word games during the sessions. She then began a series of frightening drawings, many of which she drew while shuddering. These were evidently her nighttime worries. They were robot monsters that chased frightened little girls. She acknowledged by nods or writing that these were night fears, and she indicated how sad she felt by adding tears to the girl's face. All sorts of sharp, sticking projections came from the monsters; they were often drawn in haste with much anxiety. (The therapist had the impression they alluded to the surgeon–doctor.) We began collecting these pictures and put them in a special "talking" folder for use when Amy would be able to talk. Amy was quite eager to place these important drawings in the folder. The therapist pointed out to Amy during this period how much a *part* of her wanted him to know her worries and help her get rid of them, but that another part stopped this—the part that kept her from talking.

The idea of adding drawings to the talking folder pleased Amy, and she brought a new series of drawings. These were huge animals, like dinosaurs and alligators, with open mouths. These mouths were at times so large that they extended beyond and could not fit on the page. But though these were only frightening or aggressive animals, the accompanying affect was primarily pleasure and growing excitement. Red birds began appearing in her drawings, flying in squadrons, and all had the characteristic of the open mouth. Amy controlled the mounting excitement of these drawings by abruptly stopping the activity and going to her compulsive play. But even in her defensive play, eating was the major theme. Amy carefully seated all of her doll family around the table and made huge amounts of food out of the clay. She divided the portions equally and proceeded to stuff each doll with the excessive food. When she went back to these bird drawings, she giggled and laughed. Over a series of sessions, she began creating a mural; this was filled with fleeing red birds with open mouths. Behind them were some hunters who were firing bullets from their guns. When the therapist asked why the hunters were after the birds, Amy wrote in enormous letters, large enough to cover a page, to "EAT THEM."

The therapist came to feel that as Amy developed more positive transference feelings, she was struggling with impulses of oral incorporation. He began to tell Amy the story of the gobble-gobble feelings. Sometimes girls become afraid when they begin to like places and people they came to. This was because the gobble-gobble feelings came up inside. They would worry, in their pretend games, that because of their liking feelings they would want to eat everything all up, even to swallow up the people they liked. Even though the gobble-gobble feelings were from long ago and were *only ideas*, sometimes they were such a worry that they made children keep their mouths shut very tight.

As earlier with the scissors material, Amy seemed to show a similar mechanism. At first she showed the eating, oral, engulfing impulses that she feared in herself. Then the impulses were projected onto the hunter in the mural and onto the therapist who sought to eat the birds and who began to frighten Amy in her sessions.

Elaboration of the Concept of "Transference"

Much of the treatment work with Amy was done through the transference. There are a variety of types of transferences in child work: (1) character transference, (2) transference of past relationships, (3) transference of current relationships, and (4) the therapist as an Object of externalization. Amy evidenced all the abovementioned varieties, and we shall examine them in the course of this chapter.

Character Transference

Character transference is a *habitual* mode of relating to classes of people that is inappropriate to these people but emerges from significant past experiences. Amy's habitual mode of relating to new adults was to be terrified. She reacted to people, like her new therapist, as to the dreaded authority–doctor who would hurt her. Amy had evidently been terrified at the start of treatment; she had submitted to the dread experience by taking the therapist's hand, as she had earlier submitted to the terrifying hospital surgeons. In current situations, she became frightened, submissive, and frozen. She habitually reexperienced all new unknowns in terms of the traumatic (in her mind) hospitalization. This became a habitual mode of relating.

Transferences of Past Relationships

"Transference of past relationships" refers to derivatives of meaningful and significant relationships of the past that emerge in the treatment situation because of the psychotherapeutic work. Again, they are inappropriate reactions to the therapist. The past experience is repressed, but the effects of the experience produce current disturbances in the form of symptoms or troubling behaviors, etc. The process of the therapy helps to revive the wishes, fears, memories of these past experiences through the living relationship with the therapist. This differs from the "character transference," which is global, expressed with many people, and usually evident at the start of treatment. The "transference of past relationships" usually emerges slowly in the course of treatment under the pressure of the repetition compulsion (discussed earlier).

In the above clinical material, Amy developed a number of "transferences of past relationships" to the therapist. We are aware that Amy had a significant fixation in the anal phase of development. She unconsciously retained her words as she had earlier sought to retain her bowels in her struggle with her mother. The history clarified that, provocatively, she had avoided the toilet and acted in defiance of the mother. This form of relating was lived out in the treatment. Amy provocatively showed the therapist that she had words, as she spoke loudly outside the office and up and down the corridor. She defiantly withheld her words (earlier her feces) from the therapist within the office, thus repeating in action the earlier repressed experience with her mother. The therapist identified what Amy was experiencing (her "Little Miss Opposite" feelings, which were very strong.) He also clarified that the pleasure of the "Little Miss Opposite" feelings had a major cost—she could not communicate important ideas and worries with the therapist because of her retention pleasure. The effect mobilized some internal pressure in Amy to communicate. Work with Amy on this transference manifestation allowed Amy to learn about an important characteristic in herself (her pleasurable word retention) and to make it somewhat ego-alien (undesirable), since it also inhibited communication that she wanted.

A second form of "past transference" emerged in relation to oral conflicts and expressed a primitive fear. The very young child wants to possess totally the mother, and under the aegis of the oral drive, this can take the form of "eating the mother up." (One often sees this impulse expressed by mothers, who fondly say to their child—"You look so cute today, I'm going to eat you up.") As Amy became fond of her therapist, her oral (red birds with gigantic mouths) incorporative wishes from the past emerged in the treatment. She repeated these repressed wishes from early childhood. The therapist identified what Amy was experiencing (her "gobble–gobble feelings"). He also interpreted that these oral wishes (to devour lovingly) could be very frightening and contribute to the elective mute symptom.

As noted earlier, work within the transference has the potential for special therapeutic advantage. The patient vividly experiences the affects that are identified and discussed, and this provides greater opportunities for change. For example, Amy vividly felt her intense "Little Miss Opposite" feelings around words as well as her pleasure in defying the therapist. Simultaneously she experienced the problem of being unable to tell him about her troubled nightmares because she wanted him to take them away (the therapist highlighted this problem in her retention). Amy then sought vigorously to talk (draw) and to alter her symptom. The immediacy of the transference allowed these conflicting affects to emerge and be understood. The effect of this work allowed Amy to talk more freely everywhere, with the exception of the therapy itself.

Clinical Material

As the positive feelings for the treatment increased, and as her wish to show the therapist her problem drawings grew, there was also an increase of already great guilt within Amy. There were many feelings of being disloyal toward her family. She became very provocative at home, deliberately courting punishment by such open acts as standing on the living room chairs; this was followed by frightened questions such as "Do you still like me, Mommy?" The therapist could handle some of these problems with Amy directly by interpretation. She had a big worry that, as she began to like him, her mommy would not like her so much. But the parents themselves reacted strongly. The lateness returned rather consistently, and there was a critical cancellation with little reason at a point when Amy was making a particularly strong effort to communicate. (This was immediately after Amy announced on a weekend for the first time that she wanted to talk to Mr. Chethik.) In the session after the missed appointment, Amy dramatically removed all of her pictures from her "talking folder" and took them home. There seemed to be very strong "going away feelings," the therapist noted with Amy. She was obviously worried that the treatment might soon end, and we learned shortly after that that her fears were not totally unrealistic.

The mother herself was quite upset by Amy's actions. She cried and felt responsible but seemed to indicate that she was growing more depressed herself. Several days later the therapist received a call from the father who said in a faltering tone that they had failed to inform him (the therapist) Mrs. B. was pregnant. Not only was Mrs. B. pregnant, but she was in the latter part of her sixth month, although this was not easily apparent because of her obesity. It then emerged that the parents (especially the mother), for the past months, had had growing questions about whether she could realistically carry the burden of the treatment with the added demands of her new baby, and this question was looming larger and larger. It seemed to come as a great relief when we were able to work out a new schedule so that the therapist could see Amy late in the day, and the father, by changing his work schedule, could take on the responsibility of chauffeuring Amy. At that point there was a positive shift in the mother–child relationship and striking changes in their interplay, which are discussed below.

During the beginning of the second year of work, the earlier teasing and anal withholding seemed to reappear strongly. Amy sang again in the hallway as she approached the office, but silence ensued when she entered. When she did write to explain her pictures more fully, she wrote in such small letters that it was impossible to make out the words. In addition, she had all the members of the doll family talking to each other in tiny, whispering, inaudible voices, but no sound came out directly so the therapist could hear it. At this point the therapist began to attempt to reconstruct for Amy the earlier toilet-training situation. He felt that Amy was showing him in the office an old struggle, her old feelings that she had had when she was 2 and 3 years old when her mother used to chase after her to get her to go on the potty. Then she used to hide under the bed and in the closet. It must have become an exciting, teasing chase with her mother. Now, it seemed, she was trying to make a very exciting, teasing chase here. She was trying to have the therapist chase after her words. The therapist also mentioned that she was coming to see him the *same time* every day to talk, and that *must* remind her of the special potty time that her mother had each day—when Amy was supposed to make. Now 5:00 P.M. every day must feel like a new potty time for her. She was supposed to "make" her words for me. There were times, we knew, when Amy used to put her BMs *everywhere* except in the potty, where her mother wanted her to; and now she was showing her therapist that she could talk *everywhere* except in the right place—here in the office. It seemed that the old 2- and 3-year-old feelings were controlling Amy very much.

Amy became preoccupied with the toy bathroom furniture; she stuffed the toilet full of clay, and she had each member of the family go to the potty several times a session. She then began a game in which she attached many items together with clay. The purpose of the game was to move the long attached train without losing any of the parts. The therapist talked with Amy about the worry that little girls had when they were small, the worry about losing their BMs in the potty. When children were really young, they felt that their BMs were very important to them, and very, very precious. They had a big wish to keep them and they did not want to see them going out of them. Could Amy now have this worry about her words? She had given up her BMs, but maybe now she just did not want to give up her words.

In this period Amy made her most active direct attempts to bring up words. There was a strong desire to tell the therapist about some pressing worry. She opened her mouth to say something, and quickly covered her mouth with her hand. This was a striking struggle, and her anguish and terror were difficult to watch. When she failed and no sound came out, she went to the table to draw the worry instead—e.g., the robot monster or a witch—and wrote to tell more about the worry. These desperate attempts to bring out words were repeated throughout the treatment; at times she turned pale, used her hand to pull something from her mouth, or writhed on the floor in her efforts. The anxiety was terribly severe, and Amy was most frightened.

After about a year and a half of treatment, the therapist spoke with Amy and her family about the fact that he would be leaving the community in about 6 months. We decided to postpone a decision about further treatment until the end of our work. Amy reacted by temporarily withdrawing into severe compulsive play, but she directly spoke of her sadness and anger at home.

In the last phase of the treatment, Amy seemed to focus on her problems of excitement. Throughout the treatment Amy had struggled with many feelings about having a male therapist. Amy showed a marked sudden increase in excitement related to her father. She seemed constantly to find things to fight about with him in the waiting room. She would act like a puppy dog, sitting in front of him, climbing on the furniture, and at times climbing directly on him. Sometimes I also could hear the commotion her sisters and brothers were making with the father while Amy was in her session. Amy's drawings reflected this theme—little animals climbing higher and higher, one on top of the other; or a big elephant was lifting little ducks on his back. A new consistent game with the dolls was introduced, in which a man in one car was chasing children in another car in a big race. The accompanying behavior was giggling, much bodily twisting and turning, and at times holding of genitals. The therapist noted how much excitement there was when her father brought the other children. Sometimes we could see he did not stop them, and they could get very excited. The therapist thought Amy must also worry that things might get too wild and excited in the office and that he might let her do things the way her father did. Maybe it was hard for her sometimes because the therapist was a man, like her daddy. But he reassured her that he would not let things get too exciting in the office because he knew this would scare her and not help her.

During another period of animal climbing drawings, Amy brought in a picture of a boy. This was Alfred, her 9-year-old brother, whom she wrote she *hated*. A series of drawings showed him attacked by the robot monsters and thrown into the sea to a nest of hungry sharks. From the mother, the therapist learned that Amy was doing acrobatics and exercises with Alfred, and at times she was provoking Alfred to wrestle and fight. The mother then felt she would supervise and limit their play.

During this period, the therapist became the direct object of Amy's excitement. She was much more coquettish in her general manner, and she began to come to the sessions much better dressed and groomed. A new femininity emerged. Sometimes her dress accidentally slipped too high. She had renewed desires to play tic-tac-toe and word games, but she was so apparently excited that the therapist had to stop the games, telling her that they just seemed to make her so excited. She attempted to have the therapist touch her or stop her physically by scribbling on the desk or attempting to take a chair out of the office, but an anticipatory interpretation that she wanted to make an exciting fight seemed to stop her at the moment.

Pregnancy and birth fantasies were present. Amy drew a series of pictures showing how a cornstalk grew from seed planting through maturity. She presented the therapist with elaborate drawings of Easter eggs, writing on the back of the page "Mr. Chethik." The therapist noted sadly that she showed she had many questions and thoughts about how things grew, but it was hard to understand all her ideas from the drawing alone. At this time she sought sexual knowledge from her mother directly, which enormously pleased the mother.

On one occasion she wet herself as she approached the office. The therapist wondered with Amy if one of her problems that kept her from talking was her big worry that so many excited feelings would come out. She showed by her wetting that she sometimes had a very hard time controlling these exciting feelings. Maybe she was afraid that a whole flood of excited words and ideas would come out if she opened her mouth.

During the second year of our work, Amy's general adjustment markedly improved. Slowly her speech inhibitions lessened and disappeared outside of the treatment. She became increasingly able to participate in class, including volunteering and contributing her own ideas to the group. She made many friends in class among the girls, and spoke to, visited, and played with a number of them after school. She began to talk with neighbors for the first time and found much pleasure in being able to call extensively on the telephone.

The most striking area of change was the difference in her relationship with her mother. Her mother felt she understood Amy much more, and extensive and sympathetic discussions occurred between them. Amy discussed her night fears and dog worries with her mother. For a period of time she responded to her mother's sensitive remarks by sobbing in her lap for protracted lengths of time. It was, indeed, with her mother that she worked on our final separation. She was particularly worried that the therapist was leaving because she had so consistently been unable to talk with him. Amy showed increased desires to help her mother in the kitchen; she learned to cook and shop, and she became a major mother's helper for the new baby in the family. The family decided not to transfer Amy to another therapist but instead had Amy's older brother (who had learning problems and problems in sexual identity) enter treatment. Amy's gains appeared to be stabilized during her latency years, which was the period the therapist was still able to keep in contact with the family.

Elaboration of the Concept of "Transference"

In the second year of treatment, Amy continued to bring in a variety of transferences, which were the principal media for the therapeutic work.

Transference of Past Relationships

There was further work on Amy's anal fixation, and a "working through" of the links between the retention of bowels earlier in her history and the current retention of words ("working through" is the elaboration of an earlier insight through further exploration and interpretation). In the past Amy had had a special potty time each day when a battle of wills was waged between Amy and her mother. She retained her bowels and soiled later. In treatment, Amy came to feel that the 5:00 P.M. daily session was the time for her to produce verbally, and she defiantly and unconsciously retained her words. When the therapist interpreted the maternal transference (past) that had emerged in the therapy, Amy again desparately sought to speak. It was clear that Amy wanted to talk, and the insights from the past mobilized further efforts. (Indeed, after this work she became increasingly freer to talk outside her sessions.)

Another aspect of Amy's anal period of development was reconstructed in this period of psychotherapy. In the past, Amy had had a fear of the bathroom, which is common to children. She worried that her feces were a part of her body, and these would be lost forever when she put them in the toilet. This fear reemerged symbolically in her sessions as she repeatedly played out building long attached "trains" out of clay without having any parts break off. The therapist interpreted the meaning of this repeated game and linked this worry to Amy's current fear—the fear of her loss of her words (this anxiety was similar to the anxiety expressed by Jonathan in his racetrack play in Chapter 3). She had the childlike idea that if her words came out, she would lose precious parts of herself.

Transference of Current Relationships

A major source of transference (inappropriate reactions to the therapist) is the displacement of current internal issues in the relationships with family members onto the therapist. The child patient often expresses forbidden affects experienced toward parents or siblings within the safer confines of the therapy hour. There are two major sources for these displacements: *reality conflicts* stemming from current family involvement and conflicts that emerge from *current developmental phases* that are appropriate to the age level of the child. Amy gave evidence of a number of these displacements.

A major *reality conflict* was Amy's markedly ambivalent relationship with her mother, where love and hate were often felt, as well as the fear of abandonment. Her mother also had reciprocal ambivalent feelings and wishes to get rid of the burden of her daughter. These aspects of current feelings were lived out in the transference. As Amy became more positively attached to her therapist, she began to fear the rage of her mother and the possibility of abandonment. She reacted by stemming the flow of her productive drawings and removing her material from the office. The therapist described her "going away" feelings. Rather than face the anxiety of loss of the mother, she actively began to abandon the therapist and the process they had built together. Some of the current issues in her relationship with her mother were being expressed within the therapy, particularly the fear of abandonment. The therapist was able to verbalize the worry that Amy had that if she liked him too much, she would lose her mother. But it also allowed the therapist the opportunity to work generally with Amy on her feelings that her mother would go away because she was an angry, dirty girl.

Another source of current transference phenomena stemmed from conflicts related to Amy's *current level of psychosexual development.* In the latter part of Amy's treatment, oedipal conflicts emerged stemming from her relationship with her father. She felt enormously excited being with her father, and these affects were exacerbated by the difficulties her father had in physically limiting his daughter (e.g., she climbed all over him in the waiting room). In the original diagnostic formulation, there was no evidence of oedipal conflicts. This did not mean that Amy did not experience conflicts on that level, but earlier, the preoedipal struggles predominated. It appeared that as Amy was able to work out some of the oral and anal anxieties that had constrained her, the emergence of phase-appropriate conflicts became evident.

Amy displaced many of the feelings about her father onto the therapist. The transference relationship became very sexualized. She became coquettish in the office, sought physical contact, experienced many genital sensations (her wetting). The therapist was able to discuss her excitement, her sexual curiosity, and slowly underscore the naturalness of these emerging womanly feelings. He was also able to make further links between Amy's muteness and her fear of her excited affects. Perhaps Amy had to keep her mouth closed so that a flood of exciting, sexy feelings, which were scary to her, would not come out.

It is interesting to note that the elective mute symptom that Amy developed illustrated the concept of "multiple determination." In psychodynamic theory, the concept of "multiple determination" means that a series of conflicts get attached to a particular symptom, often a series of conflicts from a number of phases of development. Amy's mutism had contributions from all the developmental phases. Her fear of her biting wishes (both hostile and loving) expressed the oral elements. Her enormous wish to retain her products reflected the anal components. Later the worry about the strength of her excitements reflected the oedipal aspects of her speech inhibition. Therefore, in the course of psychotherapy, in order to help a patient find symptomatic relief, the therapist will often need to work through the multiple roots of a problem.

Therapist as an Object of Externalization

The last general type of transference is the (inappropriate) use of the therapist as an object of externalization. In this process, the child splits off one aspect of an internal conflict onto the therapist, and the patient experiences some relief (usually from anxiety). This is a typical process in adolescence. Many teenagers experience intense derivates of sexual impulses, and rather than struggle with an internal conflict (e.g., I shouldn't live out these feelings), they "externalize" the control pressures (superego components of the conflict) onto the parents or other authorities. They repress their own guilt and see instead parents "guilt-tripping" them. This mechanism, strictly speaking, is not a form of transference but a close ally. The therapist is attributed with feelings that are inappropriate to him, but rather than the source of this attribution stemming from significant relationships of the past, they derive from current splitoff feelings within the patient.

In the earlier scissors material play sequence during the first year of treatment, Amy initially began to experience angry, biting affects reflected by the chopping scissors near her mouth. As these affects became more intense, they became more conflicted—Amy's conscience reacted to these unacceptable feelings. She then externalized (in this case, projected) one aspect of the conflict—(the impulse) onto the therapist. She became frightened that the therapist would bite her or yell at her and wanted to avoid her sessions. Although she experienced an actual fear of the therapist, she was relieved of the tension of an internal conflict, since these forbidden affects were no longer a part of herself.

Much of the psychotherapy with Amy took place in the transference (expressed in the relationship). She reenacted significant relationships and events of the past and present in her relationship with the therapist. The events and experiences that significantly shaped Amy emerged in the treatment and became available to be understood. This emotional reenactment and availability to treatment makes transference work a very important phenomenon in the psychotherapy process.

In the work with Amy, there was one area that remained unresolved at the end of treatment. Whereas it is clear that the treatment focused on dealing with the neurotic conflicts, the intractability of the speech problem within the transference suggested that there were some features in Amy's personality that were perhaps border-line. (This form of pathology is dicussed and illustrated in Chapter 7. They appeared to involve a failure to neutralize instinctual energy and deal with some aspects of magical thinking. Amy retained a belief in the magic of words and thoughts—her talking was still equated with killing and destructive power in the transference. Therefore, although she was primarily a neurotic youngster, there was also evidence of more primitive features.

COMPARING THE OLDER
AND YOUNGER CHILD PATIENT

As the child develops chronologically, many ego functions mature. Thus, in the older child patient (latency period of development), cognitive functions significantly develop, and secondary thought processes mature. (For a comprehensive discussion of these functions, see Charles Sarnoff's book *Latency*.) This development includes a number of ego functions such as the capacity for self-observation, capacity of abstraction, and a capacity to tolerate greater anxiety because of the consolidation of the defensive structure. Latency-aged children tend to utilize play somewhat less and can use verbalization more extensively.

With the prelatency child, the therapist needs to be aware of the limited capacity of the child's ego and (as noted earlier) will often need to function as an ego auxiliary for the child. One theme that is explicit in the young child cases already discussed (Amy and Mark) is the role of helping the child *develop* a capacity for verbalization of affects. The therapist identifies Amy's oral incorporative feelings as her "gobble-gobble" feelings, her passive-aggressive impulses as her "Miss Opposite" feelings, and Mark's impulsive aggression as his "lion feelings." He is helping these young children find new words for affects that are only expressed in action. In that way, part of the function of the therapist working with the young child is to facilitate development.

Another significant ingredient in work with the young child is the close identification with parents. The young child patient is affected more by the parents' concept and fantasy of the child. This was evident in the cases of Amy and Mark in the mother-child relation-ships. Amy's mother identified Amy with the mother's disturbed sister. Mark's mother fostered a strong self-representation (the rebellious child who would never submit). In these cases, direct work with the parents about their image of the child needed to occur for the child to proceed in his treatment. Therefore, in work with the young child, the parent work is more significant.

BIBLIOGRAPHY

Arlow, J. A. (1961) Silence and the theory of technique. *Journal of the American Psychoanalytic Association* 9:44–55.
Browne, E., Wilson, V., & Laybourne, P. C. (1963). Diagnosis and treatment of elective mutism in children. *Journal of the American Academy of Child Psychiatry*, 2:605–617.
Loomie, L. S. (1961). Some ego considerations in the silent patient. *Journal of the American Psychoanalytic Association*, 9:56–78.
Sandler, J., Dare, C., & Holden, A. (1973). *The Patient and the Analyst*. New York: International Universities Press.
Sandler, J., Kennedy, H., & Tyson, R. (1980). *The Techniques of Child Analysis*. Cambridge, MA: Harvard University Press.
Sarnoff, C. (1976). *Latency*. New York: Jason Aaronson.
Wright, H. (1968). A clinical study of children who refuse to talk. *Journal of the American Academy of Child Psychiatry*, 7:603–617.
Zeligs, M. A. (1961). The psychology of silence: Its role in the transference, countertransference and the psychoanalytic process. *Journal of the American Psychoanalytic Association*, 9:7–43.

6

Treatment of
Character Pathology*

Before one begins to think about the process of treatment of character pathology, it is helpful to understand some of the theory of character and character pathology. How would one define the concept of character itself? Fenichel (1945) describes it as the consistent, organized part of the personality, the habitual mode of adjustment that the ego has developed. Others have similar concepts. For example, character is defined as the basic core of the personality (Abend, 1983), or those aspects that denote the individuality of its possessor (Stein, 1969). In summation, character is the personal stamp of an individual, which has a regularity, a stability, and an enduring quality.

Character traits and neurotic symptoms have often been contrasted. Character traits are typically described as "ego-syntonic" (qualities felt by the individual to be an intrinsic part of the self), whereas neurotic symptoms are described as "ego-alien" (qualities felt by the individual as something to get rid of and in the way). For an individual, his character traits are so basic to him that they are taken for granted. Neurotic symptoms are usually a cause for complaint and seen as a foreign body. For example, Fred (Chapter 4) had a number of obsessional neurotic symptoms. He had to "check and recheck" his math; he had to be so conscious about not losing his

---

*A version of this chapter, "The Defiant Ones," by M. Chethik, was published in *Journal of Clinical Social Work*, Spring 1987, Vol. 15, No. 1, pp. 35–42.

place as he read that he could not concentrate on the content. But he was pained by these symptoms and wanted to be rid of them. He therefore felt they were on the periphery of his personality and not part of the "real Fred" who should be without these bothersome qualities. In contrast, the fighting and general belligerence of Mark (Chapter 1) was much closer to a character trait (a general counter-phobic stance). Mark was proud of his "lion feelings," this toughness and "masculinity." This quality in his personality protected him against any imagined onslaught from the outside. His hypermasculinity was felt by Mark to be his essence and central to him. Again, character traits are described as ego-syntonic in contrast to neurotic symptoms, which are experienced as ego-dystonic or ego-alien.

When we turn to children and the concept of character, one has to take into account the ongoing development process. Character is a result of a relatively completed developmental and integrative process, which is not fully consolidated until all major ego and superego functions are stabilized (Abend, 1983). This is achieved, some authors note, by the end of adolescence. Nonetheless, it is clear that children are in the process of developing character traits, and we usually describe these qualities as "on the way" to character formation or character pathology, rather than fully completed.

The term "character pathology" or "character disorder" is used when a habitual mode of adjustment an individual has developed has taken a pathological turn. Typically when most people think of character disorders, the image that is conjured up is that of the antisocial personality. Actually there are *two* major categories of character pathology: the impulse-ridden character disorder and the neurotic character (Fenichel, 1945).

The "impulse-ridden character pathology group" is defined as those individuals whose habitual mode of adjustment is instinct expressive, and indeed, it does describe the typical antisocial personality. In these children or adults, their egos habitually allow the expression of immediate pleasures. They cannot delay gratification, and their consciences have not effectively built the reactions and inhibitions that one would expect in the course of development. These individuals become the psychopathic adults, the addictive personalities (alcoholics, drug users, etc.), and individuals who have major social conflicts (impulsive aggression, fighting, destructiveness, stealing, etc.). In a metapsychological appraisal, these people evidence a fragile ego, have limited defense formation, require restraints to be imposed from the outside, do not accept the limits of reality, and typically evince little sublimation potential (the ability to work productively) (Michaels & Stiver, 1965).

In contrast, the neurotic character group is delineated by the fact that their habitual mode of adjustment was dominated by massive conflict in their development. Typically these adults and children develop a *fixed and pervasive defensive structure*, which permeates the entire personality. Thus, a youngster who is "on the way" to becoming an obsessional character (one type of neurotic character) would have these obsessional qualities "spread" into every aspect of his functioning. In the obsessional character, the control mechanisms would not only be evident in his rituals or obsessions but would also be found in his posture, bearing, and physical gait. His speech could be rigid and precise, etc. Thus, the obsessional qualities would not be localized in various symptoms but would be extensively expressed throughout the personality.

In general, the treatment of individuals with character pathology is more difficult than that of neurotic patients. Confronting behavior or qualities that are part of the character is typically very threatening to these patients, because these qualities are central to their functioning. They often feel that their whole sense of "being" or sense of self is at stake. Therapeutic alliances are thus difficult to build, and there is particularly strong resistance to the recognition of their basic pathology.

In this chapter, we focus on the most typical kind of character problem we find in childhood, where there is a mixture of impulse-ridden and neurotic character elements. The most common referrals to psychiatric and outpatient clinics for children are the fighting, defiant, and "out of control" youngsters who are very action oriented. This type of young patient exhibits trouble at home with discipline, problems with peers through provocation, and, characteristically, many behavior issues in school. Throughout his early years, this action discharge mode is often in evidence. A significant percentage of these children are potential character disorders—they are "on their way" to consolidating a permanent antisocial character pattern in adolescence or young adulthood.

In attempting to understand this group of children, Freud's (1937) discussion in *Analysis Terminable and Interminable* seems particularly relevant. He describes a group of adult patients for whom "quantitative factors" in their personality make treatment very difficult; they struggle with the *excessive strength* of their instincts because of constitutional factors or developmental experiences and find it much harder at every stage of development to "tame these instincts." He further discusses two major implications for development caused by this struggle. These patients characteristically have a *low threshold for frustration of instinctual wishes* and thereby tend toward immediate discharge of tension. Second, they have a low threshold for the *tolerance of anxiety*. Many of these defiant children described above show problems with quantity of instinctual drive, low frustration, and problems in tolerating anxiety. These aspects in their development represent the impulse-ridden components of their character problems.

In addition, these youngsters also develop massive defensive structures. Particularly prominent is the mechanism of "identification with the aggressor" or the defense of "passive into active." The mechanisms are typically used in childhood, when the young, helpless child plays being the "boss" or "teacher" or powerful superhero. He copes with his feeling of helplessness (the natural state of many children) by temporarily turning passive into active, where he is the ruler or commander rather than the child who must comply.

From the developmental histories of these defiant youngsters, we can see that they use these particular mechanisms in a pervasive way. Often this emerges in the process of superego (conscience) development. In order to build the conscience, the child has to internalize the parental prohibitions. For these children, the parental inhibition stirs enormous anxiety, and they feel massively threatened, helpless, and weak. They "cope" with this threat by the mechanism of "identification with the aggressor"—they transfer themselves from the person being threatened to the person making the attack. They ward off being defenseless and helpless by becoming the attacker. This pattern becomes a vigorous and pervasive defensive mode that seems to permeate the whole personality.

The purpose of this chapter is to (1) describe these youngsters, (2) provide a diagnostic appraisal, (3) highlight some of the typical treatment problems, and (4) discuss techniques that have been developed to deal with the massive resistances these children employ. Fortunately, many of these children have not fully developed the "armor plating of the personality" (Reich, 1963) that comes with time. Their defenses are not as solidified as those of the adult, and anxiety as an affect still remains therapeutically available. The principles of treatment with these children have a good deal of application to the treatment of character pathology in general.

These issues are discussed through the presentation of Roger L., a handsome, energetic, and extremely defiant late-latency-aged youngster.

PRESENTING PICTURE, HISTORY, INITIAL SESSIONS

One was immediately impressed with Roger's precocious "macho" quality and his premature manliness. He had a swagger, a tough gait, and cursed easily and fluently in his initial meetings with his therapist, though he was only 10 years old. Roger was the middle child in a sibship of three; a sister was 2 years older, and a brother 4 years younger. He came from a middle-class, educated, professional family. The parents were concerned about their son's intense rages. For example, Roger reacted with fury to his father's demands: "turn down the radio" would provoke a loud blasting of rock and roll music; "close the car window" would be met with an increase in the flow of air. Roger was often in trouble in school: he fought constantly, often losing out to older children, but always taking on a "dare." His fighting had led to detentions and a series of suspensions from school. He could provoke his teacher by greeting her with "Hi, stupid" as he entered the classroom in the morning. At age 10, the parents were already worried about his major attraction to the Lepke gang in the neighborhood, a group of young tough adolescents who were noted for their interest in drugs and minor vandalism. Generally the parents were strong effective people, but with Roger, the father was often provoked into counterrage (yelling, screaming), and the mother developed a placating, accommodating role to avoid trouble.

In the history, Roger was remembered as a very active baby, enjoyed by the family. As an energetic toddler, his mother found him hard to pursue at times, but although Roger was vigorous, he seemed happy and alert. He was, however, very frightened during the process of toilet training, especially avoiding the potty, and it took him 6 months to accomplish this task at 2½ years of age. The mother felt she was putting little pressure on Roger and was surprised by his struggle. Both parents felt it was striking that he became very frightened and somewhat alienated from his father at that time, particularly afraid of his father's deep, loud, booming voice and his mustache. However, by age 3½, the pattern of defiance that was described above began and generally spread. Roger now did not fear his father; he defied him. He fought the daily demands with a characteristic "No, I won't. You can't make me." Accompanying Roger's counterphobic stance during the years were shortened periods of symptom formation. Sleep problems, enuresis, and tics were evident periodically, lasting, at times, for several months.

From the onset, Roger knew he was coming to see a therapist because of his "bad temper." He described how he was beset, however, by hosts of classmates who provoked him, and one could only expect that he would defend himself. Similarly his brother and sister provoked him, and he was forced to retaliate. It was clear that as he described his active forms of revenge, a characteristic smile of pleasure came over his face.

He was angry at his mother, who was always hovering and worrying about him and who thought he was terrible. He wished she would "just get off his back." With pleasure he described some of the boys of the Lepke gang; he felt much pride that he was a fully accepted member although he was the youngest. He spoke of the huge collection of *Playboy* magazines the group accumulated.

Roger told his therapist, during the evaluation sessions, he was not going to see him. He was boring and probably charged too much, and he could not make him stay. He ended these initial sessions, however, by relating a recent nightmare—a dream in which his mother's severed head was rolling in the living room. He was visibly anxious and agitated as he described the dream. The leap from defiance and opposition to anxiety and neediness could fluctuate from moment to moment; this was characteristic of Roger in the early months of our work.

DIAGNOSTIC EVALUATION

I. Drive Assessment

The outstanding feature in Roger's presenting difficulties was his problem with aggression. He had a "hair-trigger" temper; he was exceedingly provocative and driven to prove his "toughness." The major source of *aggressive drive difficulty* appeared to be at the phallic level of development. Early conflict emerged in his relationship to his father, who appeared as a major threat and "castrator" in the perception of Roger. Roger appeared to react intensely and massively to early feelings of shame, humiliation, and smallness in relation to his father by extensive counterreaction. Thus, we see the massive defensive process. There was also some suggestion in this history that Roger was struggling with the impulses of cruelty and sadism, which are the aggressive drive components of the anal phase of development. His struggle with his father emerged during his toilet training at age 2½. An additional contribution to Roger's problems with aggression appeared to come from his endowment. He was described as a vigorous, energetic youngster from the beginning of his life, which suggests a strong constitutional inheritance of instinctual drives. This endowment could contribute to the aggressive conflict at all stages of development.

Despite Roger's impulsive behavior and his apparent unconcern for others in his attacks and disregard of rules, there was indication of a relatively higher level capacity for *object attachment*. During his early years, there was a good and "happy" interplay between parents and child. Roger also appeared to evidence the affect of guilt in the evaluation. He was very disturbed about his dream in which his mother's head was severed. It appeared that he felt guilty about the aggressive impulses directed at his mother that were manifested in the dream, although this was expressed as anxiety and agitation.

II. Ego Assessment

In many ways, Roger gave evidence of good ego functioning. Despite his behavior problems, he performed well at school academically and scored well in achievement tests. Basically, his ego functions were well developed—perception, memory, secondary process thinking, ability to abstract, etc. He also had a capacity to work at tasks (academic work) when his conflicts were not involved (e.g., his masculinity was not threatened). In the evaluation, however, there was some suggestion of ego weakness at times in relation to the strength of Roger's aggressive drives. He evidenced prominent accessibility to his aggression and found significant pleasure in his ability to intimidate peers (e.g., his classmates or siblings).

A very prominent feature in Roger's ego functioning was his response to internal conflicts with aggression. It appeared that Roger's phallic aggressive wishes promoted an anticipated anxiety response—that he would be attacked by a powerful authority (the castrator father). Roger appeared to have an enormous anxiety about castration during his development. Roger responded to his "threat" in a massive way. He used the defense mechanism of *identification with the aggressor* (or *turning passive into active*), and this defensive process became prominent, indeed, a central mechanism in Roger's life. In fact, at the time of the evaluation, Roger could be characterized by his antiauthority "macho" personality.

III. Superego Assessment

Problems in superego development seemed to fit into the above picture. In his development, Roger did experience the affects of shame, humiliation, and guilt that normally led to the internalization (taking in) of the prohibitions of parents and other authorities. However, with Roger, the intensity of the feelings of shame, humiliation, and guilt led in another direction. The anxiety that these affects produced were so powerful that Roger had to defend against them. He identified with the threatening object (father) or the subject of the anxiety, and transformed himself into the threatening figure.

An important distinction between potentially psychopathic youngsters and neurotic characterologically disturbed children is whether the affects of shame and guilt are experienced at all, since these affects are the "building blocks" of the conscience. Roger did experience these affects and then warded them off. One of the tasks of treatment was to help Roger experience them more readily, and this is discussed later in this chapter.

In the histories of youngsters like Roger, it is often difficult to reconstruct the early contribution of "nurture" and "nature." Whereas it seemed that Roger's instinctual endowment was a significant factor in his life-long problems with aggression, the therapist had some lingering question about the capacity for parental empathy during these early years. These parents were clearly thoughtful, psychologically minded people at the time of the evaluation. However, in reviewing the toilet-training history, it seemed that they appeared *intent* on pushing for accomplishment despite their youngster's fears and intense reactions. Did this indicate some inability to assess their child's intense anxiety during this period? These questions about parental contribution are often difficult to assess fully.

COURSE OF TREATMENT

Clinical Material

Roger was seen twice weekly for about 1½ years, and the course of the psychotherapy is described as it unfolded. During the early months of treatment, Roger highlighted his delinquent exploits in a highly pleasurable, excited, and heroic way. He thoroughly enjoyed the Lepke gang activities: they developed techniques as Peeping Tom's; they had continuous rip-off plans for stealing from supermarkets, drug stores, etc. They had a constant store of liquor, cigarettes, and pot, which they used in the group. They were involved in guarding the "turf" of the neighborhood, letting no alien young adolescents use the playground or ride bikes on the streets. They enjoyed attacking the rich. For example, throwing eggs at Cadillacs was great sport. Similar feats were described at school: Roger discussed his techniques with spitballs, his protection of vulnerable girls against the older kids, etc. His greatest contempt was for the frightened and weak boys. He noted, with contempt, that the "punks" and the "fags" that populated his school made him sick.

Roger appeared to have a number of motivations in providing this "heroic" material. He was pleased with the exhibitions of his exploits. He was also defiantly testing out the therapist to see if he would react with sanction and admonition. It was important for the therapist to maintain his relative neutrality. The gang attachment was part of an important pattern that the therapist and Roger would need to understand as the therapy went on.

Very occasionally there would be a session in marked contrast to the unfolding of these daily exploits. Roger would then be extremely agitated and markedly upset. For example, he was beset by thoughts that his father would have a car accident or die slowly of a heart ailment. He hated these thoughts and wanted therapy to get rid of them right now. He felt they would drive him crazy. He wanted to get away, to change schools, or move to another area where peace and tranquility could reign. The few occasions that guilt and anxiety reached consciousness were intolerable feeling states for him. The therapeutic task was to link this isolated misery with his more typical aggressive pleasure.

The therapist began to find occasions to make important connections. For example, the Lepke group, along with Roger, had been harassing an older couple in the neighborhood, a couple that Roger really liked. He had delivered papers to them and cut their lawn. In their harassment, the gang would ring their doorbell and hide. The pleasure was watching these people sputter and get increasingly upset. Roger was responsive to the therapist's observation that he felt bad attacking these people, but a very important feeling drove him to join the harassment. *No matter what, Roger could not stand being accused of being a chicken. He would always act to wipe out any hint of babyish "punk-fag" feelings in him.* This theme of wiping out any potential "punk-fag" feeling no matter what the cost became a very familiar refrain. He often reacted to his mother's concerns about getting into trouble by yelling at her and breaking something. Again he could slowly hear from the therapist that he felt her message was that he was a helpless little boy. His furious response was to show that there were no "punk-fag" feelings in him. His father's rules, on some occasions appropriate, always made him feel like a "little shit," and he was forced to act to wipe away that feeling. In fact, the therapist suggested again and again, his daily exploits were to quiet the inside "punk-fag-chicken" worry. On one occasion in this period, Roger acknowledged that when he had been little, he was afraid he would be drafted into the army and killed in a war, and also afraid that his father was a member of the National Guard. He seemed to listen when the therapist responded that *all* little kids were frightened as they grew up when they looked at the big giant father, the father who was a mustache man, and that doesn't really make them "punk-fags."

Similar themes permeated the transference. He could get mad with his therapist whenever he wanted to, he declared. He did not have to listen to a shrink or anyone who told the lies that his therapist told him. Many sessions were filled with acts of defiance. He walked out of the office on occasions, or lit up a cigarette. Not only would he leave at will, but he also announced he would never return. The therapist became adapt at spotting the need for the "tough Lepke gang" stance during the treatment hour. He told Roger that internally, he needed to think about what made Roger need to be tough. Perhaps Roger was upset with the therapy because he had told the therapist about the army worry or that he was "complying" too much by coming to his sessions on time. These acts could carry a "punk-fag" valence for Roger and stimulate the intense affect of shame. Roger would then react with his characteristic defiance. The therapist began to articulate these dynamics within the hour, as it occurred in the transference. For example, on one occasion, after a good series of sessions, Roger spit repeatedly into the wastepaper basket and snarled for the first 20 minutes. The therapist commented that the "Lepke gang was certainly here today in full force." He thought that maybe they showed up because Roger had become worried about what was happening in treatment. Things had been going too well. If things continued this way, what would happen to his "bad temper"? The therapist wondered if Roger worried that without his Lepke temper, he would feel weak and helpless. Roger translated, "You mean I might be worried that I'm going to become a pussy. Naw, I'm not worried about that," and he smiled broadly. And Roger calmed down for the rest of the session.

Discussion

What techniques did the therapist employ dealing with the character mode that Roger employed extensively? The therapist understood that Roger's driven "acting out" behavior was primarily based on conflict—he could not tolerate feeling small and helpless, and he was driven to erase that internal image.

The concept of *defense analysis*—repeated, repetitious interventions aimed at working through maladaptive behaviors that are pervasive resistances—is the key intervention with children with character pathology. Some of Wilhelm Reich's early work on character analysis (1963) is especially applicable. If we look closely at the above clinical material, we can delineate a series of interventions in the process of *defense analysis* with Roger. This process involves four steps: (1) making the particular behavior (character trait) explicit to the patient's ego; (2) making the ego-syntonic behavior (character trait) somewhat more alien to the patient; (3) making the underlying motivation for the behavior conscious to the patient; (4) making these motivations, formerly frightening, acceptable to the patient.

Initially the therapist defined Roger's behavior. The therapist *confronted* and *clarified* the action in question: "Roger often needs to act tough"; "Roger needs to defy adults, break rules at home and school"; "Roger needs to prove he is as tough as the older kids."

Roger's general stance and the associated behaviors were explicitly brought to his attention. This quality became defined as Roger's "tough Lepke-gang stance" and became a metaphor in the treatment hour.

A major early goal in the work with Roger was to make some of this explicit behavior *ego-alien*, though it previously had given him great pleasure. Feelings of unpleasure that Roger experienced (loss of self-esteem, guilt, loss of parental love) were affects that emerged but were *split off* from Roger's acts and not seen as connected. It was enormously helpful to clearly link some of the dreadful internal consequences that Roger experienced with Roger's daily behavior. Thus, the therapist clarified that Roger's provocation (with the Lepke gang) of the older neighborhood couple *did* make him feel very guilty. He felt bad later and uneasy with himself. Similarly, the anxiety dreams about Roger's father's health often emerged after Roger had given his father a very hard time. He seemed to worry that his troubling behavior with his father could seriously effect the older man and hated himself for the problems he was causing. Similarly, he often seemed to be very upset after a big blowup with his mother. The internal and hidden cost of his driven exploits become clearer to Roger and tarnished the sense of pure pleasure to the action–macho image.

The prominent and repeated *interpretations* were the therapist's comments that Roger's tough behavior pushed away the *normal* helpless internal affects of childhood. As noted above, the process of "identification with the aggressor" warded off a sense of weakness and helplessness, which had induced shame and humiliation. Slowly verbalizing the self-images that Roger feared (the punk–fag fears) and providing an acceptable developmental context for them were critical elements of the treatment process. Any command or request by parent, teacher, or therapist was seen by Roger as an attack on his self-esteem, an attempt to bring him to his knees. These "humiliations" made him need to act defiantly quickly. Slowly, Roger came to accept that although he could feel small (be given an assignment by a teacher or a chore by his father), the "small" feeling was typical for all children and young boys. He, however, tended to experience these requests as an enormous put-down and reacted to them as a major slight. In order to *work through* Roger's defensive overreaction, this interpretive theme was repeated very often in the course of the work. This was particularly effective in the transference—when Roger became tough in the session, the therapist searched for the material of the hour or the previous hour that could have provoked a sense of humiliation.

Why is the therapist primarily limited to *defense analysis?* Much of the focus of the work is intended to deal with extensive variations of a particular form of maladaptive behavior. Since Roger used this central defense pervasively, repeated intervention became necessary. In addition, children with character pathology do not tolerate extensive reconstruction of the past history that originally fostered the need for the pervasive defensive reaction. One can speculate that the reason Roger's phallic and oedipal struggle with the "castrating" father became so intense was that his underlying dependency needs and feminine wishes were particularly prominent factors in his development. One could also speculate that for children like Roger, the early experiences of childhood would be even more beset by intense anxiety than with neurotic children, since they resort to the massive defensive reactions. Intense anxiety states interfere with the development of cognitive functioning and growing verbal and symbolic capacity. These factors can make it more difficult for a reconstructive process to take place in children with character pathology.

COURSE OF TREATMENT: CONTINUED

Clinical Material

The work with Roger during the first year did not only involve identifying his need to act to ward off helpless affects. He also had many difficulties just containing stored-up rage. We witnessed an already familiar pattern, an outbreak of rage and later apparently unconnected self-loathing. For example, on one occasion, the whole family attended a piano recital for Roger's sister, who was an accomplished musician. Later, in celebration at a restaurant, Roger had made an incredible scene, defiantly yelling at a minor request by his father. He ended by screaming, "I hate families," and the L. family was forced to leave the restaurant abruptly. When the therapist discussed the event with Roger (the therapist had received the "news of the week in review" from the parents), Roger focused on his father's rotten behavior. However, his characteristic smile of pleasure emerged when the therapist attempted to reconstruct his feelings of the afternoon: how much he must have hated his sister, his wish that she would make a mistake during the concert and screw up, and how good it felt to finally ruin her day and get all his angry feelings out. The therapist predicted that he would later have a strong "black sheep" feeling. Roger responded immediately by talking of a dream he had recently had, about a dog the family had onced owned. In the dream the dog had "pissed and shit" all over the house and was taken by the collar to the Humane Society by the father. It was clear Roger felt that he was the incorrigible dog who would be thrown out of the family and killed. The themes of his constant daily rage with those close-knit family members, his intense pleasure at upsetting them, his strong feelings of being the outsider became very familiar ideas.

Roger began to speak more of his internal life. He talked about stories and books he had read. Prominent was the story of a white boy raised by Indians, or a child who lost his parents in World War II and survived in a concentration camp. When his feelings of being the abandoned orphan were discussed, Roger told his therapist of his conviction that he was really adopted and that he had often searched the house for his "papers." He came to identify these upsetting "black sheep" feelings and also began to realize that his daily rage *did* make people treat him differently in the family. Roger developed an increasing awareness that his own behavior and the parental counterreactions promoted his sense of being different, adopted, rejected. With this material, after a year of work, Roger's behavior began to change. He began working with his father, doing heavy "manly" construction work on the house, and redesigning furniture for his room. His father found him an energetic and amazing worker.

During the last 6 months of work, there were many behavior fluctuations in a good–bad Roger, with increasing periods of control. He still had numerous problems on the school playground and smilingly told his therapist he had a magnet in his pocket that attracted fights. The therapist noted that it was hard for him to tolerate the feelings (the identity) of being good. The therapist coined the phrase, "a fight during the day keeps the punk feelings away." A sudden disruptive episode with a teacher he was beginning to like was respresentative. Mrs. G. was a teacher of German extraction, and one day he came to salute her with "Sieg Heil" in the classroom and answer all questions with "Ja Wohl." It slowly became clear that he had become increasingly fond of her, was being used by her as a class monitor, and that he was overwhelmed with a "goody-two-shoes" feeling. His reaction was to disrupt the needy, caring, and tender identity.

Roger increasingly discussed feelings that made him embarrassed. He had some current worries. He was still afraid of the army and was relieved that there was no draft any longer. At times he had bad dreams. After seeing *Jaws* (the movie) he was beset by shark dreams. He recalled more childhood night fears of a white hand trying to choke him or pirates who cut off limbs with a sword. Attempts to move into underlying sexual anxieties and masturbation were met with intense resistance. For example, when the therapist brought up the idea that often guys' concerns about damaged limbs had to do with their fears of touching themselves, Roger could not work with that kind of internal material. But Roger's daily self-observation increased. He reported potential "dares" that the former (before treatment) Roger would get involved in. For example, in the past he often would break up some football play of older boys, intercept the pass, and run off. While he had similar urges, he now refrained. He knew the urge was just to prove that he was not scared and that became a stupid idea because he would always get beaten up.

With Roger's sustained good functioning, there was pressure from him and parents to stop treatment. At termination, it was suggested that there might be flare-ups in the future and that the therapist would be available for any crisis work.

Discussion

In the above treatment material, there was an important shift in the course of the work. Roger himself actively identified his provoca-tive-defiant patterns and self-observed the process. For example, he commented that he had been tempted to provoke the older kids on the schoolyard but refrained. The patterns became more ego-alien because he was much more aware of the "black sheep" consequences (his own punitive superego). However, when the therapist pointed out his fears of tender, caring feelings (e.g., toward the teacher) that promoted acting out, Roger could only tolerate limited exploration of the threat of his "soft" feelings.

In the later stages of treatment, Roger could tolerate the thera-pist's descriptions and verbalizations of his primitive rage and de-structiveness. For example, the therapist reconstructed the proud recital day—Roger's hatred of his sister, his wish that she would err during her performance, and his desire to ruin the celebration at the restaurant. The therapist added a human dynamic—Roger had these feelings because he was jealous, and these are common sibling experiences. The purpose of verbalizing these constructions and providing a context for them was to modify Roger's own overly harsh internal reactions to these destructive wishes.

There are some important counterreactive tendencies and issues within the therapist that typically emerge with these youngsters when confronted with sustained defiance and provocative behaviors. What are the internal reactions of the therapist to having smoke blown in his face, having "asshole" written on all available newsprint, and having the theme of uselessness of therapy constantly elaborated on? Three major counterreactions are stimulated within the therapy with children like Roger. One common reaction is rage, which is often handled by expression in some direct or subtle way within the treatment or by suppression of the "unacceptable" feelings. For example, fueled by the natural anger these patients evoke, it is not uncommon to make a direct, forceful intervention. On one occasion, the therapist was describing how isolated Roger's behavior was making him from his peers. He became aware that in his description of the rejection Roger was experiencing, he was "twisting the knife" so Roger could fully experience the pain. On self-examination, the motive for this "intervention" was revenge.

Another major reaction is a subtle admiration for these youngsters who, on the surface, appear as though they are afraid of nothing. Partly, the therapist is impressed with their evident "masculinity." A third typical counterreaction is fatigue as a reaction to the provocation coupled with a desire to shut off the search for an empathic response. The transactional dynamic is that the defiant child presses the therapist to repeat the past relationships—provocation of the adult authority and angry counterreaction. The feelings of having extended onself, "gone the extra mile" for the youngster, are often intense internal reactions that can lead to a cessation of the therapeutic process. The therapist's understanding of the patient's internal dynamics, therefore, is vital for his dealing with the counterreactive trends. For instance, when Roger walked out of the treatment office telling the therapist he had better things to do, it became clear that he was trying to make the therapist feel small and helpless. Something was happening currently that had induced these unacceptable feelings (smallness, helplessness) within Roger, and Roger was attempting to reverse the situation in his characteristic way. The therapist could then use this information (Roger's attempt to externalize his feelings of helplessness) to understand Roger's current struggle. Such mechanisms are common transference paradigms with these youngsters.

The difficulty the therapist typically has in sustaining his empathic capacity with the intensely defiant child patient brings us to some of the diagnostic considerations discussed earlier. We discussed some of the "nature" and "nurture" contributions to the pathology of these children. Children like Roger are typically described as "intense," "active," and "driven" from birth, and this speaks to the heightened instinctual endowment one often finds in these youngsters. They also approach each developmental task intensely. Thus, when Roger struggled with the developmental issues of autonomy and limits, he appeared vigorous and defiant (rather than frightened and terrified at times) to his parents. Although the parents reacted somewhat with force (e.g., toilet training) rather than understanding, can we say there was a major failure of parental empathy that caused the developmental interference in Roger's growth? In my experience with youngsters like Roger, it is clear that they often need unusually tolerant and empathic parents to fare well in development, and typically adequate parents often do badly with these children who need more.

SUMMARY

In summation, there are a number of important similarities, differences, and limits when we compare treatment of the children with character pathology and neurosis. The work with many children with character problems is a form of insight-oriented, uncovering treatment. Essentially, in the work with Roger, the therapist helped him to gain insight into the unconscious motivation of his character pattern. In this sense, the psychotherapy was "uncovering" and "interpretive" (bringing into consciousness what has been unconscious) as with neurotic children. However, there are many differences. In work with character pathology, insight is primarily limited to *defense analysis*, and there is a minimum of *content analysis* (exploring the underlying wishes and fantasies and placing them in a historical context). In the treatment process with Fred, the neurotic youngster (Chapter 4), there was a good deal of treatment of the defenses (resistances) when the work on his mechanisms of intellectualization, isolation, etc., was analyzed. In addition, however, Fred engaged in major content analysis and more fully explored the roots of his aggression, dependency wishes, sexual, and masochistic longings using memories and dreams that reconstructed the past. This fuller exploration is much less available in work with children with character pathology.

BIBLIOGRAPHY

Abend, S. (1983). Theory of Character. *Journal of the American Psychoanalytic Association.* 31:211–224.

Eissler, K. (1948). Ego-psychological implication of the psychoanalytic treatment of delinquents. *Psychoanalytic Study of the Child* 5:97–121.

Fenichel, O. (1945). *The Psychoanalytic Theory of Neurosis.* New York: W. W. Norton.

Feranczi, S. (1942). Gulliver fantasies. *International Journal of Psychoanalysis* XXIII:221–228.

Freud, A. (1946). *The Ego and Mechanisms of Defense.* New York: International Universities Press.

Freud, S. (1937). *Analysis Terminable and Interminable* (Standard ed., Vol. XXIII). London: Hogarth Press.

Johnson, A. M., & Szurek, S. A. (1952). The genesis of the antisocial acting out in children and adults. *The Psychoanalytic Quarterly* 21:323–343.

Michaels, J., & Stiver, I. (1965). The impulsive psychopathic character according to the diagnostic profile. *The Psychoanalytic Study of the Child* 20:124–141.

Redl, F., & Wineman, D. (1951). *Children Who Hate.* Glencoe, IL: Free Press.

Reich, W. (1963). *Character Analysis.* New York: Noonday Press.

Rexford, E. N. (1952). A developmental concept of the problems of acting out. *Journal of the American Academy of Child Psychiatry* 2:6–21.

Rexford, E. N. (1959). Antisocial young children and their families. In: L. Jessner & E. Pavenstead (Eds), *Dynamic Psychopathology in Childhood* (pp. 186–220). New York: Grune & Stratton.

Stein, M. (1969). The problem of character theory. *Journal of the American Psychoanalytic Association.* 17:675–701.

7

Treatment of the Borderline Child

In the following two chapters, the focus is on the treatment of children with borderline and narcissistic disturbances. The pathologies represent the more severe psychopathologies of childhood, and they tend to be viewed as disturbances centering in early object development (the early relationship with the caregiving adult). Therefore, in order to understand the treatment strategy with these youngsters, it is helpful to review some early object relations theory so that the therapist can have a conceptual framework of this period of development.

In addition, we also describe the treatment process with the disturbances. With the severe pathologies, treatment techniques tend to be "supportive" rather than "uncovering" as those employed with the neurotic child. When the patient is more fragile, it is generally disruptive to functioning to "uncover" the instinctual life. The supportive techniques are aimed at "shoring up" or building the ego. This is done by stabilizing and fostering the development of ego functions (e.g., reality testing) or the specific ego defenses.

Therefore, as we examine the case of a borderline child in this chapter, there are two major themes: (1) understanding this youngster's pathology in light of problems in early object attachment and separation, and (2) examining the ego-building and supportive techniques the therapist can employ in dealing with the borderline patient.

A REVIEW OF EARLY OBJECT RELATIONS THEORY: THE DEVELOPMENTAL CONTEXT FOR BORDERLINE AND NARCISSISTIC DISTURBANCES

In the past 35 years, the pioneering work of Margaret Mahler (1952, 1968) (elaborated by Furer, Settledge, and Pine) focused on the early phases of development of the infant, particularly in relation to the progression of attachment and separation from the object (caregiving individual). The object relations theory (the course of attachment and separation from the caregiver in the first few years of life) that has emerged has a similar structure to drive theory (course of the sexual and aggressive drive). In drive theory, there is a progression through natural phases of development (oral, anal, phallic, oedipal, latency, adolescence) for the child to traverse. For the best outcome in development, the child needs to move successfully through conflicts at each specific phase of development. Arrest or fixation (a lack of progression of the sexual or aggressive drive) in any phase can create the basis for pathology in adulthood. For example, severe problems in the normal oral phase can be the basis for eating disorders in adolescence and adulthood (for example, bulimia, anorexia, obesity). Problems at the oral phase can produce a fixation, which is expressed in later life through a variety of symptoms or behaviors. For example, having a very depressed and absent mother as an infant can produce an anxiety about starvation. This "oral anxiety" can then become a preoccupation throughout life, a fixation at the oral level, because of the intensity of the early problem. In early life, the youngster could attempt to deal with this difficulty by overeating. Later any anxiety could produce the "symptom" of overeating. We would then see the legacy of the early fixation in this individual's adult psychopathology expressed in obesity or an ever-present anxiety or preoccupation with food.

In a similar way, Mahler outlines the process (phases) of early attachment and separation that the infant and young child must progress through. Arrest or fixation along this continuum of development provides the legacy for the severe developmental pathologies of childhood.

The following is a condensed summary of this progression. In the early weeks of development up until 2 months of age, all infants experience the "normal autistic" phase where they are, as yet, unattached to the object (mother). At this point, the infant has no connection to the object, and the beginning connection becomes stimulated by the care and ministrations of the caregiver. The normal autistic phase is seen by Mahler as an objectless phase.*

In normal development, under the aegis of the pleasure principle (the adequate care, feeding, playing, etc., with the child that is experienced as pleasurable to the child), the child "attaches" to the parent figure. The nature of that early normal attachment is a symbiotic one, where the infant cannot distinguish himself from the object. This second early phase of object development is called the "phase of primary narcissism" (Freud, 1914) or the period of "symbiotic union" (Mahler, 1968). This normal phase has a number of characteristics. During this phase, (1) the child cannot distinguish between self and other, (2) he experiences a growing sense of omnipotence and magic gratification, and (3) all good experiences are part of the emerging self, whereas bad experiences are expelled outside of the self.

In these early months the child cannot separate out the physical boundaries between himself and his mother. For example, by 9-10 months, he may be aware of the word "nosey" and know which part of the body this refers to. However it is not until a number of months later that he can distinguish between "his nosey" and "Mommy's nosey." At the phase of symbiotic union, there is a natural fusion of the child's and the caretaker's physical boundaries.

The child also experiences omnipotence and a sense of magic gratification at this stage of development. Most mothers are very sensitive to their babies' needs, and they have learned their babies' signals and cries. They can often distinguish among the hungry, the need-to-be-changed, and the I-want-to-be-held signals. The young child experiences these ministrations and gratification of needs as magic, and he experiences an early sense of omnipotence (if I have a need, it will be met).

The world surrounding the young child is conceived as "all pleasurable," and he expels any frustration to the "outside" or the nonself. We speak of this period as a time when normal "splitting" occurs, where the "good" world is central to the self, and the "bad" world is protruded to the outside. Since the *phase of primary narcis-*

---

*In the more recent infant developmental literature, researchers describe very early active connection to the environment and objects. For further information, the reader is referred to Stern and Sander (1980).

sism or *symbiotic union* is part of the normal experience of development, there is a natural legacy for all individuals to recreate this early
Garden of Eden, where no frustration and endless gratification exists. For example, one of the facets of the "perfect vacation"—lying
on the beach surrounded by the warm sun and sand, no daily cares,
perfect meals, etc.—seems to embody a return to the characteristics
of the period of primary narcissism.

If major problems occur in this phase of development (because of
internal organic factors within the child or major problems in the
environment), there can be an arrest or fixation in this symbiotic
phase. An early form of childhood psychosis is the "symbiotic-
psychotic child" (Mahler, 1968), one of the severe developmental
psychopathologies. These children have marked disturbances in their
body boundaries. For example, one such child patient of the author
feared that his facial characteristics might change. He was afraid to
look into a mirror because his face could turn into the face of his
mother. Another child was afraid to go into the water since he could
not see his legs. He feared these extremities would cease to exist if
they weren't in sight. There was no sense of solidity to his physical
self. These children often have similar problems with boundaries
outside of the body, physical boundaries in space and size. They fear
that buildings can disappear or rooms can suddenly change. There is
often no solidness to the world at large for these children. These
fears reflect the difficulties in fusion, characteristic of the period of
symbiotic union. The pathology of these children is severe and falls
into the realm of childhood psychosis. With the perceptional distortions they develop, there are marked difficulties in the function of
reality testing (the ability to know the difference between an internal
and external perception or thought). It is primarily the function of
reality testing that distinguishes the psychotic from the nonpsychotic
individual.

Slowly, beginning in the latter part of the first year, the child
normally progresses from the symbiotic phase to the period of
separation–individuation. This encompasses a number of steps or
subphases (hatching, practicing, rapprochement, libidinal object constancy) that are achieved by the end of the third year. In this process,
the child moves from the magic world to reality and from the normal
narcissistic stage to a shared world with objects (parents, siblings,
and peers). There are a number of tasks the young child must achieve
to make this effective transition into reality: (1) a gradual giving up

of the sense of omnipotence, (2) the ability to separate self from object, as well as (3) the capacity to synthesize the "good" and "bad" aspects of the object and the self. Much of the impetus for separation-individuation comes from the child's ability to locomote (crawling, standing, walking) and the enormous pleasures derived from the sense of mastery in self-achievement through action in reality. For example, when a toddler sees a ball across the room that he desires, and he crawls or walks to get it himself, he experiences an internal pleasure of accomplishment of his own action. This internal pleasure of the autonomous self grows and becomes the force for separation from the object and fosters the sense of individuation.

During the past 10 years, infant observers and researchers have modified some of Mahler's conceptions, particularly of the earliest infant phases. Most researchers now question the existence of a "normal autistic" phase and indicate that the infant is social and active from birth. They see the initial period from birth to 2 months of life as a phase of normal emergence or awakenings rather than an objectless one (Stern, 1985).

Similarly, in the period of 2 to 7 months, the period of "symbiotic union" prior to separation-individuation, there are also modifications. The processes of fusion of self and other as well as the emergence of the individual self are definitely observed in early childhood. However, rather than distinct phases following each other, these processes are seen as occurring and unfolding simultaneously from the early months. Whatever the timetable, the processes of symbiosis and separation-individuation do occur.

Early interferences in the separation-individuation process (constitutional factors, severe illness in childhood, major problems in parent-child relationship) can affect this progression and lay the foundation for further severe pathology in childhood. Problems in the separation-individuation phase can be the breeding ground for "borderline" and "narcissistic" disturbances (Chethik & Fast, 1970; Chethik, 1979; Settledge, 1977; Meissner, 1978). Borderline pathology reflects a partial transition out of the process of symbiotic union. The borderline child has become able to separate self from other, and he therefore has no problems in body boundaries or in the boundaries in reality. He does not exhibit the psychotic processes evident in the symbiotic child, according to many authors. However, he fails in several other tasks. The borderline child retains "splitting," and objects and self-representations must be divided into "good" and "bad." In addition, some aspects of magic and omnipotence are also maintained.

It is helpful to explicate the meaning of "splitting" more fully. "Splitting" is a normal mechanism in early childhood. The young child naturally pushes away any images of the angry mother (she is not my mother; she is someone else), and he retains a feeling of safety with only positive images of the mother. This is reflected in the children's fascination with fairy tales, tales young children love because they reflect their internal struggles. The good Fairy Godmother is the symbol for the all-giving mother who provides everything, whereas the evil Wicked Witch or the Wicked Stepmother (*Cinderella, Hansel and Gretel*) is the repository of all of the frustration and projected punishments by the object. The world is divided into good and evil. The young child "splits" the maternal images into these extremes. During separation–individuation, a task for the growing youngster is to become increasingly able to put together these diverse images of mother and to retain some aspects of both. The images of the angry mother or the grouchy mother must become part of the overall caregiver who is the provider depended on. The ability to achieve this reality view of the object depends, in part, on the quality of frustration by the object—how she disciplines, withholds, and demands—as well as on the subject's own internal equipment. The borderline child *fails* to accomplish this developmental task. Clearly, the vast majority of children achieve this step.

With this background, we can now follow the presentation and the treatment process of a borderline youngster, Matthew, a 10-year-old youngster in a residential treatment center.

PRESENTING PICTURE, HISTORY AND DIAGNOSTIC THOUGHTS

Matthew was placed at Sagebrook treatment center because of chronic problems that made him unable to function in the community. Essentially in the classroom he had been seen as "strange" and "always in his own world." He muttered sounds, seemed unable to learn (he had spent years in the "special education" program), and rarely spoke to the teacher. At times, without any apparent provocation or predictability, he had become agitated, terrified, and had acted impulsively, totally disrupting the classroom. On these occasions, he had been very hard to contain.

Similarly at home, he withdrew into the "safety" of his room and had fought any excursions outside of the house. The growing isolation and withdrawal had concerned the parents increasingly.

In the residential center, a similar picture emerged in the first few months after placement. Matthew was quickly nicknamed "Cartoon Boy" by the other children in the cottage. Each day would find him totally engrossed in himself in a corner of his room, producing his shows and cartoons. The cartoon was introduced by the appropriate Looney Tunes melody; one heard the sounds of the chase, the scuffling, the ultimate victory of his characters, and the cartoon was clearly over when the last few fading bars of the introductory melody were repeated. His hero, Popeye, was represented by a little plastic toy figure, who vigorously fought off pursuing monsters and attacking tornadoes with great animation. When the demands of the day interrupted Matthew's cartooning—for example, when he was called to lunch—he managed to announce "intermission" and very tentatively and fearfully proceeded to join his cottage mates in the dining room.

During his early years, Matthew seemed to evidence a constitutional vulnerability. His mother, a wholesome woman who cared very adequately for two other siblings, described a nightmare-like first year of development for this child. At first Matthew had been unable to suck. He had cried constantly during the day. Often his distress reached screaming intensity without any evident source of irritation or frustration. The parents finally found that the only way to soothe him was to drive him endlessly in the family car. Even when he slept, Matthew was obviously fussy and troubled.

Throughout the first year, Matthew was tense and stiff when held in his mother's arms. He arched his back away from her, and she found herself unable to calm him. Mrs. L. had trouble with feeding. As the year progressed, Matthew refused to chew and would not take liquids other than milk and cocoa.

At age 4, his mother described him as an "albatross around her neck." She could not limit him. At the supermarket he ran throughout the store pulling items off the shelves and jumping and climbing over counters. The mother was unable to visit with anyone when accompanied by Matthew, because he was restless and needed constant supervision.

At times, Matthew yelled and screamed in a very infantile way, and tantrums, produced by very minor frustrations, were an everyday affair. With Matthew present, the mother found it very difficult to share her attention. He seemed jealous and interfered with her when she was on the telephone. Matthew also refused to do anything for himself—he refused to try to unbutton his jacket and waited for Mother to take off his hat and coat.

In contrast to his usual wildness and distractability, within the limits of his familiar room Matthew could play for hours. He could sit and listen to his records over and over again and play with a group of plastic soldiers for long lengths of time. However, his mother experienced an uneasy feeling because at these times, in the course of this play, Matthew would often let out a peculiar shriek for no apparent reason. The mother also noted some of Matthew's occasional efforts to restrain himself. He doubled up his fists and made squeezing noises as if to keep himself from breaking things.

Discussion

Matthew presented evidence of a longstanding developmental disorder. In their histories, borderline children typically show major disruption in the first year of life. Matthew's history revealed early disturbing feeding experiences and major problems with the ability to be soothed and gratified by objects. Throughout his childhood, Matthew showed profound problems in three major areas of development: drive development, ego development, and object relations development.

I. Drive Assessment

Matthew, like many borderline children, struggled in an attempt to deal with primitive pregenital aggression (Kernberg, 1975). In normal development, when a child can give up the early mechanism of "splitting" into good and evil, it is implict that the "evil world" and the aggressive world is less frightening. For example, the images of the angry or grouchy mother can become part of the good mother he depends on, because the angry mother is not so frightening. This is not true for the borderline child. The "bad" outside world continues to retain the early primitive terror. This terror continues to plague the borderline youngster as he develops.

Matthew attempted to handle this frightening world through his "cartoon" fantasy life. This appeared to serve two functions: he withdrew from the real "frightening" world into his own fantasy life, and within the fantasy world, he sought to master the dangers. His fantasy life was filled with aggressive monsters and tornadoes, a representation of the "split-off" bad world of the narcissistic phase of development. He magically mastered the danger by becoming Popeye, superstrong to overcome every adversary when he swallowed the can of spinach. He retained the magic solutions typical of the narcissistic period of life. Thus, borderline children struggle continuously with primitive aggression and do not achieve the neutralization (dilution) of the aggressive drive that we see in normal development.

II. Ego Assessment

Matthew's presentation and history evidenced the generalized weak ego functioning that is commonly associated with many borderline children. It is generally the task of the ego in normal development to handle and negotiate the "threats" to the self that come from either internal or external sources. For example, by age 4, the normal child is expected to adapt to a new nursery school situation and function and learn therein, despite being separated from the mother. The young child's ego can typically cope with the potential threats of this new environment. Bigger or aggressive children will not be overwhelming, since the average child can place trust in the new mother substitutes in the school.

Most borderline children do not have the ego capacity to adapt to new surroundings. At age 4, Matthew was constantly overwhelmed by a feared threat in any new surround. He became restless, agitated, driven, and out of control in the supermarket, even in the presence of his mother. All new stimuli terrified him, and he felt safe only in the close confines of his room. He appeared to be constantly traumatized and had no effective adaptive or defensive system to negotiate the daily environment. He had built a wall of isolation and fantasy (cartoon world) that increasingly physically separated him from the world. He clung to outside objects (mother) to manage him, to function as an auxiliary ego, and to provide a source of safety.

Object Relations Assessment

Borderline children typically relate to objects on a "need-gratifying" basis, which is an early form of object tie associated with the narcissistic or symbiotic processes of development. The "all-good" object will fulfill all wishes, and the helpless child is totally dependent on the object for survival. This form of relationship is retained by the borderline youngster often throughout childhood, and forms of this interaction are retained by the borderline adult.

Throughout Matthew's history, mother was forced to serve as his need-gratifier. She had to provide constant attention, and even the telephone (taking attention away from Matthew) was perceived as a threat. Matthew was anxious about any independent step he would need to take since it would separate him from his mother. Therefore, mother had to button his jacket, etc., well beyond the time he could physically cope with this skill. Borderline children often experience panic and terror with the separation from the "object" who keeps them safe, and they are also coersive with the object. They demand the attention because they fear that if the "object" shows independence, the object can leave them.

Often these children will also withdraw from objects because of the perceived pain and lack of gratification in the real world and real attachments. They "people" their fantasy life with the omnipotent, protective, need-satisfying objects they seek. For Matthew, Popeye was a protector with his magic strength. The perceived frustrations of the real objects pushed Matthew to develop an extensive fantasy world and to develop a schizoid-like posture by his withdrawal into a narcissistic fantasy life (the cartoon world). This is a typical solution for many borderline children.

Matthew was seen initially over 10 years ago. He had had a number of neurological work-ups, including an EEG and neurological exam. There was no overt evidence of brain damage. In recent years, however, there has been more extensive development of diagnostic tools to pick up subtle brain malfunctions. A youngster like Matthew would also currently receive medication trials to augment psychotherapy, since there has been the development of effective drugs to help these youngsters. Perhaps a trial of a minor tranquilizer would be used in conjunction with hospitalization (residential treatment) and psychotherapy.

We now focus on the typical psychological treatment problems the therapist faces in work with the borderline child and the techniques and interventions he is often called on to employ. These are illustrated by the treatment of Matthew:

1. The emergence of the narcissistic fantasy life of the patient.
2. The problem of the lack of repression.
3. The coersive quality of the object tie.
4. The problems of the lack of structuralization.

COURSE OF TREATMENT

Dealing with the Narcissistic Fantasy Life

Clinical Material

When treatment began, Matthew sat in the far corner of the therapist's office with his back to the therapist. Only roars, grimaces, and screams were emitted as the course of the cartoon progressed. Matthew was clearly terrified of the therapist. He surrounded himself by his cartoons, and there was no recognition that the therapist existed for many weeks. The therapist, from his own growing extensive knowledge of cartoons from Saturday morning TV watching, began identifying the specific characters from across the room. The therapist wrote up a movie program of each session. All the varied cartoons were listed in order of presentation, and since Matthew had a vast variety of characters, he would pack in as many as 20 cartoons in the 50-minute hour. Matthew left the corner of the room and, responding to the therapist's interest, unfolded the program on the therapist's desk. He corrected the therapist's titles and named each cartoon. They collected the programs in a special drawer, and Matthew took pleasure in reading the old programs as well as developing new ones. This introduction took a period of 4 months.

After this long period, Matthew decided on a change—he would include some full-length features in his movie house. He particularly wanted to add an adventure serial, and it became highly desired that the therapist have a prominent role. In the film, the therapist was the big protector, as he and the little boy took on very frightening elements. They faced spooky and haunted houses together, high winds and hurricanes, bad doctors who gave terrible shots. He produced a long film called World War II. The therapist (directed by Matthew) saved Matthew from torpedoed boats, artillery fire, and strafing fighter planes.

After about 8 months of work, the therapist introduced his own variation into the program, the idea of a documentary. Any good movie house must have a documentary, he proclaimed. He insisted that this documentary contain the essential element of a documentary—it had to reflect and record a true event. Although Matthew eagerly agreed at first, he subtly fought and tested out the new rule. For example, Matthew at first brought in documentary weather reports. On a lovely spring day he described the deep snow, slippery walking conditions, etc. Or he described the different fish he saw on a visit to the aquarium but added wings to the fish and made them fly. The therapist pounded on the desk, noting that this was a violation of the documentary idea, and the weather and fish reports were not accepted until changed.

Documentary "true" talks assumed a more prominent role in the sessions. They began to reflect real affect. Matthew introduced the documentaries entitled "Homesick," "Home Sweet Home," "Learning about Sagebrook," etc. Matthew described his feelings of loss of home, his present terror, and his questions about the institution.

In his documentaries about Sagebrook, an observing ego began to grow, and some aspects of a therapeutic alliance (rather than the earlier omnipotent protecting relationship) emerged. As "Cartoon Boy" he felt he did not have any friends in the cottage; he felt very lonely, and he wanted boys to like him. Matthew noted that he hated the name "Cartoon Boy," and he made his own special contract with the therapist that cartoons would eventually be stopped. He even fixed the specific date several months hence. Matthew then brought a new film—a "Sports Reel"—into the sessions, in which he vividly became a great baseball hero and football giant. The therapist interpreted that he had a big wish to be liked and play with the other boys and develop his skills. Changes in Matthew's sessions were reflected in his daily life. He fought his cartooning and narrowed the cartoon time spent each day in his room. He practiced baseball and football with the child care worker he felt close to, and he began to participate in cottage meetings.

Discussion

The work within the psychotherapy reflected only a small part of the treatment work at the time. Matthew's beginning turn toward reality and self-observation could not have occurred without a concurrent

and very active "milieu therapy" (Bettleheim, 1971). To use Nos-
phitz's term, the child with massive ego weakness must be "en-
globed" by treatment—not 1 hour three times per week, but consistently for many hours each day. The residential treatment center or
hospital setting provides the opportunity to utilize fully this enveloping form of therapy. The therapist needs to work closely with the
milieu to help them understand the internal life of the child so that a
strategy can be devised to deal with the child's underlying problems.

Matthew was frightened by his own destructive potential and that
of the environment. In cartoons, the characters he identified with
met and mastered each projected danger. His withdrawal separated
him from the unpleasant and frightening reality as his attention
centered itself on his fantasy life. He denied his internal helplessness
through magical omnipotent means: Popeye, when overwhelmed by
danger, always had available a can of spinach that produced the
strength to cope with all threats. For Matthew, cartoons warded off
the unpredictable reality.

The function, then, of our early milieu work was to make the reality
predictable and concrete. With help from the therapist, an outer
stabilization and structure was provided in Matthew's daily life. The
child care staff actively preplanned with Matthew what was in store for
each day. His schedule was described at first on almost an hourly basis;
he was helped to learn which staff members went off duty, and who
came on to work. Any change in routine, or visitors, or furniture
alteration, whenever possible, was discussed with Matthew before. As
Matthew had earlier listed his cartoon schedule, he now wrote out the
daily cottage schedule, and his ability to anticipate events and changes
allowed him slowly to become a fringe member. Only with this consistent milieu backdrop, actively initiated and supported by the therapist,
could the work and progress in the psychotherapy continue. This
process of interpreting the underlying anxieties to the milieu, and
creating a structure to counter these fears, is a very essential part of the
work with many borderline children.

In helping Matthew work toward reality *within* the psychotherapy, it was also initially critical to understand the function of his
fantasy world. As noted above, Matthew was struggling with "split-
off" terrors he was unable to integrate. He attempted to cope with
the world utilizing the mechanisms (magic, omnipotence) of the
small child during the narcissistic stage of development. The therapist slowly *joined* his world by identifying and explicating his "car-

toon shows." Over a period of time, they collected over 100 cartoon show programs. Attempting to gain entry to the fantasy life and being admitted by the borderline child is often a necessary and critical initial step in the treatment process. The fantasy life of the child is often the most highly invested (cathected) area in the child's psychic existence, and the initial task of the therapist is to become an important part of that internal life.

Matthew, deriving increasing pleasure from this growing *mutual* movie production, decided to expand and include the therapist in full-length feature serials as well. He used the therapist in these productions as a narcissistic, need-satisfying protector. In the adventures Matthew had the therapist rescue the little boy from sharks, tornadoes, and bad doctors. This had a similar dynamic as the cartoon world, since together they fought the "split-off" evil world, but Matthew was establishing a strong libidinal (loving) tie to the therapist.

As their relationship grew, the therapist began to slowly demand that Matthew incorporate the real world. He noted that whereas every movie house has cartoons and full-length features, the really good theaters also had documentaries. The therapist began to function like a facilitating parent who helps his frightened toddler to integrate aspects of the "scary" world. Although Matthew fought the documentaries at first, he gradually developed them fully in his "Home Sweet Home" and "Learning about Sagebrook" stories. The real world became somewhat less frightening under the protection of the therapist. Matthew then slowly decided to give up the "cartoon world" totally because of his desire to please and identify with the therapist as well as his growing awareness of the isolation caused him by cartooning. In addition, the real relationships at Sagebrook were beginning to provide pleasures that his fantasy world could not. This process parallels the strides the young child makes within the context of his libidinal attachment to his parents. The initial psychotherapeutic task with many borderline children is to develop a significant libidinal connection within the context of the treatment process. This can be achieved by fostering a connection within the central fantasy life of the child.

The Problem of the Lack of Repression

Clinical Material

After Matthew had successfully controlled cartoons, much more direct aggression appeared. Matthew often, in his postcartoon period, broke up the office. He kicked at the furniture and threw toys and crafts around the office. On campus, he seemed to direct his physical attacks toward younger girls, attempting at times to scratch and choke them. Following these open attacks he would show much self-abuse—throwing himself into the mud, banging his head against the wall, and asking to have his fingers cut off to keep him from scratching.

His theme in therapy was that his "madness" was coming out. The madness came in the form of every-night dreams, dreams that filled the entire night and that he had to relate fully in his sessions. At first, in his dreams, little girls got hurt. They tripped, damaged their knees, and had to go to Mt. Sinai Hospital for an operation. There, however, was a special rock near the hospital; the rock became a rock monster, rolled into the hospital, and bashed and battered little girls until they were all dead.

The little girls, after a period, changed directly into one specific little girl, Matthew's sister, Judy, whom he described as having long, black hair. In his continuous dreams, Matthew tricked his sister into entering a rocket alone. His mother, sensing danger, tried in vain to stop him. The rocket flew into space, crashed into meteorites, and broke apart, and Judy was killed. For long periods, as she rode into space, the wild flight made her scream and yell. There were variations in the dream in which Matthew was able, at times, to trick his mother into entering the rocket to take the fatal trip. In his sessions, he vigorously played out the rocket trip, smashing the rocket against the wall, mimicking the screams, and, at points, directly stabbing Judy and his mother after the rocket crashed.

Matthew made many excited side comments as the material flowed. For example, he said "Don't look, it's a very bad game," or "Shut your eyes and don't listen." He could not decide whether it was an adventure or a nightmare, a pleasure or a scare, and he would forcefully fight any interruption of his flow of fantasy for a long period of time. When the therapist attempted to control the outflow of material, Matthew would scream, "You talked, now I don't have time to finish my dream." "You don't want to hear my dreams," and this remark would precede a tantrum and acting out in the office. At times, however, there would be an overt plea, "Can you get me into control, Mr. Chethik? If you can control me, I can control the rocket."

During much of this period, Matthew proclaimed that it was very hard to stay at Sagebrook. He felt he could not stand to be there, and he constantly noted he just had to return home. The rocket dreams were often followed by punishment dream episodes. Matthew and friends were chased by mummies (not mommies), and they were biting mummies. They caught the children, stripped them, and bit at parts of their bodies. The children would manage to escape, opening a trap door to the center of the earth. However, as they were going down a long tunnel, lava began to pursue them. As the lava flowed in one direction, the boys turned to run in the other direction, but the dangerous mummies quickly appeared at the exit.

Discussion

Often borderline children become overwhelmed by their aggressive fantasies. Because of problems in their ego functioning, they are unable to repress (keep unconscious) their primitive rages and sadistic impulses. They feel overwhelmed and experience the anxiety of going crazy (my "madness" is coming out, said Matthew). With the borderline child, there is little reflective or observing ego to address one's comments to at these moments. The major purpose of treatment, when this quality of drive material emerges (as it often does with a borderline child), is to *bind* the material and to bring it under some control of secondary processes.

When Matthew gave up a major defense of withdrawal into fantasy (his cartoon world), he had to deal with the "split-off," aggressive world he had avoided facing earlier. When he experienced the aggression toward his mother and sister (in the rocket fantasies), his ego functioning deteriorated. He regressed markedly into severe acting out of these feelings, and there was a loss of impulse control. His anxiety became overwhelming and, during this period, primary process (primitive) thinking dominated his consciousness. Magically, he feared his thoughts were *actually* hurting his mother and sister, and he wanted the therapist to control his thoughts. One saw, in Matthew, an extensive (though temporary) breakdown of reality testing, wherein he was unable to distinguish between internal thoughts and external consequences. During this period, Matthew experienced a lack of repression, a flooding of primitive thoughts, cognitive disorganization, and concretistic thinking. The therapist used a variety of supportive interventions to help Matthew cope with this disorganization.

Several therapeutic techniques seemed most useful in work with Matthew. At first, the therapist dramatically insisted on talking and commenting on the material, structuring a 10-minute thinking period in each session when the reflective ego processes of the child and the therapist dominated. The therapist pointed to his watch when the therapist (thinking) time would begin. The therapist used Matthew's pleas of "Can you control me?" to show him clearly his fear of the material, his fear of being overwhelmed.

The therapist helped Matthew to clarify internal and external danger, the difference between thought and deed. When Matthew, for example, sought desperately to leave Sagebrook for home, the therapist interpreted his need to reassure himself that mother and Judy were actually all right. He could then point out to Matthew to show him how often he seemed to make such a big "mix up"—a really strong mistake. He pointed out that when Matthew came up with strong killing ideas and mind thoughts, he actually became afraid that these ideas would come true in real life. This was a major confusion, a major mistake. How could blowing up Judy in the office hurt her at home? It is important to point out that this was done *dramatically* by the therapist. His facial expression indicated disbelief that Matthew could make this confusion; he hit his forehead in disbelief.

The therapist could also acknowledge with Matthew that he was describing many internal angry-killing feelings toward sister and mother. He noted that all children, as they grew, carried not only love feelings for their family but also very big angry, killing feelings as well. When a new younger sister comes into the family, boys hate them. The purpose of these generalizations was to provide Matthew with some understandable source for the frightening fantasies and affects he was experiencing (to distinguish them from his term "madness"). It also served to show Matthew that his affect could be a form of accepted and understood communication.

In this period of treatment, one could see the effect of Matthew's weak ego functioning in relation to the aggressive drive. The therapist used a variety of *supportive interventions* to "shore up" Matthew's faulty ego.

Functioning as an "Auxiliary Ego"

Matthew, at first, could not control the outpouring of his aggressive impulses expressed toward sister and mother. The therapist, as an auxiliary ego, insisted on a "10-minute thinking time" in each session, which had the effect of limiting the onslaught of the overwhelming material and created the ego opportunity to observe and understand it. One could say the therapist "threw" his ego into the breach to dam up the flow of instinctual material.

Rebuilding Ego Functions

In this period, Matthew suffered a temporary breakdown of the ego function of *reality testing*. The therapist powerfully addressed this problem by bringing into consciousness repeatedly how Matthew acted as though his internal thoughts (killing ideas toward sister/mother) were having a real effect (he ran to the telephone to find out if they were all right after his sessions). The effect of confronting and discussing these distortions helped to reestablish more effective functioning. Matthew could observe this distortion in his thoughts as the therapist described Matthew's action.

Using "Binding" Interpretations

The therapist interpreted that the rage toward Matthew's sister was the expression of jealousy and a form of sibling rivalry. He explained how little boys feel when a baby sister is born and how these rival, killing feelings were reemerging currently, since he was in an institution and his sister was home. The effects of this *binding* interpretation (as noted earlier) are not to elicit more material but to give Matthew a human context and history for these disturbing feelings, in essence, to sum them up.

During this period of work, the therapist needed to work actively and dramatically. It was necessary to use dramatic action (e.g., "You really think, Matthew, that flying your rocket into the wall will hurt your sister," said with clear disbelief) so that the idea conveyed would be very clear. This process is reminiscent of a mother making a dramatic point to a young toddler who had done something unsafe. For example, she might proclaim with intense gestures that the stove is "HOT, HOT, HOT" so that the danger is clear. At points of severe regression the interventions need to be clearly emphasized with borderline children.

The Coersive Quality of the Object Tie

Clinical Material

Matthew, as do many borderline children, felt unsafe unless he was in the proximity of an object that he endowed as protective. This need markedly limited his ability to be on his own.

Matthew's limited "reality span" troubled him greatly. He was aware of his need to linger around the child care staff, to touch them at times when he spoke to them, and to be in their shadow. The other boys ridiculed him about this, and he felt the ridicule was justified: his habits did make him feel babyish. Matthew also used the therapist as a protective object. He "touched base" as often as 10 times per day by coming to the therapist's waiting room and feeling close and safe on those occasions. Matthew decided to experiment—he would not visit the therapist's building as often as he had been doing, and when he came for his appointment he was determined he was going to enter through the side instead of the inviolate front entrance he always had to use. No longer, he was determined, would he take the same path going to school every day; even though it was longer, he would try walking all the way around campus. For a period, we found Matthew experimenting somewhat inappropriately—he would suddenly walk out of class in order to try being alone.

On another occasion, Matthew brought in some school problems that seemed to ruin his day. They had been learning about Paris in class, and he had become very frightened. We came to understand that Paris was in France, and Europe was separated from America by a large body of water. This made his big "getting lost" worry very strong. Matthew's new defenses seemed to begin to go to work as he attempted a new solution. He associated all the foreign landmarks of Paris with familiar landmarks within the United States. The Champs d'Elysee was similar to a broad street in Detroit, the Arc de Triomphe was similar to the Washington Square Arch in New York. The Eiffel Tower reminded him of electrical transmitters he has seen near his home. The effect of these associations was to bring and attach the foreign with the more familiar, and the separation anxiety seemed to abate. This was a complex system to make the unfamiliar more familiar, and Matthew began to use it often to cope with object loss. It became an increasingly effective system that allowed him more independence. All trips to new places, which had been fright-

ening earlier, now became possible when Matthew made his familiarizing associations.

We saw over a period of years that Matthew's reality span, his safety
perimeter, grew larger and larger. His earlier need to touch the
protecting adult directly became much more symbolic. He came to be
able to go on pass into the community, to attend public school, etc., as
long as he knew that when in a crisis he could reach an adult. He kept
several phone numbers in his pocket—he could use them if it became
necessary. Again, as all staff became aware of the underlying anxiety
that Matthew had with object loss, many devised creative mechanisms
that would allow him to take more extensive independent steps.

Discussion

The extremely cumbersome system that Matthew devised to handle
his social studies problem (Paris) provided a view of the extraordi-
nary amount of energy necessary for this youngster to cope with
object loss. It was nonetheless a more effective pattern than his
earlier method of attaching himself to his protecting object. By
continuing to use this process of familiarizing associations, Matthew
was presently able to move further away from his need for direct,
immediate "refueling" objects.

How did he develop this greater capacity? Some of the supportive
treatment techniques seemed to play an important role.

Confrontation and Clarification Leading to Mastery

Although the interventions of confrontation and clarification are the
preparatory steps for interpretation with neurotic children, they can
often serve a major function in supportive psychotherapy as steps
leading to mastery.

Matthew became increasingly concerned about his pride (he did
not want to be called "Baby Matthew"), which was interfered with by
his marked separation fears (he clung to staff to feel safe). His
conflict (his wish to be accepted was inhibited by his fears) was made
explicit to his ego on many different occasions. The therapist drew
his attention to the multiple situations in which his "getting lost"
worry came to the foreground and how it limited his ability to play
with the other kids. As these conflicts were depicted, Matthew
sought to master his anxiety by taking measured steps from the

protective object in doses that he could tolerate. Thus, in relation to the protective therapist, he decided to visit the waiting room less often, changed the familiar path to the office, etc. He was delighted at times that he could control the scared feelings and not run to find the therapist. As his separation tolerance grew, he took further steps. No unconscious interpretation (e.g., his fear of annihilation) as one uses with neurotic children would have been effective or appropriate.

Dealing with Poor Structuralization

Clinical Material

In the last 2 years of his placement, Matthew made many strides. His academic performance improved; he was involved in some clubs and interests in the community where he contributed, and although social relationships never acquired an intimacy, he had a few contacts with peers outside of the institution. Home visits were pleasurable, and there was a growing reintegration with his family. He was very engaged and busy in his therapy sessions, which he came to use in a particular way.

Matthew developed an extensive system, which he described as "charting." He designed many actual charts with the therapist. Charts were built for school progress, club activity, and mood swings. The graph that followed the course of his moods over the week showed a range from the highest category "calmness" to the lowest category "blow-up," and he reacted with pleasure and received full praise when he had managed a steady, placid week. Acknowledged achievement seemed to serve as a stimulating reward.

The need to anticipate potential upsets, as he extended himself further, became singularly important. Matthew developed an early warning system—"What did he need to know to be adequately 'on guard'?" He made long written lists of potential problems. For example, when summer camp began he anticipated that he might get worried about insect bites, poison ivy, spiders, etc. He thought that his "getting lost" worry might come back again. These "worries" were written down and studied before going off to camp. Before travel vacations with parents he prepared for car accident thoughts, noise of the subway, reactions to tall buildings. A heavy amount of homework and a harsh command from cottage staff were also "on guard" inducing situations and were written on his study lists. He searched for physical factors as well. He knew he became upset with a stiff neck or sprained ankle, and special watchfulness of oneself was necessary at those times.

Role play became an important device to augment his ability to cope with a new situation. He played out how he would react when teased by peers he met in his clubs; he preexperienced sitting through a long church service at home, and practiced and repracticed in the sessions how to find his way to all the classes and the locker room in the junior high he had begun to attend.

Discussion

In this last period of work, Matthew and his therapist developed coping skills that allowed Matthew to extend markedly his perimeter of safety. A number of supportive interventions were used that enhanced Matthew's ego functioning.

Developing Signal Anxiety

One of the major developmental lags evident in borderline children is their anxiety intolerance. Matthew either withdrew from the frightening, anxiety-provoking world or he panicked. In this treatment period, he extensively used trial action, anticipation, and role play, which all helped him develop an "early warning system," a form of signal anxiety. If he could preexperience frightening contingencies, he would "expose" himself to the new, unfamiliar environment. He also found a growing ability to tolerate stress as long as it came in anticipated situations. He began to use his intellectual capacities to cope with anxiety-producing situations.

Building Defenses

In conjunction with his increased ability to anticipate frightening stimuli, Matthew began to develop contingency plans to cope with these possibilities. For example, if he became frightened of some children in his new classroom, he could walk down to the principal's office. These new rules were memorized, and they allowed him to extend his perimeter. This kind of work in coping with the challenges of growing independence had the quality of compulsive-like defensive systems. He was using his increased intellectual capacity to do this preplanning and mapping out. It allowed him to master his environment adequately for the first time, and it was fostered by his work in his psychotherapy.

SUMMARY

In the process of psychotherapy with borderline children, the therapist has two major tasks. He initially must find an effective way of establishing a libidinal (meaningful) connection. With many borderline children, this means finding a method of *joining* the narcissistic fantasy life the youngster is attached to. (As with Matthew's cartoon world, this process is also described in the next chapter.) The effective alliance allowed the therapist to help Matthew move from his narcissistic world toward an investment in reality.

The second major task of the therapist with the borderline child is helping that youngster with fragile ego capacity to deal with reality. The fragile ego capacity means that the therapist will need to deal with eruptions of impulses, breakdowns of ego functions (reality testing), excessive dependency on the therapist, and a general lack of adequate defenses. The author has described a variety of supportive interventions in which the primary goal of the treatment was to foster and enhance the ego functioning of the borderline child.

It is important to underscore the concept of supportive work with a youngster like Matthew, rather than "uncovering" psychotherapy. For although many of these children have "access" to their instinctual life, the reinforcement of an internal exploration and expression will often promote severe regression. To young practitioners such an exploration may be very seductive, since it usually involves "good material" (e.g., Matthew's rocket dreams). Most borderline children, with fragile ego resources, cannot tolerate dealing with their internal aggressive life.

BIBLIOGRAPHY

Bettleheim, B. (1971). The future of residential treatment. In M. Mayer, A. Blum (Eds.), *Healing Through Living.* (pp. 192–209). Springfield, IL: Charles C. Thomas.

Chethik, M. (1979). The borderline child. In: J. Nosphpitz (Ed.), *Basic*

Handbook of Child Psychiatry, Vol. II (pp. 305–321), New York: Basic Books.

Chethik, M., & Fast, I. (1970). A function of fantasy in the borderline child. *American Journal of Orthopsychiatry* 40:756–765.

Freud, S. (1966). *On Narcissism*, Standard Ed., Vol. 14. London: Hogarth Press.

Kernberg, O. (1975). *Borderline Conditions and Pathological Narcissism.* New York, Jason Aronson.

Mahler, M. (1952). On childhood psychosis and schizophrenia, autistic and symbiotic infantile psychosis. *The Psychoanalytic Study of the Child*, Vol. 7 (pp. 286–305). New York: International Universities Press.

Mahler, M. (1968). *On Human Symbiosis and the Vicissitudes of Individuation.* New York: International Universities Press.

Meissner, W. W. (1978). Notes on some conceptual aspects of borderline personality. *International Review of Psychoanalysis* 5:297–312.

Noshpitz, J. (1971). The psychotherapist in residential treatment. In: M. Mayer, A. Blum (Eds.), *Healing Through Living.* (pp. 158–175). Springfield, IL: Charles C. Thomas.

Pine, F. (1974). On the concept "borderline" in children: A clinical assay. *The Psychoanalytic Study of the Child* 29:341–368.

Settledge, C. (1977). The psychoanalytic understanding of narcissistic and borderline personality disorders. *Journal of the American Psychoanalytic Association* 25:805–834.

Stern, D. (1985). *Interpersonal World of the Infant.* New York: Basic Books.

Stern, D., & Sander, L. (1980). New knowledge about the infant from current research: Implications for psychoanalysis. *Journal of the American Psychoanalytic Association* 28:181–198.

8

Treatment of the Narcissistically Disturbed Child

The narcissistic disorder, like the borderline syndrome, also has its roots in the separation-individuation phase of development, although it is seen as a less severe disturbance (Mahler & Furer, 1968). Many of the problems evident with borderline children emerge in this disturbance. The narcissistically disturbed child shows similar difficulties in object development. He has a poor capacity for intimacy. The mechanisms of "splitting" of objects into good-bad terms, the processes of devaluation or idealization of self and objects, are commonly evident in this disorder. Many of the early problems of pregenital aggression occur in this pathology as well. However, children with narcissistic disturbances do *not* have the severe ego defects in thought processes, reality testing, and judgment that characterize the borderline disturbance (Settledge, 1977). These children generally have good work abilities and can effectively learn intellectually. These ego capacities allow them to use psychotherapy more effectively, and they are often capable of being treated with a variety of uncovering as well as supportive interventions. It is not well understood what has occurred developmentally that would differentiate these two groups of children. Several authors speculate that with the narcissistic disturbance, the problems occur later in the separation-individuation subphases (namely, the rapprochement subphase), whereas problems that lead to borderline disturbances occur earlier in the practicing and hatching subphases (Settledge, 1977; Kernberg, 1975).

In this chapter, the early psychotherapeutic work with Tom (a youngster with a narcissistic disturbance) illustrates some of the similarities and differences in the treatment between the two syndromes. The focus is primarily in three areas: (1) similarities and differences in the developmental histories, (2) similarities and differences in the capacity to adapt to the real world and its demands, and (3) similarities and differences in the treatment process of these two syndromes.

BACKGROUND, HISTORY, AND SYMPTOM PICTURE

Tom's early life had been dominated by pain. He had undergone constant pyloric spasms during the first 18 months of his life, and all medication had seemed ineffective. His chronic pain had been evident—he had grimaced, was often doubled up, and had cried constantly, particularly in relation to feedings. He had fought feedings and vomited a good deal, suffered diarrhea, and gained little weight during that period.

Nearly all developmental milestones reported had been delayed or were not achieved at all, especially those in the interpersonal realm. Mrs. G., Tom's mother, recalled no early smiling, no sense of unfolding mother–child dialogue within the first year, no stranger anxiety, and poor attachment behavior. Often in pain, Tom had held onto his mother tenaciously, had clutched her, and had dug his fingers into anything he could grasp on her person. Because of the pain he had experienced much of the day, he could make little constructive use of toys. During the first 18 months, he had played little with them except to throw them or bite into them. Gross motor development had been interfered with. Tom had developed his own unique means of propulsion. Again in pain, he had dug his heels into the household carpeting while lying on his back, and he had pushed himself backwards with intense momentum throughout the house. On many occasions, he had crashed into furniture.

It is important to note how the parents handled this trying youngster during this period. The mother recalled that she had been unable to calm Tom, and she had felt absolutely terrible about her ineffectiveness. Her self-condemnation was felt even more intensely because her husband could be somewhat more effective, although he had typically been busy and absent. Mrs. G. seemed to have been a remote and self-absorbed mother, overidentified with her son and unable to handle him without intense anxiety. She could acknowledge many feelings of her past wish to be rid of this impossible child, and particularly she recalled the desperate longing for some peace from her child's constant irritability.

It was apparent to all members of the family that the extreme pain had abated when Tom was about 18 months old. But the parents questioned whether Tom had ever recovered from the trauma. Essentially from that point on, Tom was described as a "stoic" youngster. He was easy to handle and never made demands on anyone in the family. The parents reported that it seemed as though Tom had developed a "shell-like" buffer between himself and the world.

Tom seemed to erect a characteristic posture, which varied little; he was pleasant, compliant, often with a slight fixed smile on his face. Tom had never developed any friends. He played near his own older brothers, who developed a protective attitude toward him. He never ventured off the family property, which served as a safe surround and perimeter. Occasionally schoolmates visited him, but play or relationships were not sustained, and he seemed to be uninterested.

Tom enjoyed reading and devoured a good deal of the extensive family library. Tom developed a positive relationship with his father, but primarily in the form of teacher–student. The father spent much time with all of the children explaining the natural phenomena they experienced in terms of his extensive scientific background. Tom was evidently quite bright, scored superior in IQ and achievement tests, yet the same theme of nonengagement was evident in class. He completed none or few class assignments, never spoke or volunteered in class, and clearly drifted off mentally somewhere during the school day. At times he would also wander back home from recess without comment or explanation to the teacher. He did not arouse anger in the teaching staff; rather, he stimulated rescue fantasies, for although he seemed lost, he was felt to be shy and appealing, and teachers longed to make contact with him.

Mr. and Mrs. G. had sought treatment for Tom because they began to realize that he would not "grow out" of his isolation, and he was falling behind in school because of his chronic lack of investment. In this therapist's early work with Tom, he proved somewhat of a diagnostic dilemma. He did not evidence the generalized ego weakness and the difficulties in thought process that many borderline youngsters possess, but he seemed to articulate clearly the object relation dynamics that is generally associated with the borderline syndrome.

Discussion

Tom, like Matthew, had evidenced major problems in infancy. His early feeding pattern was filled with enormous difficulties, and there was evidence of striking problems in the process of attachment to early objects. Thus he, like Matthew, had experienced the real world as a painful and unsafe place. Both youngsters had utilized severe forms of withdrawal to handle this frightening reality. Whereas Matthew (Chapter 7) had built an extensive cartoon world, Tom had withdrawn into a compliant, buffer-like shell. Tom had "split-off" safe and limited areas and had thus avoided the dangerous world outside; the safe perimeter had been represented by the boundaries of his home. He had gone through the motions of attending school and associating with peers but had returned quickly to his home and avoided the "hostile" world.

If we compare the early histories of these two youngsters, Tom illustrated a quality of ego functioning to handle the perceived aggressive assault from reality that was not evidenced with Matthew. Matthew was generally overwhelmed by stimuli, and his attempts to negotiate his day were very inadequate. He panicked, deteriorated into tantrums, and desperately clung to safe objects.

Tom's ego, in contrast, had appeared able to erect a powerful defensive system at an early age. There had been a massive effort directed at "coping" when, at 18 months, he had withdrawn from the painful world. Tom had erected an extensive character defense to ward off "pain" from objects and the world. He had not been overwhelmed by anxiety: throughout his childhood he had been able to use signal anxiety and to master his internal aggressive impulses. The problem in the development of trust and seeing the world as a "good-enough" place had remained central for Tom. He had developed a schizoid-like character defense* that had protected him, but

---

*"Schizoid-like character defense" is used descriptively. Many narcissistically disturbed children cut themselves off or withdraw into an extensive fantasy world, which serves as an imagined island of protection. This withdrawal separates them from relationships and appears "schizoid-like."

this defensive posture had also produced many problems in development. It cut him off from objects and had severely limited his experiences.

TREATMENT (PHASE I)

Tom was a little over 11 years of age when we began psychotherapy. The initial treatment period was dominated by Tom's wooden compliance. He was listless, with little energy, and used a minimum number of words. He made a thin attempt to be serious and appear involved in the ritual of treatment. He volunteered little; in fact, he would go to inordinate lengths to use the specific words and ideas in his answer that the therapist had used in his question. For example, if the therapist noted that Tom had had some problems in school and did not hand in any assignments, he agreed he had school problems, and they were because he could not hand in his assignments or papers. The therapist's words seemed to be safe for him to use. As the hour wore on, the veneer of interchange quickly abated. Tom drifted away, mouthing silent words. With some embarrassment, he would occasionally verbalize them: "Sza, szu Dupres," but he had no associations. Or he would become involved in slowly moving his leg. Again, with some hesitancy, he would describe a complex set of levers he imagined that was controlling and setting his leg in motion. Or he would quickly move his eyes and follow his thumb. He explained that he was not sure if his thumb moved when he was not watching it, and therefore looked quickly to catch the movements. At first, the therapist was concerned about the mechanisms of body deanimation (loss of human features) and fragmentation that Tom was experiencing. However, all of these body preoccupations seemed to be an attempt to organize, order, and explain how his body was integrated. The therapist felt that Tom listened closely when he noted how much Tom was trying to put his body together. When he was very young, he experienced intense and exploding pain (the therapist explained the spasms), which must have made him feel he was totally falling apart.

Tom presented a picture of enormous isolation. On the weekend, he could watch 14 hours of TV, and although he had an idea he might go sledding, he dismissed it since his knee hurt. He had a special way of drifting off in school, and he did not know what had actually been said in class. He would fix on the movement of the tip of his pencil and be lost in that fragment of motion. He enjoyed his bedroom and liked to develop plans where his sleeping area would be hidden from the view of the doorway; it would be contained as a room within a room within a room. Similarly, he was devising an underground hide-away fort in the woods (though within his property line), which would be virtually inaccessible. He had also been uncomfortable at night as he slept, but he had recently rigged up an opaque shower curtain that surrounded his bed, and he slept more peacefully. Tom, the therapist felt, was seeking to be held, surrounded, nestled, and only then could he rest comfortably. It was as though he longed for the comforting breast without pain. This was indicated by the "womb-like" qualities of his images—the enclosed sleeping area, the room within a room, the enclosed underground hideaway, the shower curtain sealing off his bed. In addition, Tom's history would suggest that with the early mother–child bonding interferences resulting from pain, the longing for early comforting might continue to persist.

The Henry stories* the therapist developed together with Tom slowly provided a greater avenue into his internal world. A pleasure world appeared that centered on Sun Valley, an area he had visited for several summers. Henry entered into a huge mine shaft and came out after a long struggle to a beautiful valley. He lived there in peace, within a small house, and endlessly watched the wildlife, the vegetation, and light around him. On another occasion he followed the flight of a golden eagle as it soared over the countryside. Later stories included wandering through the woods, touching the deer he had befriended, and walking in the company of two dogs he had known. His stories had no beginning, middle, or end. They were captured still-life scenes that he described in detail. His rebirth fantasy through the long mine shaft led to a pleasure world of pastoral peace and beauty. He seemed to identify with the freedom of the golden eagle, who could avoid and limit his attachment to the earth. But there was a strong sense of a total endless pleasure world, his Garden of Eden, where no pain or displeasure ever entered.

---

*Older latency-aged children usually have difficulties becoming directly involved in play, since they feel that play is "babyish." They will often develop stories (fantasies) and a story line when the therapist suggests that "imagination" will help to understand worries. This was how the Henry stories came to be born in the work with Tom.

The threat to Tom seemed to be the state of being in need, for with the tension of need, an object (caretaking person) was necessary. Internally for Tom, being in a state of need brought back the early feeding, mother–child situation that had brought enormous pain. Our Henry stories often led us to view the Nepal Man. Henry passed this old man who sat endlessly in a religious trance. Because of his inactivity, he could survive on the juice of one orange every other week. At times when the Nepal man was going to move his hand to reach out, he would squeeze it in a particular way with the other hand, stop the motion, and create a temporary paralysis. Similarly, Henry passed an old woman who sat trying to thread a needle. Although she was shaking with age, she never stopped and evidenced no frustration or need for help.

When Henry finally turned to people, the objects were typically empty. Henry wandered into an old warehouse that was filled with rusty cans and parts of old tools. He picked them up, one by one, and examined them. Finally, he came to a room with a bed in it. When he lifted up the cover, he was confronted by a skeleton in the middle of the bed. Sir Henry went back into time to the years of King Arthur's knights. He rode, and facing him on the highway was the figure of the Black Knight. He was still, and Henry attacked with his lance. The Knight clattered to the ground, and when Henry lifted the iron mask, there was nothing but blackness inside. On another occasion Henry rode down the Colorado river in his kayak. Vultures circled overhead. He was frightened and moved to a cave for safety. No one lived there, however, and he could only faintly make out the writing of some dead civilization on the stone walls.

Discussion

Tom, like Matthew, recreated aspects of a symbiotic world. At first, he had sought to establish an "all-good" world. He had set up a warm surround through his "room within a room" and his underground hideaway. The Sun Valley fantasies, where he was comfortable, were like the protective enveloping objects of early childhood. These appeared to represent times in Tom's early life when he had felt comfort and a sense of peace and tranquility. This fantasy life had the features of the early omnipotent period of primary narcissism. This pastoral world was "all good." Everyone lived in harmony and peace, and therefore there were no demands to stir up aggression. Tom was primarily attached (cathexis) to this fantasy world, and he went through the motions (like Matthew) in his existence in the outside, real world. Borderline and narcissistically disturbed children, who have early problems in their infancy with objects, develop the need for a safe "cocoon." Matthew constructed his cartoon world where he mastered danger. Tom used his skills to develop this Sun Valley world. It was to these internal worlds that the bulk of investment occurred, since these controllable worlds provided the greatest pleasure. The outside world was minimally invested. Tom went through school and handled the routine of the day minimally, because reality represented the painful and threatening world. In similar fashion, Matthew had announced "intermission" from his cartoon world when he had to join his peers for activities at Sagebrook.

In the above material, Tom also explicated some of the features of the "bad" split-off world. He described the objects, and his people were empty. The skeleton in the rusty warehouse, the empty interior of the Black Knight, the images of the cold cave, vultures, and the writing of the dead civilization depicted Tom's internal representations—the bad objects that inhabited his world. They were cold, dead, and unavailable. These objects represented life in the outside world, and therefore Tom remained primarily attached to his early narcissistic life. The intense negative infantile experiences had fostered this "splitting" into the two diverse worlds. It appeared that when he was an infant, there had been some pleasurable experiences in being held, etc., and these provided the traces of the "all-good" world. Clearly the "all-bad" experiences had occurred when Tom was fed and he had experienced the intense pain. He had been unable to take the important developmental step in childhood of integrating these "good" and "bad" worlds, and the need for "splitting" of objects was maintained.

For Tom, to be in a state of need represented a great threat. The Nepal Man lived in a trance but developed a problem when he became hungry (and then needed objects for food). He reached out for food and contact but then stopped himself by "paralyzing" his arm. Tom appeared to relive the early hungry–eating experience in childhood, when he needed to be fed but had used enormous energy to contain himself because of the anticipated pain he would experience.

The Nepal Man was the epitome of the self-contained stoic man, the man who could survive on the juice of one orange every other week. The trembling old woman was a similar self-contained figure who arduously struggled to thread a needle but never turned to others for help. These images were self-representations and ego ideals for Tom. They described precisely the adaptation that Tom had achieved—they created the shell-like buffer between themselves and the real world, even though they did have needs. By the barriers Tom erected between himself and objects, he effectively minimized the pain of the real world. And his daily life clearly reflected the distance he had established between himself and the major aspects of the real world.

Both Tom and Matthew handled their perceived painful worlds by withdrawal into fantasy. However, there were major differences in the quality of their fantasy lives. Many aspects of "secondary process thinking" (the ability to abstract, use metaphor, and symbols) were evident in Tom's thoughts and ideas. Tom had an extremely rich capacity for verbalization and extensive speech, in comparison to the almost nonverbal quality of Matthew's cartoon world. Tom's characters involved extensive use of symbol formation and metaphor rather than the extensive need for direct action that characterized Matthew's play. Creative and synthetic functions were available to Tom, and he could integrate the images of his imagination from his extensive reading and intellectual gifts. Tom had the capacity for sublimation that was not evident with Matthew. It is not unusual that adults with narcissistic disturbances develop successful work and career capacities, whereas borderline adults rarely achieve success in the work area. The difference appears to be in the quality of their respective ego functioning. Matthew's cartoon format had the young child's quality of play where fight and victory (e.g., Popeye and Bluto) provided a sense of magical triumph. This was in contrast to the subtlety of the Nepal Man's characterization in Tom's imagination, who represented a complex self-representation where the issues of food, need, and stoicism were vividly described.

This different level of ego functioning allows the therapist to utilize a greater amount of *uncovering techniques* in the treatment of the child with narcissistic difficulties. During the above period of work with Tom, Tom slowly experienced greater ambivalence about his extensive isolation. The hours spent in his room, the time away from other people, the solitary perimeter he had developed made him feel "lonely" and "bored" a lot of times. Tom and his therapist began to develop a *therapeutic alliance* in which they shared a similar therapeutic goal. They could commonly attempt to understand the need for Tom's extensive withdrawal from reality and perhaps even alter some aspects of this isolation.

When Tom's "Henry stories" described the idealized scenes of Sun Valley, the therapist began to make both *interpretations* (providing the unconscious meaning of the material) and *reconstructions* (putting these meanings into the context of the past history). He discussed with Tom the comforting world he had to create and cling to because of the exploding pain he had experienced as a very young child. In contrast to the pain, Tom had constructed a soothing world. And, the therapist added, he continued to create this soothing environment currently by the special surround in his bedroom and the hideaway fort on his property. He acted as though the past painful threat still currently existed.

When Tom brought the images of the empty and unavailable objects in his life (the rusty warehouse, the skeleton, the Black Knight, etc.), the therapist again slowly interpreted their meanings. For example, the "little boy" in Tom had come to "learn" (because of the pain in eating) that those who fed him were felt to be cold and dreadful and that the outside world was terrifying. Perhaps these past feelings had made him feel that all people currently were similar. Thus he avoided adults, teachers, parents, peers, and went through the day with a minimum of interaction.

As the creations of the Nepal Man and the trembling old woman appeared in metaphor, the therapist interpreted Tom's enormous fears of reaching out to objects. Both images expressed strong needs for help, but their need to isolate themselves from others persisted. This was exactly how Tom functioned at home or at school. He feared that if he asked for help, he would again experience the intense pain and hurt. This worry came from his feelings as an infant rather than the current reality. The thrust of these interventions began to produce an important shift, which occurred in the next phase of the psychotherapy.

TREATMENT (PHASE II)

Phase I encompassed the first year of treatment. During the next 4 months of our work, there was a slow erosion of Tom's complacency and an expanding tension. Tom felt at times like a "caged animal," searching throughout his house for something to do but finding little. He could no longer sit around passively, and his major complaint was his enormous boredom.

Initially some memories came. These were thoughts that came naturally. They were of pleasant moments spent with his older brothers. He recalled riding in the back of a truck with them, going into town. He remembered camping with his older brother's friends. He recalled the campfires, singing, and the food they ate. He remembered a long walk into town from his home in Sun Valley and how, when he was frightened of the saleswoman in a store, his brother helped him buy the candy he wanted. Clearly, I noted he was now feeling more lonely, and the memories he had were of the few times of loving, close moments with people in his life.

He began to make forays into the city, beyond the perimeter of the land surrounding his home. But he complained that the climate in town was not right. This city was not his kind of place. It was highly polluted, and he longed for Sun Valley. He told me of worries that there were muggers in the city who were out to kidnap him and hold him for ransom, since he came from such a wealthy family. Yet he increasingly drove himself to get into the city each weekend.

Transference elements emerged more clearly in his sessions. Tom elaborated a playful preoccupation that had been growing. There was a major plot going on that pleased him to think about. He was marked for murder. His mother was an important member of this conspiracy, but she would give no indication of being part of this evil group. The therapist was also a member, recently hired, and part of the therapist's purpose was to brainwash him so that he would not be as vigilant as he needed to be. He could be assassinated on any street corner of the city. He imagined himself with a machine gun as he rode through town, blasting away at the attackers. When he walked through the city he carried (in his imagination) a variety of concealed weapons he had access to at a moment's notice. These ideas were embellished and elaborated over many weeks. The pleasurable aspects of this affectively distanced scenario were that as he traveled through the city, he was not bored, but in a state of excitement and adventure as he played out these themes.

In new Henry stories, people were now clearly included. Henry had found a group of kittens which he brought home to care for and nurse. They had been abandoned. But Henry's mother had an intense allergy to cats and would only allow them to be housed in the garage. The result was that they wandered away at night and were lost.

Despite the negative connotations of the indifferent or hating objects, Tom was evidently growing much closer to his therapist. One day, when discussing future plans, instead of talking about his wish to be a physicist like father, he slipped and said "psychiatrist" like father. The therapist noted the slip and commented that Tom seemed to have good fatherly feelings about him. On another occasion, noting that the therapist had been rather silent for several sessions, Tom said he knew why the therapist was really being quiet. In a most intense way, he said the therapist wanted to give him a chance to come out of himself, to let what was really inside of him emerge. The therapist's silence, therefore, was experienced as a loving, interested, and empathic silence.

The newer aspects of the internal Tom were simultaneously filled with aggression, and there was a growing availability of *real affects* as he brought more internal material. He dreamt of a party where his mother was preoccupied with the guests downstairs. She came up to say good-night to him, and he noted a bloodstain on her white blouse. Later he realized he held a knife. As he described the dream, Tom clenched his fist and rage permeated his face. Another dream fragment was of a vampire bat. He commented that while these bats were seen as ugly and disgusting, among the bats themselves they were quite acceptable. He then noted that he felt ugly and angry. In a third dream in this period, he was an observer of a witches' coven from a balcony. There was much activity within the group as they scurried back and forth. He realized as he watched them that they were making plans not only to practice evil among themselves but to affect the world at large. He noted that when he awoke, rather than being frightened by the group, he was fascinated and liked the idea of the power they had. He was smart; wouldn't it be terrific if he had the power to run the world?

Some breakthroughs occurred in Tom's reality functioning. He began to enjoy school and his work there. He felt he now had new energy for his assignments, and for the first time he volunteered in class. He was terribly pleased with the fact that when he gave a thoughtful answer the teacher smiled and others approved. Several people spoke to him for the first time, and he was invited to eat lunch at the popular table. In addition, he related he did something with his mother he had never done before. While they were driving, he thought of a funny program he had seen on television. He wanted terribly to tell someone about it. He related the TV incidents to his mother, and she laughed. As we discussed this interchange, it became clear that this was the first time he could remember bringing something of himself to his mother. He invariably only answered questions people asked him and never brought aspects of himself into any encounter. In addition, it was hard for Tom to believe that he could really make someone laugh—that he could have a real impact on the real world, mother, teacher, and students in his class.

Discussion

In the above phase of psychotherapy, Tom (like Matthew) emerged from his isolated world as it became more ego-alien. Earlier it had protected him, but now he felt like a "caged animal." Therefore, he made forays into the "polluted" city and in doing so began to deal with some aspects of the dreaded aggression he had "split off" and avoided.

What provided the impetus for change and the initial moves out of his isolated world? A major aspect was the effect of the growing positive transference and libidinal (loving) relationship to the therapist. Evidence for this emerged in his slip (wish) to be a "psychiatrist," his comments on understanding the therapist's relative silence at times, the increased sharing of his internal life, and his growing investment in the treatment. The pleasurable relationship with the therapist restimulated the *need* for relationships and underscored his intense loneliness. Thus, the good attachment memories of contact, closeness, and warmth with his brothers emerged in his associations. We can also speculate that his transference capacity to engage with the therapist had an earlier basis—his positive ties to his father. The effect of this experience in treatment was to make him increasingly dissatisfied with the impoverished, isolative world he had created. Thus he became a restless "caged animal" at home, seeking more contact and relationships. But as he attempted to give up his enclosed world, he reexperienced the earlier dreads and anxieties that he had defended against. What would happen when he needed people and sought contact?

What led to the development of the positive transference? Again it is helpful to use Freud's concept of "repetition compulsion." In the process of psychotherapy, the patient will experience past events that were centrally conflictual and repressed (cut off from conscious awareness). The above material indicates that Tom earlier sought and valued positive and loving attachments, and he recreated this in the treatment. The therapist was then in a position to point out this intense current conflict (a repetition of the past). For example, when Tom brought the vignettes about his brothers, the therapist commented that he seemed to enjoy being with other people and that this contact gave him a lot of pleasure. Now, however, he seemed to live in a way that really cut off people. Highlighting the conflict contributed to Tom's pressure to alter his current separation from the world.

As Tom grew increasingly dissatisfied with his schizoid-like withdrawal, the "unintegrated" all-bad aggressive world reemerged. The city he initially sought to enter was polluted and populated with muggers, kidnappers, and murderers. His mother was the personification of all evil, and even the therapist could become an "all-bad" object joining the conspiracy. The attacking world of early childhood that provided the intense pain reappeared. As the threatening world emerged, Tom at first warded off his internal fears and counterrage by making his forays into the city a game. He described *playing* that he carried a machine gun and other weapons to kill the assassins.

As Tom brought on this aggressive world, the therapist had opportunities to make a number of interventions—interpretations of defense and content and reconstructions that were slowly helpful to Tom. The therapist did a significant amount of interpretation linking Tom's vision of the current hostile world (e.g., the polluted attacking city) to the world he had experienced as a little boy when he felt attacked by the continuous "outside" pain. As he felt he was attaching the past to his current perception of the city, he became less frightened of leaving the perimeter of his home. The therapist also interpreted the meanings of the "plots" against Tom conceived by mother and others. The therapist linked the current distrust of mother and her murderous intent to the feelings of a little boy. Tom had constructed, with the pain he had experienced, that he was being poisoned by an evil witch with every feeding. The therapist also touched on the counterrage any little boy would feel. Tom was destroying all the assassins with his machine guns. When a child felt he was being poisoned, he would not only be frightened, he would also want to kill everyone in sight, and especially the evil witch-mother who he imagined was continuously giving him the poisonous feedings.

One of the major problems facing children with borderline or narcissistic disturbances is the life-long difficulty they have in integrating the rawness of their pregenital aggression, both emerging from the self and projected onto the outside world (Kernberg, 1984). As Tom became more comfortable with the "playful" game-like murderous feelings he could attribute to himself in the city family, he allowed more real affect to emerge. He experienced the rage toward his mother in the party dream, he felt intensely like the ugly and angry bat, and he vigorously identified with the witches who wanted to rule the world for their evil purposes. The therapist continued to describe the intense feelings of a "poisoned" (perceived by Tom) little boy. The little boy would want to seek revenge against his mother and the whole world. He would seek to bloody (blouse) the clean, deserting mother. In his angry imagination, he would want to become an ugly vampire bat (oral destructive rage) and repay the object world for his early sufferings. Could the witch's coven be his inside idea of the plans the mother–witches were hatching to torture him with every feeding? Tom listened intently to these constructions of his emotional early life.

As noted above, as Tom's aggressive fantasies emerged and were made less pernicious through the treatment, the real world became less frightening. School, peers, and home became less formidable, and he invested increasingly in his relationships and learning. In subsequent periods of work in the psychotherapy, intense rage affects broke through, often directed against both the therapist and himself. And as these affects were understood, Tom's investments in reality were further enhanced. In later years Tom's isolation was significantly altered, but it was the therapist's assessment that his capacity for intimacy remained somewhat limited. For example, he related to peers around interests rather than as people.

SUMMARY

From the two cases described (Chapter 7 and 8), it is clear that there exists a range of severe pathology in childhood. Both children evidenced some similar features in object relations difficulties and in the early separation–individuation phases of development. However, there existed a wide difference in ego capacity and achievement in these children. Such differences substantially alter the treatability and prognosis. Children like Tom, who exhibit good ego functioning, have the capacity for a significant degree of insight-oriented psychotherapy. Those like Matthew can be helped to master poor adaptation primarily through supportive and ego-building techniques.

In reviewing the treatment process with Tom, we can see many similarities to the uncovering process with the neurotic children. The primary intervention was through interpretation and reconstruction. The major difference in work with narcissistically disturbed children is not the modality of treatment itself but the specific content that the therapist needs to understand. He needs to become familiar with the early developmental process of infancy and toddlerhood and the nature of the early interactions with the primary objects. These aspects of the early history will arise in the symbolic material of these children (e.g., Sun Valley, Henry stories). Additionally, the therapist needs particularly to understand the role of aggression and the adaptation through the mechanisms of "splitting" and the construction of the all-good/all-bad worlds these children make.

BIBLIOGRAPHY

Abend, S., Porder, M., & Willich, M. (1983). *Borderline Patients: Psychoanalytic Perspectives*. New York: International Universities Press.

Fast, I. (1970). The function of action in the early development of identity. *International Journal of Psychoanalysis* 51:471–478.

Fast, I., & Chethik, M. (1972). Aspects of depersonalization experience in children. *International Journal of Psychoanalysis* 53:479–485.

Kernberg, P. (1984). The psychological assessment of children with borderline personality organization. Presented to the American Psychoanalytic Association, New York.

Mahler, M., Pine, F., & Berman, A. (1975). *The Psychological Birth of the Infant*. New York: Basic Books.

Meissner, W. W. (1984). *The Borderline Spectrum*. New York, London: Jason Aronson.

Pine, F. (1985). *Developmental Theory and Clinical Process*. New Haven: Yale University Press.

Settledge, C. (1977). The psychoanalytic understanding of narcissistic and borderline personality disorders. *Journal of the American Psychoanalytic Association* 25:805–834.

9

Focal Psychotherapy

Thus far the topics in this section of the book (Part II) have focused on children with longstanding developmental problems. Neurosis, character pathology, narcissistic, and borderline disturbances have had their roots in the preoedipal or oedipal phases of development. The purpose of the treatment of these children has been to produce "structural change"—change within the structure of the personality affecting the drives, ego, or superego components. For example, in our discussion of the treatment goals of Fred (obsessional youngster, Chapter 4) we discovered his symptoms had primarily been caused by severe superego reactions to his "unacceptable" aggressive impulses. The purposes of the treatment was to produce structural change, to make the internal impulses more flexible to Fred by modifying longstanding harsh superego reactions that Fred developed. To achieve this structural change goal, the uncovering that was required necessitated several years of intensive psychotherapy. Similarly, in the case of Matthew (Chapter 8, borderline youngster), the goal of the psychotherapy was to develop the quality of ego functioning (structural change) that could allow this child to function in the real world. Components of the ego (e.g., signal anxiety, defenses) had to be built through the therapeutic process. Again, this required a period of lengthy psychotherapy. Thus, when we normally think of producing structural change through treatment (altering longstanding patterns of psychopathology), it is almost implicit that the treatment will be both intensive (more than one time per week) and of long duration (usually several years).

There are, however, many situations that children experience that place a strain on their development but that do not require extensive psychotherapeutic intervention or major internal changes within the child. These experiences are typically stimulated by focal stress events in the child's life or family life, and they have the potential of derailing the developmental process or have already produced some recent changes in the child's functioning. These are often classified as "reactive disturbances," a disturbance in reaction to a stress event. The following is a possible list of such events in a child's life, but certainly not an exhaustive one:

1. Death in the family (parent, sibling, relative).
2. Divorce within the family.
3. Surgery to child or other hospitalization.
4. Major physical or emotional illness of a family member.
5. Major illness of child.
6. Suicide of a family member.
7. "Life crisis" of a parent (job, affair, etc.).
8. Birth of a sibling.
9. Extensive separations from the caregivers.
10. Family dislocations.

For some children who are well integrated, these events will cause only transitional stress that will be mastered after a period of time. For these youngsters, no professional intervention will be needed. Others will show marked and persistent changes stemming from the crisis. Many children are affected indirectly, less by the event itself (e.g., death of a sibling) and more by the parental reaction. Often there is an alteration of the parent's ability to function as a parent. For example, a depressed mother dealing with the death of a child in the family may have little capacity to deal with the other growing siblings. The parental change may constitute the primary developmental interference for the child.

When it appears that the child's reactions to these events or changes in the parents go beyond a transitory period, an evaluation is indicated, and "focal psychotherapy" may be the appropriate recommendation. This intervention can be directed at the child, parent(s), or both. Typically these treatment experiences are shorter than those involving children who require structural change, and it may last from several months to less than 1 year. The purpose of this chapter is to illustrate this intervention and to discuss generally some of the differences in the process of this work.

THE PREPARATORY PROCESS

All of the above stress events have been extensively written about in the clinical professional literature. These reports are both general (e.g., typical reactions to divorce, death, illness) and case reports (specific courses of treatment of these children). It is usually very helpful to become familiar with the clinical literature* as one proceeds with the evaluation and treatment of a possible reactive disturbance. In the evaluation process, this can help the therapist distinguish between a transitional reaction (normal) and a pathological one. It can orient the therapist to the specific components of an event that are generally troublesome for youngsters (e.g., loyalty conflicts, reconciliation wishes in divorce). The literature also provides information on how these events will affect the child at the *specific developmental stages*. Different developmental stages will alter the child's experience. For example, the extended absence of the caregiving mother because of illness will affect the 2-year-old male toddler differently than the 6-year-old "oedipal" boy. The 2-year-old will primarily struggle with issues of loss and survival, whereas the 6-year-old will be more concerned with affects of guilt about his impulses (sexual, primarily) that "drove" (his perception) the mother away. The 6-year-old will be better able to use other objects (e.g., father) to deal with loss than the 2-year-old who is still in the throes of the dyadic dependency.

In the course of this chapter, we follow several cases, focusing first on a child who was reacting to divorce and then on a child who was reacting to the death of a parent. The material illustrates the evaluative process and the course of treatment.

---

*A particularly helpful clinical *index* that surveys the literature was compiled by I. N. Berlin, *Bibliography of Child Psychiatry* (1976). It carries the most relevant readings until 1976.

CASE 1: IMPACT OF DIVORCE

Richard was a blond 6½-year-old boy who had become increasingly depressed and lethargic following the marital separation that had occurred 1 year earlier. The parents described a youngster who was developing well until the family crisis had occurred. For example, Richard had done well in kindergarten and was considered very bright. He now appeared "unmotivated" in first grade and worked below his ability. Although he had many friends in school and in the neighborhood, his wish to play with others had dropped off markedly. He had been an affectionate and cooperative youngster with both parents earlier. He now rarely interacted enthusiastically with either parent, and he had become withholding regarding chores and tasks around both the mother's house and father's apartment. The changes were striking and appeared related to the marital disruption. In the evaluation sessions with Richard, he was somewhat sad, but primarily sullen and uncooperative. There was clearly a suggestion of intense anger, which he was unable to express directly, verbally, or in play.

Diagnostic Considerations (The Preparation Process)

As noted above, it is initially helpful to familiarize oneself with the available current literature regarding the "interfering" event. There is a considerable body of articles and books on the impact of separation and divorce on children within a psychodynamic framework, including authors such as Wallerstein and Kelly (1980) as well as work by Kalter (1977) and McDermott (1970). Generally, divorce is considered a developmental interference that will always create significant internal stress within a child. The child will need to deal with four major affects stimulated by the marital disruption: (1) anger/ rage, (2) loss/grief, (3) guilt/self-blame, and (4) fears.

Children are typically *enraged* internally because they feel cheated by the disruption in the family life and their sense of security. The rage may become evident and acted out (for example, expressed by defiance or direct antisocial trends). The anger may feel very threatening, since the child may fear further loss; it may then be defended against intensely (evidence of this may emerge in symptoms such as phobias). One child had to avoid watching TV, since he might see direct aggression expressed, and he would be filled with intense anxiety. The aggressive *wishes* were repressed, and the expression of them (even on TV characters) became a source of fear.

According to the literature, there is usually a substantial *real loss* the child experiences. The quality of the parental relationship with the father (typically the noncustodial parent) changes, and there is also a major loss in the sense of family (Lohr et al., 1981). Direct depression or depressive equivalents emerge within the child and need to be internally handled.

Guilt is a very common affect children experience in the throes of separation and divorce, and usually it has several sources. Most young children have the egocentric fantasy that they were the central reasons for the divorce. This kind of self-blame often causes loss of self-esteem (a sense of badness) and needs for punishment. *Loyalty conflicts* very often further the feelings of guilt. It is not unusual for there to be a good deal of rancor between the parents, and many children feel torn between them. Children often feel pressure to agree to disparaging ideas that one spouse expresses toward the other, while at the same time they internally try to maintain a loving connection to the disparaged partner. This struggle causes a sense of disloyalty and guilt.

Many *fears* abound for children during marital separation and divorce. Although they may fear abandonment by the separated father, they are often concerned that the mother will take a similar abandonment course. Thus, we often see clinging behavior and separation anxiety symptoms. The fears of survival are prominent, expressed in concern about money or preoccupations regarding food.

With the preliminary material regarding Richard, what kinds of hypotheses can we generate regarding his internal struggles, which have altered his behavior over the course of the year? Richard is "unmotivated" in school, less interactive with peers, distant from both parents, and withholding regarding responsibilities. Several possible conflicts suggest themselves. Richard does appear to be struggling with his anger stemming from the divorce experience. His withholding patterns in school and at home can be a form of passive aggression, and this is partly confirmed by the sullen, uncooperative stance Richard assumed in the evaluation sessions. Richard would also be struggling with depressed affects that "depleted" his energy to work and interact.

As noted above, in this initial assessment process, it is helpful to refine further one's understanding about the impact of the event specifically in the context of the child's developmental struggles. Richard was still in the phallic–oedipal phase of development when the marital separation occurred, and there is further literature that describes the problems of divorce on the "oedipal" child (Neubauer, 1960). The normal oedipal male child naturally competes with his father, and his mother becomes a sexual object. How would a separation and divorce affect a child during this phase? According to the literature, the major developmental problem is that the divorce (typically the father leaving home) often "confirms" for the oedipal boy that he was indeed the "victor" in this triangular struggle within the nuclear family. Often this "victory" produces intense anxieties when these frightening wishes appear to have come true. The preliminary material with Richard raised several hypotheses involving his oedipal struggles. Richard appeared to withdraw from his mother, and the close affectionate relationship disappeared. Did this withdrawal indicate that Richard's "sexualized" feelings indeed became very frightening to him, and he therefore sought to distance himself from his mother? Similarly, we found that Richard's interaction with his father lost its spontaneity since the separation. Did this change indicate that Richard became fearful of the normal, competitive feelings a youngster would express with father? Did the problems with his competitive wishes also inhibit the intellectual progress in school, where competitive feelings are heightened?

The decision was to take Richard into focal psychotherapy to attempt to deal with the impact of divorce, which was clearly impeding his ongoing development. Richard was seen one time per week for a period of 6 months. The mother was seen biweekly, and the father was seen on a sporadic basis (approximately one time per month).

Course of Treatment

In the opening treatment sessions, Richard elaborated intense competitive play. Two army sides emerged, reinforced by tanks, cars, and armored vehicles. Strategy then developed: fake decoy attacks, elaborate spy schemes, smoke screens, and air reconnaissance. Richard also had an array of special weapons that his opponent was without. He had a huge snake that took the entire opposing army to subdue, and it needed the total strength of all the troops to remove the enormous sac from its head; Richard also had a jet streamer, a special plane equipped with flame throwers that no enemy barricades could stop. And, most powerful of all, he had black monsters available to him who had "poison prickers" that penetrated and stopped enemy soldiers and thereby killed them.

This play gave Richard and his therapist the opportunity to explore a number of themes. The therapist noted how much Richard wished he himself would have a superspecial pricker. When he thought of the super prickers that grown-ups and daddies had, he seemed scared, since this meant that grown-ups had super powers. Richard laughed and noted that only orange juice came out of his pricker. He brought in chemicals from his chemistry set and made many mixtures in his sessions. When the therapist spoke of his wish to have special chemicals in his pricker like daddies, Richard confided that he loved to wet his bed—it was very warm. Whisker, his cat, always slept with him, and that was how Whisker had baby kittens. The therapist could empathize gently, over a period of time, with Richard's wish to be as full-grown as a daddy, and do all the things that a daddy did. It was hard for him to still be a small boy, and it made him sad, angry, and scared. Sometimes he had to make believe that he had all the power and that he was the boss.

In this initial work, Richard's intense anxiety over underlying powerful feelings of competition with his father emerged. Richard's envy and fear of his father's power and abilities, represented by his focus on "prickers," was interpreted, as were the accompanying sad feelings of being so little compared to his father. Clearly therapeutic work of this sort is common with children irrespective of whether their parents divorce. However, the interruption of an ongoing, emotionally central, relationship with his father intensified the conflict and made the fantasies less amenable to new and qualitatively different realistic experiences with father. Without father there to "test out," as it were, the veracity of these fantasies, they retained all of their original force.

Richard then began a long series of stories, which he called "Dungey House." In his stories there was fighting between a mother and a father. A baby listened to the ruckus while he was still in his mommy's stomach. The father did not want the baby, but the mother did. This was the reason they fought. The baby crawled out, smacked the father with his fist, and ran away with the mother to his special

"Dungey house." The house was old, broken down, and cheap. There he tenderly planted a full garden to take of all their food. He cut wood for the fireplace, and mother and father got a "divorcement." The Dungey stories and adventures continued but often did not have the happiest ending. For example, the police came because the baby was declared a runaway. They put a chain around the baby's neck and took him away, even though the mother fought desperately to save him.

The Dungey stories brought forth one of Richard's hidden conceptions of the marital disruption. He had felt that his destructive behavior, his jealous wishes were responsible for his parents' "divorcement." His beginning phallic–oedipal urges together with an egocentric cognitive view of the world, both in ascendance at the time of the separation, resulted in this self-blame and ensuing guilt. He and his therapist, in the context of the Dungey stories, began to clarify some of the realities of the history of the difficult marriage and parental fighting. The stories understandably ushered in rich oedipal material—his tender and caring feelings toward his mother emerged not only in the stories but in reality as well. Richard also confided that he often sneaked into his mother's bedroom when she was gone and picked the lock of her jewelry box. Then he could see her wedding ring and all the gold that was there.

Slowly, stories that had a different and more empathic view of grown adult men began to emerge in a new series, called the "Old Man Fogey" stories. The Timberlee Hillbillies, a group of young toughs, attacked Old Man Fogey's house. They chopped down dead trees, which crashed against the roof. They threw wood into his chimney, which shocked him and ruined his fire and made his life generally miserable. Yet, these were only in the order of pranks. When Old Man Fogey was actually trapped by a fire in the house because of faulty wiring, the Hillbillies climbed on top of each other to reach an open second-story window and rescue the old man. They then cooked a huge pot of soup to warm up the survivor and shared the food together. Richard also introduced a wise old owl in his puppet play, who soothed the impulsiveness of an irrepressible monkey who constantly stole jewelry and who also soothed the viciousness of primitive father–tiger puppet, who was out to tear the monkey apart. The wise old owl effected continuous compromises, showing the little monkey how he could work and acquire many treasures and teaching the tiger to have some pleasure from the playfulness of the immature puppet.

Other activities became part of each session. There were many highly pleasurable, new-formed, and highly skilled competitive games. Complex forms of "tic-tac-toe" were introduced by Richard that became furious battles. Also, both therapist and child participated in hangman, a special word-guessing game. Richard saved up the longest possible words he could imagine to stump his therapist with—"hamburger," "television," "somewhere." And his therapist countered with even longer word puzzles—"sometimes," "nobody," and "Mickey Mouse." And this intellectual battle in therapy had its reverberations in school, where Richard began to work avidly.

Discussion

At the start of treatment, Richard began to have problems dealing with phallic, oedipal, and early latency-aged issues that he seemed to be handling well prior to the marital disruption. He appeared to stop his development commensurate with the age he experienced the interference of the parental divorce and the partial emotional loss of his father.

Richard's case illustrates the derailment of development caused by the divorce experience and an applicable form of focal psychotherapy. Richard's initial terror of his own phallic, competitive drives was sufficient to cause inhibitions in both his assertiveness at school and his tender feelings towards his mother. Instead we saw the regressive withdrawal from his mother and an inability to use his intellect at school.

We saw these presenting complaints and their underlying conflicts as related to affects stimulated by parental divorce. For Richard, the affects and conflicts evoked by the divorce included a *sense of anxiety and self-blame* for having caused so major a life event as his parents' divorce, an underlying feeling of *intense guilt* over besting his father in the competition for who would "win" (i.e., live with) mother, an *anxiety over fantasized retribution* for this forbidden victory, and *sadness* over losing his father when he moved out of the family household. An inhibition of phallic competition, the inhibition of affectionate feelings toward his mother, was invoked to cope with these painful affects. The fact of living in a one-parent household with his mother and seeing his father only once a week potentiated these conflicts and made them more difficult to resolve. The reality of living with his mother without father present fueled his forbidden unconscious oedipal wishes and made having affectionate feelings toward his mother nearly impossible. At the same time, when his father became emotionally less central in Richard's life, Richard's frightening fantasies of the angry, overwhelming, and vengeful oedipal father could not be tested in ongoing interactions with him.

There was a very marked shift and growth in a 6-month treatment period. While the therapeutic relationship had many traditional aspects (e.g., the therapist interpreted the unreality of frightening, unconscious fantasies, the therapist interpreted defenses of expressing safe affects to ward off painful affects), the major aspects of the therapeutic relationship had a special quality. Under the direction of the patient, the therapist became an aggressive competitor: at first he was fearsome and terrifying, but under the aegis of a growing libidinal context in the therapy, the competition in play became increasingly highly pleasurable and interesting. The feared, vengeful castrations became modulated by the reality experiences with a newly available object, and Richard became increasingly comfortable with his own aggression. He became generally more cooperative and able to use his aggression in learning.

Similarly, if we follow the course of object and superego integration in the therapy, changes emerged through the new attachment in therapy. Grown men, who were at first one-dimensional attackers who took little children away with a chain around their necks, slowly became full people. Old Man Fogey could be hurt and needy, and Richard could empathize with his pain. The wise old owl in his play represented a strong man who was kindly and thoughtful as well as powerful. Richard identified with the therapist. He became much less harsh in his own superego prohibitions. The self-representation of the irascible monkey does not have to be torn apart by the primitive, angry, oedipal father or locked in jail, but he can be "forgiven" since he is in the process of growing up. Richard's conscience became more tolerant and realistic about his impulses.

These developmental tasks—the greater comfort with the aggression, the resumption of affection in object development, the modulation of superego prohibitions—are the changes that occur in normal growth only if adequate objects are available. Richard could continue this normal unfolding when he united with a new object who served the integrative function his father could no longer provide, within the focal psychotherapy.

CASE 2: A BEREAVEMENT REACTION

Sandra was evaluated at age 8½, a year and a half after the abrupt death of her mother. Her mother had died in a car accident, in which her mother had been a passenger. A friend of the family had been driving the car and had also been killed in the head-on collision, which was the fault of the driver in the other vehicle involved in the accident.

There had been a period of shock and numbness (disbelief) for all the family members, including Sandra's father and brother Jason (1 year younger than Sandra). Memories of the few months following the death were clouded, but the father felt that both children showed moments of intense sadness, weeping, and loss.

Sandra had done well throughout her life. She had been an exceptional student and had had an array of friends prior to the death. Since the demise of her mother, she continued to be able to maintain her high level of achievement, and her functioning with friends and relatives went very well. The past relationship with her mother was described as "close" and "warm," and there were no particular periods in the past that highlighted evidence of tension or stress in Sandra's development.

About 6 months after the death of the mother, Mr. E. met a divorced woman who was approximately his age. They married after a 6-month courtship, and the two families joined together. Sandra acquired a stepmother and a stepsister, Margaret, who was the same age as Jason.

The impetus for the referral (about 6 months after the second marriage) came from Sandra herself. She talked about being frightened at night and became quite anxious as bedtime neared. She was unable to describe why she was frightened, except to indicate that she feared "bad dreams." Both parents also felt that although Sandra was polite and well-behaved with her stepmother, she maintained a reserve and aloofness from the new members of the family. The parents were disappointed with the continuing distance that Sandra experienced but would continue to let her become "attached" at her own pace.

In the early evaluation meetings with Sandra, she was appropriately apprehensive but relaxed when the therapist spoke generally about how girls are naturally frightened in this new and strange situation. As she approached discussing the night fears, she became visibly distressed and anxious and was unable to describe her fears or show the therapist about them in drawings or writing. She indicated, however, that she wanted to have a private place to share these feelings, and she implied she would be able to tell me about her distress gradually.

The therapist recommended a twice-weekly open-ended therapy, since he did not have a good understanding of Sandra's struggle. He felt she was probably dealing with some acute affects related to the death of the mother and the remarriage and thought he could provide a better perspective when he knew Sandra better. The therapist decided to see her several times weekly rather than once a week, since he anticipated dealing with the acute affects that might arise from the traumatic event. He was concerned, for example, about leaving this youngster for a full week with intense grief reactions and anxiety. The treatment lasted for an 8-month period.

Diagnostic Considerations: The Preparatory Process

From the literature on children and death of a parent, there emerges a general consensus that children do not have the capacity to deal effectively with death. Wolf (1958) indicates that only at age 10 or 11 can children cognitively comprehend the full meaning of death. Wolfenstein (1966) notes that children, if they comprehend death, are unable to mourn emotionally, to experience the painful and gradual decathexis (letting go) of a beloved parent. She noted that they tend to mourn "at a distance" and manage this episodically. Nagera (1981) adds that because of the pressure of development, children need to retain their important objects. They will recreate the objects anew, often in idealized form.

When we turn to look specifically at how latency-aged children handle the death of a parent (Sandra was 7 at the time and entering early latency), Shambaugh (1961) and Furman (1964) both speak of the tendency for children at this age to erect a massive denial. They describe case reports where all of the affects the children experience related to the death of the parent were defended against acutely. Most authors note that often some intervention is useful to enable the child to experience the dreaded affects emerging from the event and to invest adequately with present or new objects.

What hypotheses can be generated about Sandra at this point? She appeared to be an extremely well-integrated and highly functioning youngster who had a very effective ego. Why was she experiencing anxiety at the present time, 1½ years after the death of her mother? Were aspects of a denial breaking down? Was she attempting to engage the reality of the death of her mother? Was she dealing with the pain of the loss, guilt about the event, or rage about the abandonment? What were the implications of having a new stepmother? Did her needs for mothering from this new object create conflict, since they would mean "leaving" her mother and feeling disloyal?

Course of Treatment

After several weeks of treatment, Sandra began to describe an extensive fantasy she had developed that had begun to frighten her. She had created an "at will" (her words) fantasy, meaning she could develop it and think about it through her willingness to do so.

Shortly after the death of her mother, she had developed the idea that she could rise up from bed to contact her mother. She imagined that her spirit had left her body, rose above the roof, above the clouds, and then she would meet her mother. This meeting was located on a large cloud area and had an ethereal quality. Mother characteristically wore a special beautiful long robe, and she also wore lovely jewels. Mother and daughter visited from a distance, and all was totally quiet. They never touched each other, and there was no need for speaking since they could read each other's minds. There was a "glowing" quality to their surround—mother "glowed" and the house she lived in in the background "glowed." The details of the fantasy grew and had been continuously embellished over the past 1½ years.

Sandra was very upset as she recounted the fantasy world and its history. She was very anxious and spoke almost inaudibly. Things had begun to change. She told me that she was more frightened recently because she was "visiting" more frequently. What had started out as a fantasy she had induced once or twice a week had now become compelling and was something she had to do almost every night. Now she often felt that she did not want to start the dream, but if she concentrated she could hear her mother call her, and she "rose up." The feeling that she was losing conscious control of this fantasy and its production created the terror that forced her to seek help from her parents (i.e., tell them that she was having very bad dreams).

In reviewing this material early in the treatment, the therapist had a number of thoughts. The original function of the fantasy had been the denial of the mother's death. Through the fantasy, Sandra could "keep" her mother with her. This process of denial, as noted above, is common with latency-aged children. Through this process, Sandra maintained the object (idealized as beautiful in her glowing gown and jewelry) and also avoided the affects of sadness, rage, and aloneness.

It was also clear that contained within the fantasy was a limited acknowledgment of the death. The union was with spirits: ghost-like figures of herself and her mother were present; she rose to meet her mother "above" in a heaven-like surround; and there was a lack of human contact since there was no touching or mutual sounds.

What was creating the frightening shift in the intensity of contact with the mother? Sandra felt greater pressure to join her mother. In the fantasy, the mother now called her. How can we explain the loss of volition in invoking the fantasy and the change to a sense of dreaded obligation? The beckoning of her mother had the distinct flavor of a *conscience call*, and Sandra's superego seemed to be reacting intensely. Did she originally feel responsible for mother's death? Were there wishes within Sandra to "desert" the mother, and did this impulse create intense internal conflict? Did she have to deny her wish for more gratification from real and living objects? It was clear there was internal conflict within Sandra, and the fantasy now had a punishing quality. Joining her mother "up above" carried a death (or suicidal) implication, a severe form of self-punishment.

My intervention with Sandra was to note generally that she had developed this dream, or at-will fantasy, to soothe herself, as many children would after the death of a mother. She had loved her mother, needed her, and her dream was a special way of trying to keep her alive. Right now things had gotten very scary with this dream, and we could only *slowly* come to understand together what was happening. She needed to continue to tell the therapist about the dreams and her ideas. Sandra continued to draw pictures of her dreams and the details of this Heaven-like setting in her sessions.

During one of the ongoing visits to her mother ("called" by her mother), a mental discussion between them occurred. Mother wanted to know how the new mother was. Sandra reassured her mother that the stepmother was bad and that she still loved her own mother. The therapist noted, at this point, that she seemed to be having a really big struggle. All girls would need, more and more, some *real* mothering in their lives, but when she came closer to her stepmother, she felt very disloyal to her mother. Sandra was very upset. She described how her stepmother recently had bought her favorite luncheon meat, and Sandra had wondered a little if it had been poisoned. Perhaps, the therapist noted, she needed to find reasons to keep her stepmother far away.

A great deal of material then emerged about the stepmother, who was realistically a very wholesome person. At first Sandra was very angry. She *hated it* when her stepmother *tried* to be a mother. She felt like a stepchild, blamed for everything that was wrong, etc. Holidays were different—her stepmother was Jewish and she Christian, so they had to celebrate both Chanukah and Christmas. She was scared about even mentioning Christ at home. I wondered, from time to time, if she had to *make* the stepmother bad, so she could appease the memory of her mother. All girls her age needed to have someone close and real in their lives, but she felt this need took something away from her dead mother. With this form of repeated interpretation, a shift began to occur. Sandra occasionally permitted herself to sit on her stepmother's lap and let her stepmother comb and braid her long hair. She had to agree, for a stepmother, she was fair and did not always favor Margaret (stepsister) in disputes between the children. She liked the gifts her stepmother gave her, especially a soft feminine pair of gloves. She began to draw pictures for her new mother.

On many occasions in this period, she experienced enormous guilt. For example, she had a negative memory of her real mother—she had not smiled a lot. Sandra confessed her strong attachment to her kindergarten teacher before her mother's death. She even used to have wishes that the orange juice lady (commercial) on television would be her mother, since this lady had a wonderful smile. I noted how all children had times when they wished for other mothers, especially when their real mom was out of sorts. Memories of these natural wishes made her feel terrible since her mother had died, and these bad feelings about herself were especially strong since she was beginning to care for her stepmother.

One of the major affects that adversely affects the course of bereavement is the reaction to past aggressive thoughts and wishes toward the object, the natural ambivalence that all children experience in development. During the preoedipal years, when the mother is frustrating, there are wishes for an "all-good" mother. The natural oedipal triangle involves rivalry and death wishes toward the parent of the same sex. Latency produces the "family romance," longings for perfect parents to replace the natural parents whose faults become evident. These natural past "aggressions" are a common source of intense guilt if the parent actually dies. Sandra clearly struggled with guilt for her past "transgressions" (the attachment to the kindergarten teacher and the orange juice lady), and this guilt was intensely exacerbated by her need for and attraction to her stepmother. This underlying dynamic interfered with the capacity to detach from her mother. She also found a way to use her "at-will" dream to punish herself for these past transgressions. A formerly soothing fantasy became dreaded and frightening, driven by an attacking conscience.

After 6 months of treatment the "visits" to Sandra's mother came less frequently, and it appeared Sandra again created the fantasy when she herself missed her mother. Her acute anxiety toward nightfall abated. In one drawing of the "above" world, there was a sign on her mother's fantasy cottage. It read "HERE LIVES ISA-BELLE F. . . ." (mother's name). The therapist noted that if we removed one letter, the "V," it would read "HERE LIES ISA-BELLE F. . . ." Sandra became acutely sad and told me that she often cried when she saw a car in the street that was the same model her mother had died in.

In the ensuing weeks, Sandra was silent and withdrawn. When the therapist commented on her anger toward him, she told him that he wanted to take her mother away from her. On a recent "visit" to her mother, her mother told her not to talk to the therapist, who now looked terrible to her, even like the devil. Sandra related a dream in this period. "Old oak trees housed birds and squirrels. A lumberjack came to destroy the tree. The birds tried to peck at the lumberjack." The therapist noted to Sandra that it felt as if he were the bad lumberman who was cutting down the beautiful tree-dream that she had grown and where part of her was trying to live. The dreams she had developed were used not to keep her from feeling very sad about her mother who was gone.

With her stepmother, Sandra began to visit her mother's actual grave site for the first time. She looked at photographs of her mother and experienced much sadness with the members of her family. In the sessions themselves, she recalled birthdays with her mother and special foods her mother had cooked for the children. There were also poignant memories of coming home from school after the mother's death and calling out for her mother in an empty house. She had called "Mommie, Mommie, Mommie" and only heard her echoes in the house. Some of these memories evoked intense sadness in both Sandra and the therapist.

As Sandra's relationship with her stepmother improved and there were fewer and fewer recurrences of the at-will dream, Sandra and the therapist set a termination date 1 month in advance. For several sessions in this last period, Sandra expressed great anger at her father. She had visited relatives during Easter and had had a wonderful time. They had invited her back, and she longed to go, but her father noted the family had other summer plans. She was furious. She recalled all the good times she had with her cousins in great detail. The therapist interpreted that he thought Sandra was telling how angry she was with him about the therapy. She had earlier developed a wonderful visit with her mother, and the treatment process had had taken away this wonderful soothing time she had. Sandra obviously had mixed feelings about giving up her mother-dream and the connections she had developed through fantasy.

Discussion

Prior to the death of the mother, Sandra appeared to be doing very well throughout her development. After the death, she attempted to cope with many aspects of the event by developing her "at-will" dream of union with the mother. Union fantasies with a deceased parent are not uncommon and can be particularly useful for a circumscribed period as the child attempts to come to terms with the reality of death. Children temporarily use soothing fantasies to deal with all sorts of events. For example, many children experiencing divorce evoke reconciliation fantasies of their parents to deal with the immediate crisis of separation. Slowly most children accept the reality of the divorce, or death, and the reconciliation or reunion wishes recede. Sandra's union wish with mother, however, was not abating, and she had been brought into treatment because it was indeed intensifying.

The persistence of the fantasy appeared to be fueled by several internal factors. In part it was driven by Sandra's *intense guilt*. She had felt very guilty about some of her earlier natural ambivalence toward her mother as well as her attachment wishes toward her stepmother. Any internal wish to separate from the mother (give up or lessen the fantasy) appeared to evoke enormous guilt, and Sandra denied her wish to separate by intensifying the tie. Another factor that fueled the fantasy was her fear of the affects of *sadness* as she experienced loss. To actually acknowledge the grave, the memories, the car model her mother had died in evoked very intense sadness, which was very frightening to Sandra. Keeping mother alive in the dream warded off these affects and the sense of emptiness and aloneness she experienced without her mother (e.g., the memory of calling for the mother in the large empty house).

Earlier it was noted that focal events have the potential for "derailing" the natural developmental process. Richard, 1 year following his parents' divorce, showed inhibitions in school and withdrew from his parents. With Sandra, there were no manifest symptoms or behavior difficulties 1½ years after the death of her mother, except that she experienced a growing subjective anxiety. It is clear that although she functioned well, the death (focal event) had the potential for significant developmental interference that had not, as yet, manifested itself.

What potential problems could have developed within Sandra if there had not been some intervention? It appeared as though Sandra was in the process of constructing a *harsh and punishing superego* as a reaction to the death. Her guilt regarding her "disloyalty" toward her mother was corrosive, and it was increasingly interfering with her life. Her increasing need to join her mother above (evoked by her guilt) had an element of a death wish, which her conscience appeared to be stimulating. It appeared, in the course of treatment, that Sandra's "confessions" of her affection toward other objects (teachers, orange juice lady, stepmother) allowed her to modify her intense disloyalty guilt.

Similarly, what would have been the potential impact on Sandra of the extensive use of denial (of the death of the mother)? The vividness of the fantasy and the growing incursion on her daily life raised questions about potential problems in *reality testing*. Could the need for mother (both gratifying and defensive) have fostered a growing investment in the fantasy world that would have rivaled her commitment to reality? It was also clear that the dream world that was erected could severely interfere with her ability to *invest in her new maternal objects*. She clearly needed to distance herself from any "replacement" object in order to maintain her loyalty to her mother.

Since the mourning process could not be completed in this stage of childhood, Sandra would need to continue to work through her grief at other stages as well. Separation from home, going to college, marriage might be nodal points in the future, where this youngster and the young adult could again face conflicts involving her early childhood loss. The possibility of the need for further work in the future was shared with Sandra and her parents.

CONCLUSION

How does the process of focal psychotherapy compare to long-term treatment? The treatment experiences described in this chapter were quite similar to the work with neurotic children except they were shorter in duration, moved more quickly to the underlying central dynamic issues, had less protracted periods of resistance, and the changes in symptoms or behavior difficulties occurred more quickly.

One general issue in work with children with reactive disorders is that it may be difficult for the therapist to sort out for a long period of time whether this is a case where the child is reacting to a focal event or indeed has a form of a more extensive psychopathology. Is the child reacting to an acute stress, or is there a more extensive problem? For example, this was a nagging question in the work with Sandra. When the history was explored, the therapist had questions about its thoroughness and accuracy. On the one hand, the major history provider (the mother) was absent, and on the other, the therapist wondered about the general need of the family to idealize the memory of the mother as a caretaker. Individuals who die are often recalled in idyllic terms. As the case unfolded, there was material that made the therapist wonder about the possible harshness of the real mother. Was the perception that Sandra recalled of the mother never smiling a real perception or a distorted one filtered through the child's natural ambivalence? Why did she have to "cling" to her mother so tenaciously? Was she defended against her natural ambivalence (the premise the therapist used in the work), or was the ambivalence exacerbated because of a problematic mother–child tie? These are common concerns child therapists struggle with in work with reactive disturbances.

Focal psychotherapy does not imply altering a basic insight-oriented treatment process. In these cases the processes of confrontation, clarification, and interpretation were absolutely necessary to achieve resolution of problems. Sandra came to understand the frightening, aggressive impulses she had toward her dead mother that had been repressed. Richard experienced aspects of his competition with his (noncustodial) father in the transference that had created inhibitions in his work and phallic development. These issues were fully explored, as in a long-term therapy.

Because children with reactive disorders have a relatively healthy history in development, they often evidence facets in their personality that foster an effective and rapid treatment process. Both Richard and Sandra formed positive working relationships quickly that supported the treatment process. Many of these children had a history of solid object relationships before the developmental interference and therefore developed a sense of "basic trust" before the problematic events in their lives. These children usually do not have the rigid defensive postures that are in evidence in children with longstanding problems. Although Sandra used the defense of denial in relation to her mother's death, this was not a mechanism she used extensively in her character. The resistances do not have the protracted quality we see with more disturbed children. Therefore, with the assets these youngsters had through their earlier development, they were able to regain an effective developmental course through a shorter treatment experience.

BIBLIOGRAPHY

Berlin, I. N. (1970). Crisis intervention and short-term therapy: An approach in a child psychiatric clinic. *Journal of the American Academy of Child Psychiatry* 9:595–606.

Berlin, I. N. (1976). *Bibliography of Child Psychiatry*. New York: Human Sciences Press.

Furman, R. (1964). Death and the young child. *Psychoanalytic Study of the Child* 19:321–333.

Kalter, N. (1977). Children of divorce in an outpatient psychiatric population. *American Journal of Orthopsychiatry* 47:40–51.

Lohr, R., Press, S., Chethik, M., & Solyom, A. (1981). Impact of divorce on children. The vicissitudes of the reconciliation fantasy. *Journal of Child Psychotherapy* 7:123–136.

McDermott, J. F. (1970). Divorce and its psychological sequelae in children. *Archives of General Psychiatry* 23:421-428.

Nagera, H. (1980). Children's reactions to the death of important objects. In: H. Nagera (Ed.), *The Developmental Approach to Childhood Psychopathology* (pp. 363-404). New York: Aronson.

Neubauer, P. (1960). The one-parent child and his oedipal development. *Psychoanalytic Study of the Child* 15:286-309.

Proskauer, S. (1969). Some technical issues in time-limited psychotherapy with children. *Journal of the American Academy of Child Psychiatry* 8:154-169.

Proskauer, S. (1971). Focused time limited psychotherapy in children. *Journal of the American Academy of Child Psychiatry* 10:619-639.

Shambaugh, B. (1961). A study of loss reactions in a seven year old. *Psychoanalytic Study of the Child* 16:510-522.

Wallerstein, J. S., & Kelly, J. B. (1980). *Surviving the Breakup*. New York: Basic Books.

Wolf, A. K. M. (1958). *Helping Your Child Understand Death*. New York: Child Study Association.

Wolfenstein, M. (1966). How is mourning possible? *Psychoanalytic Study of the Child* 21:93-123.

PART III

WORK WITH PARENTS

Introduction

An area that has received relatively little attention in child psycho-therapy has been work with parents. It is obvious that no child in treatment can prosper without the sanction of the parents, and it is the parental support of the treatment that *allows* the child to use the therapy experience.

In Part III, we look at a range of interventions with parents, that include:

1. Parent guidance.
2. Transference parenting.
3. Treatment of the parent–child relationship.
4. Treatment of the child via the mother.

Typically one begins all parent work with "parent guidance." Parent guidance is primarily an educational form of intervention, and varied aspects are discussed in Chapter 10. The premise in this form of work is that treatment tasks will be fostered because of an effective alliance between the therapist (his treatment goals for the child) and the healthy, adaptive capacities of the parents.

At times, however, there are problems in parent work because of limits within the parents. Some parents who are relatively more disturbed and dependent make better use of the intervention of "transference parenting" (also described in Chapter 10). This form of intervention provides "sustenance" that some parents need, and this is fully described in this section.

There are also many parents who consciously want to help their children, but whose child has some major unconscious meaning to them that fosters the pathology and difficulties in the child. The technique of "treatment of the parent-child relationship" can be utilized to provide them some insight, so that the parent can interact with the child in a less encumbered way. Chapter 11 illustrates this process, and discusses some of the difficulties and limits.

There are also some situations when parents can be enlisted to do the necessary clinical and interpretive work directly with the young child. This technique of "treatment of the child via the parent" is discussed and illustrated in Chapter 12.

10

*Parent Guidance and Transference Parenting**

In this chapter two approaches with parents are discussed—the techniques of *parent guidance* and, in the latter part of the chapter, the process of *transference parenting*. The most common and the initial approach with parents is parent guidance. This process assumes that the parent has relatively good ego functioning and that he/she identifies with the goals of the treatment. Basically, it is supportive work.

In the literature on parent work, authors describe a wide spectrum of issues that they subsume under parent guidance. Sandler, Kennedy, and Tyson (1980) discuss general goals. They see the function of parent guidance as a process to ensure "providing continuing emotional and practical support" to the child treatment. Additionally, this work should "lend support to the parent's self-esteem." Arnold (1978) describes parent guidance as a continuum from simple information or education through advice, permission, and clarification depending on what is necessary. Weisberger (1986) also specifies a number of goals and processes. Parent guidance should mobilize the familial environment to support better parental functioning, thereby relieving unrealistic and unhealthy pressures on the child. In addition, she notes that parent guidance should offer information about growth and development and give practical help with management. All authors imply

*Steven Rubin, psychology intern, provided some of the clinical material used in this chapter.

that parent guidance is not an interpretative process. Essentially the therapist works with parents' conscious or preconscious material.

Since there is a large variety of issues that fall under the aegis of parent guidance, the author suggests two general categories as broad domains for parent guidance work and lists specific areas of work within each category:

1. Issues that affect the emotional balance in the family, which would include:
   a. Working with general difficulties in either parent's life that would affect his or her ability to parent.
   b. Working on differences between parents regarding the handling of their children.
   c. Working with stresses that emerge in parents caused by the fact that their child is in treatment, e.g., a sense of failure, fear of the child's attachment to the therapist, etc.
2. Issues that center on the child patient primarily, which would include:
   a. Receiving from the parents current reality information of child and family events.
   b. Imparting to the parents a *general* understanding of child development and the internal affective life of the child.
   c. Imparting to the parents a *specific* understanding of the child patient's symptoms or behavior changes that emerge (the purpose is to help parents cope with the behaviors or symptoms or with the changes that emerge within the treatment).
   d. Clarification with parents of the problematic interactions between themselves and the child patient (the purpose is to alter parental handling by highlighting the interactions, advising changes, and providing explanations for the changes).

The following clinical examples illustrate the varieties and dimensions of parent guidance work.

CASE 1

Nathan was a 6½-year-old "hellion" who had evidenced many problems in kindergarten and first grade in public school because of his aggressive behavior with peers. Children and teachers became concerned at the intensity of his rage, which was primarily promoted (we learned in the course of his therapy) by his underlying fears of punishment.

There had been a divorce in the family when Nathan was 3, and this event had promoted a good deal of difficulty. Nathan and his mother appeared to have an enmeshed relationship that was troubling for him, and he also felt responsible for having "driven" his father away. The parents had joint custody, both in terms of decision making and physical custody. The therapist saw the parents separately, since mutual animosity made joint meetings impossible.

Much of the early work centered on the difficulties with effective discipline in both houses. Very often, Nathan simply would not comply (e.g., climbing on furniture, refusing bedtime, coming to dinner late). It became clear that both parents felt a need to "cater" to him, to give into him. His mother wondered whether he was "fragile," and his father tended to look the other way, waiting until he went back to his other home. Slowly both parents, in examining some of their motives for laxity, realized they felt a great deal of guilt about the impact of the divorce on their youngster. They felt that they had caused him enough suffering, and they were the source of his pain. With this internal understanding, and the evidence that the problems in discipline at home fostered difficulties in the community for their son, both parents developed more effective standards. This went beyond the demands for compliance and involved appropriate responsibility for a youngster his age—helping to fold his clothing and putting laundry away, getting his own glass of water, etc.

As we traced some of the divorce issues, both parents discussed some of the rage and frustration with each other following the divorce. The father described how he used to hate to answer the telephone—the mother would be calling to berate him and have yet another demand. The mother lamented her lost opportunities because of the divorce. She had supported her husband through his advanced schooling years, and they had had an understanding that she would have a similar opportunity. Now, because of economics, there was no free future. She generally felt that the burdens of being a single parent were more difficult for her to bear because of her relative financial constriction. The effect of this bitter unloading of the past (done in individual sessions) allowed the parents to work more freely together around Nathan's issues.

A major additional theme in the work in the first year with the parents was helping them to understand the implications for an "oedipal" child in the aftermath of a divorce. We were aware that Nathan was struggling with the oedipal phase of development by virtue of his age, while simultaneously dealing with the separation and divorce in his family. Two major features of the normal oedipal phase would need to be kept in mind: (1) the affectionate and sexualized relationship with the mother and (2) the heightened competitive relationship and rivalry with the father. The mother raised Nathan's "touching" problem, which she had wanted to avoid. Nathan had sought to kiss her on the lips or "accidentally" fondle her breasts. The therapist's general discussion of the intense natural sexuality of children and how it is enhanced when there is no prohibiting father allowed the mother to gain some perspective on Nathan's "excitement problem." She could also, then, use the information to take more appropriate steps with modesty. For example, she would now have Nathan take his own bath because he needed the "privacy."

When Nathan's mother broke up with a year-long boyfriend, Nathan was very upset for a number of weeks. The therapist noted that her relationship had made Nathan feel safer in the house—it had inhibited some of his excitement urges. When the mother spoke to Nathan, he intensely related his worry that he "drives everyone away—his daddy also."

Another general theme in the parent guidance was the identification of underlying issues when an aggressive crisis emerged in school. For example, on one occasion Nathan had been very attacking of several boys in his class for a number of days. "Randy almost tore my arm off," "Joshua made a deep cut on my arm," complained Nathan. When the therapist explored this behavior with the parents, it emerged that the paternal grandfather had recently had emergency surgery on an embolism that was lodged in a vein on the grandfather's leg. This had aroused much anxiety within the child. With encouragement, the father spoke to his son about the operation. Nathan voiced a number of anxieties about his close relative—"Will grandpa die?" "Will they have to cut his leg off?" And these concerns could be addressed realistically. Nathan slept peacefully for the first time in a week after the discussion, and the fighting in school abated.

Discussion

This material illustrates a number of features of parent guidance work. One aspect of the above work is *dealing with the typical problems of adults that can interfere with their effective parenting.* Both of Nathan's parents are relatively well-integrated individuals who clearly identified with the goals of Nathan's treatment and who functioned well generally in their lives. The divorce, however, had left many residual scars that interfered with their parenting capacities at times. Both parents felt very guilty about the disruption in their child's life and tried to make up to Nathan by minimizing his frustration and avoiding limit setting. The mother also, at times, made up for some of her own loneliness by an overly intense attachment to her son. When these patterns were noted, the parents could respond effectively. In addition, because of some of the past bitterness in their relationship, they found it hard to work conjointly regarding their son. The opportunity for some discharge of feelings stemming from the impact of their failed relationship on their later adjustment allowed them to put the past somewhat in perspective.

Another component of parent guidance is the therapist's ability to *generally describe the internal life of the child* so that the parent can gain some greater awareness of the developmental process. A major theme in the above material was sorting out with the parents the underlying oedipal dynamics particularly affected by a divorce. The therapist highlighted the typical sexuality of a 6½-year-old boy and his exaggerated fears of impulse expression without the inhibiting father. This glimpse of the internal erotic struggles of Nathan alerted mother to the need for more physical distance from her son, far greater privacy and modesty, and helped her understand his strong reactions to her male friends. These dynamics also helped father become the "heavy" with Nathan (he could be the prohibitor), which was a role he had until now avoided.

The therapist also helped the parents' *understand some of the patient's specific dynamics,* another aspect of parent guidance work. Nathan was a counterphobic youngster—when he became frightened (often projected fears) he "identified with the aggressor" and often lashed out. Castration anxiety was a major theme in the direct work with Nathan. There were many opportunities to help the parents understand that when Nathan became aggressive (manifest behavior), he was often frightened internally. Thus, the therapist and parents could clearly trace Nathan's attacks and arm worries to the surgery of his grandfather. Their growing ability, in the course of the treatment to help Nathan understand the "scary" roots to his hellion-like behavior outbursts enhanced the overall therapeutic process.

CASE 2

Andrew was a 12-year-old youngster whose parents became concerned because of an exacerbation of problems about 6 months before they came for the evaluation. He appeared to have become acutely depressed, expressed constant dissatisfaction with himself, and avoided investing a good deal in his schoolwork because he was "shattered by errors" he naturally made in the course of his work. The evaluation underscored that Andrew was a neurotic youngster. The primary dynamics seemed to center on unresolved oedipal conflicts, particularly a struggle with his competitive and phallic feelings emerging from his relationship to his father.

In the conjoint work with both parents, one important focus was the father's anger with his son. After a period of time, Mr. D, a business executive who commanded a large work force, acknowledged that he had an anger problem—he had high standards for himself and his children, and he was "quick on the trigger" at times and aware of his explosiveness. Thus, part of Andrew's difficulty in his competitive feelings with father and others stemmed from an external problem—the father's reality demandingness and anger that evoked counterrage and fear in his son.

Since the father cared about his son and identified with the goals of the treatment, he slowly became increasingly able to observe his interactions with his son; he also permitted both the therapist and his wife to explore these events. In board and card games at home, the father instinctively pressed his son for better performance and was aware of his angry countenance. When Andrew was having problems with math and had difficulty with his father's tutoring, Mr. D. had yelled, "You *WILL* learn to do this now," and his son had broken into tears. The father began to observe and evaluate how he had reacted when there had been minor "transgressions"—when his son's manners slipped, or when his son interrupted him momentarily when he was working on the computer, etc. He became increasingly aware of the tension and anger these experiences with his son evoked. He spoke of his own mother's ridicule and demeaning behavior toward him throughout his own childhood years and felt in some ways he was repeating something similar.

As the father became more fully aware of his patterns, he discussed with his son his own temper problem after some outbursts, and at times apologized for his overreactions. At first Andrew reacted with intense anger: "You are never satisfied with me—I hate you!!" At times, depression was evident—"You are much smarter, and I'm dumb." But after a period of an ongoing life-space dialogue, Andrew began to develop some humor and distance from his own counterrage. After losing in checkers to his father, Andrew mused "I hate your guts again, but you didn't beat me by too much." The father began to take his son to work on occasion to show him some aspects of his work environment, and he also told his son that a motor bike stored in the back of the shed would become his vehicle when he reached driving age. They would rebuild it together. Generally the father became able to modify his rage reactions against his son significantly and to acknowledge his overreactions when they emerged.

Discussion

The above clinical process with the D.'s occurred over the course of a year, while Andrew was in the process of psychotherapy. *One facet of parent guidance work is the process of helping parents become aware of aspects of themselves and their handling of their youngsters that unfavorably affect their child's development.* Although Andrew had internalized conflicts, one component of his depression/self-hatred was the external reality conflict with his father.

As a trusting relationship developed between the therapist and parents, the therapist could identify this angry, harsh feature between father and son, emanating from the father. Although such confrontations are always threatening to parents, Mr. D. had the capacity to accept this aspect of himself and follow it closely in the course of the work. Mr. D. was an effective individual within his profession and family and had the capacity for self-observation. He also clearly wanted to help remedy the difficulties his son had developed; he had, as well, an appropriate quality of guilt regarding his earlier interactions with his son. The "exposure" of these interactions with his son did not evoke the intense humiliation (and defensive denials) that we often see in parents with narcissistic problems.

In the course of the year, Mr. D. was able to significantly master and modify his pathogenic interactions with his son. The self-awareness (ego awareness) led him to become conscious of the situations that evoked his rage with his son and also the quality of his overreactions (since it was necessary for him to continue to limit his child appropriately). This monitoring process had an important effect on their interactions. Mr. D. did not need insight (to understand the unconscious meaning that his son represented) in order to make this change. Although he commented that this represented a repetition from his own childhood, this was not fully explored. The parent guidance process made explicit a pattern of interaction that Mr. D. was aware of on a preconscious level. If greater internal understanding was necessary for the change, the appropriate intervention would have been a form of "treatment of the parent–child relationship," which is explored in the next chapter.

CASE 3

Gerald was an 11-year-old youngster at the time of his evaluation: he was a member of an intact middle-class family and the second sibling in a sibship of four. He was the only boy. He had been referred for his generally "obnoxious" behavior. Nothing seemed to please him, and he felt any task or demand was "unfair." He was sullen about taking out the garbage and complained to the parents when his day was not interesting enough. He was arrogant with his few friends, bossing and ridiculing them. Although he was bright, he found his homework "boring," did few assignments in school, and acted as a clown in class.

In the early work with the parents, his mother appeared particularly anxious. Her "schedule" made it hard for the parents to show up on time for their sessions. She eyed the therapist with suspicion, seemed eager to leave quickly, wrung her hands or talked volubly and intensely. She wondered on several occasions what her son had had to say about her in his sessions. When the therapist noted some of these signs of discomfort, she acknowledged her sense of apprehension. Would the therapist find something wrong with her? He commented that parents are often concerned they have contributed to difficulties and then approach the therapy with worry that they will be criticized.

Mrs. A. confessed, as therapy commenced, that she feared she had spoiled her son. She guessed that she had tended to do too much for him. She found herself catering to his needs in a way she did not with her daughters. She always asked him what special foods he wanted included in his lunch and complied with his requests to be driven wherever he wanted to go. She was anxious about these confessions—"Have I hurt him?" "Is he too spoiled?" The therapist pointed out that she herself seemed already to have an awareness that Gerald generally had trouble tolerating frustration, and her need to give into him was probably not helpful. The mother noted that she found it hard to stand the anger he would express, and she was always worried about him.

This general apprehension about her son had other vicissitudes. Gerald tended to complain about his body (neck pains or leg pains), and Mrs. A. quickly had to check with the family pediatrician. In addition, when her husband (a rather passive and busy man) attempted to impose some limits, she invariably defended her son and found mitigating circumstances for the last transgression. Thus, the sanction was never imposed. When the therapist underscored the problems she had in imposing effective limits, Mrs. A. acknowledged her role in the sessions. She feared that she could become too angry and had impulses to send him to a military school. ("Does this mean I'm a very bad mother?" she would interpose anxiously.) She knew that in the past, as she grew up, she had been very angry with her brother. She wondered if that could be affecting her relationship with her son.

Despite the somewhat driven quality of her need to protect and overindulge her son, the awareness of these patterns mobilized Mrs. A. to alter her handling. With the major support of her husband, routines and rules were established. Allowance was curtailed for mishaps, a bedtime schedule was established, study time was enforced, and he was effectively sent to his room for his "obnoxious" outbursts and argumentativeness. Mrs. A. commented during our weekly meetings on her continued internal anxiety and her apprehension after she had set limits. However, she felt a great deal of relief when Gerald's schoolwork improved and he responsibly ran a paper route for a 6-month period.

Discussion

In the above parent guidance work, Mrs. A. brought rather typical reactions at the start of treatment. *Bringing their youngster for treatment often evokes a myriad of reactions for parents.* Most parents experience a sense of failure when they acknowledge that their child has emotional problems. They often feel internally responsible for the difficulties. Whereas some parents handle their guilt initially by attacking the therapist (they fear condemnation), many parents anxiously "confess," as did Mrs. A. When the "expert" therapist can tolerantly acknowledge some contribution to the difficulties the child has, without the attack the parent fears, parents often feel a good deal of relief.

Many parents have a preconscious idea about problems in handling their children, as we have seen in the case of Mr. D. Mrs. A was very aware of her need to cater, indulge, and overidentify with her son. The process of parent guidance allowed her to make these patterns more ego-distonic (alien to her), and to take concrete steps to better her handling. Earlier she used many rationalizations to continue "protecting" her son. As in the other case illustrations, the healthy aspects of Mrs. A's ego allowed her to mobilize techniques to effectively frustrate and limit this youngster. Although she wondered about the early sources for the difficulty in handling (e.g., her relationship with her brother), this was not a central area of work. There was no insight to her past that illuminated this tendency. Rather, her own enhanced self-observation and her desire to help her son fostered the changes in her daily interactions with him.

CASE 4

Rita was an attractive, well-dressed, but somewhat stocky 5-year-old at the time of evaluation. Her parents had brought her for therapy because of an increasing sense of panic when she separated from her mother, an inability to become "unfrozen" in nursery school, and a generalized stubborness and anger that permeated her demeanor. In the past year there had also been a steady weight gain. Rita had two older brothers (one brother, Robert, was just 1½ years older than she), and there was also a new sibling, Tanya, who was only 6 months of age. Both parents had a professional background, and the father was particularly busy and preoccupied at work, since he was struggling to achieve tenure in an academic setting. The evaluation revealed that Rita was struggling with two levels of conflict: preoedipal anger that had been evident in her toilet-training history and expressed in her current stubborness; and penis envy issues that particularly focused on her next oldest brother, Robert. Rita was seen twice weekly, and the parents were seen conjointly every other week. The parents were highly motivated to help their daughter and understand their own influences on her development, and they also seemed to have a good, mutually supportive relationship.

In the early phases of the parent work, Mrs. D. became aware of the enormous sense of burden she felt raising this large "nest of children." Although there was often much pleasure, she was quite overwhelmed by the sheer level of the daily demands, the endless tasks, and the fact that her day never seemed to end. At times, she cried unexpectedly toward the end of the day and often felt extremely fatigued. Was she depressed, she wondered? Much affect emerged when she discussed her promising past professional career. She had indeed had a very stimulating, high-paying job after college in which she had clearly been very highly valued. Currently, on occasion, her old boss came by with some task or problem that she handled on a consultative basis. The contrast, at times, to the daily "drudgery" began further to explain the fatigue and sense of depletion she experienced from time to time. She laughed when she noted that her work at home was not terribly intellectually stimulating. This general discussion began to provide a thoughtful framework for Mrs. D. She could now understand her periods of intermittent depression, although she clearly also loved being a mother. At times she had felt she was endlessly trapped by diapers, but she began to realize that as her tasks abated (as the children moved into school) she could slowly renew her professional contacts and interests.

Mrs. D. had also made few demands on her husband for childrearing since his career had reached a critical juncture. But it emerged that Professor D. was often only a "play daddy." For example, when he came home late in the evening (a number of times per week), he took several of the children out of bed, since he missed them. The excitement, stimulation, etc. undid the sleep preparation routine, and chaos could ensue for another hour. Mrs. D. was internally very resentful on the one hand, but she also felt the children and father needed each other. These discussions began to highlight the lack of support the mother felt she received from her husband, in areas of discipline, routine, and sheer general child care. The father noted humorously that perhaps this explained some of his wife's sexual withdrawal at times when she said, "I'm too tired." The couple began to make changes that were mutually agreeable—for example, father could come home for dinner every night, spend time with the children, help "bed them down," and then return to the office. But he realized he could also bring certain of his work tasks home.

At times, Mrs. D. would observe that she had felt tense with Rita, and a sense of alienation. She did not experience this with the other children, and this distance upset her. As we looked at the weekly incidents, a pattern seemed to emerge. Mrs. D. would stay in the bedroom with Rita saying goodnight until Rita would "allow" her to leave. At times, she felt estranged when Rita was talking very loudly and angrily to her. It became clear that Mrs. D. had a good deal of difficulty firmly limiting and making demands on her daughter. We found that Rita had virtually no chores, whereas the older boys worked appropriately within the house. Mrs. D. preconsciously anticipated any potential difficult confrontation with her "stubborn" daughter and worked assiduously to circumvent a blow-up. She also feared, the therapist noted, her own anger toward her daughter. All agreed that the demands, frustrations, and blow-ups were necessary, and it was underscored that if she became less afraid of her child's emerging anger, this would be a reassurance to her daughter. Mrs. D. became increasingly able to insist that Rita work with her around dinner preparation, setting the table, etc., and she did not "give in" to Rita's protests when she left her in the bedroom after a reasonable "tucking" in.

Throughout the work with Rita, certain behaviors became highlighted at home as they became an internal focus within the child's psychotherapy. During a particular period of work, Rita's demand for food and stealing of food became prominent. The parents worried further about weight gain—should they put her on a diet, should they lock the cupboards, etc.? The therapist indicated the natural feelings all children have in relation to siblings: they often feel deprived when there is a new baby and feel (often imagined) deprived and thrown out by the mother. Food becomes a source of solace, because it brings the feeding mother back. Mrs. D. then recounted some of the current subtle aggression that Rita felt toward the baby. Rita held the baby and hugged her too hard, or the mother would find a penny in the crib that Rita "accidentally" left there. Because Mrs. D. was a resourceful and intuitive mother, in her next appointment she described a new game she had played with Rita. When she was diapering Tanya, Rita had begun some baby talk. Rather than discourage this or react with guilt as she had earlier done, she entered into a game with "baby Rita." She cooed back to her, made believe she fed her with a spoon, etc. Rita loved the opportunity for temporary regression, in play she renewed the baby status she had lost, and the rapport between mother and child was reconnected.

During another phase of work with Rita, she became somewhat accident prone and preoccupied with any injury. The slightest scrape or splinter made her very upset. The parents were again concerned, and the therapist had a chance to explain body feelings that many girls had as they developed. At times, girls did not feel as good as boys and feared this was affirmed by their observation of their bodies. The therapist explained that all girls at one time or another feared that their lack of a penis made them inferior and that they were wounded or hurt or not fully developed. Thus, there can be a preoccupation with injury and damage at different times. Both parents described the recent ferocity in Rita's interactions with her older brother Robert and her jealousy if the father did special things with the boys and left her out. The father was clearly even handed with the children and felt his daughter was pretty and charming. The explanations helped the parents gain some distance with some of Rita's jealous outbursts.

Discussion

In this case, the parent guidance work had a wide scope. Several factors initially had interfered with Mrs. D.'s parenting capacity at this stage of her life. The sheer burden of raising four relatively young children and the inability to mourn the loss (perhaps temporary) of her profession were contributing to her feelings of fatigue and despair. It was very helpful to Mrs. D. to become aware of her internal struggle—the trapped feelings she had in rearing her children and her rage toward the "play daddy" father who was busy and preoccupied. Whereas the clarification of the internal stress was helpful to the parents in making direct changes in the mother's life (having the father more available, structuring time when the mother could be away, etc.), it also "normalized" the negative feelings that Mrs. D. would experience at times with her children. She came to feel significantly less burdened by her difficulties and did not need to give to her children in an unremitting way.

It became clear in the course of the treatment with Rita that one factor that contributed to Rita's problems with anger was the difficulty Mrs. D. had in the comfort of her own anger. This internal difficulty within the mother exacerbated Rita's own rage and her anxiety about *her* aggression. She felt unsafe and feared her impulses. One part of the parent guidance was to make Mrs. D. *aware of her own problem and how it affected her handling of her daughter*. As this became evident to Mrs. D. by her inability to limit the goodnight rituals, provide demands through chores, etc., Mrs. D. confronted these issues. Despite her internal apprehension, she faced her daughter's tantrums and rage when she demanded help around the house. In this form of parent guidance, Mrs. D. did not explore her history, the origin of her fears, the particular reasons Rita was singled out for the mother's anxiety. Within the limits of parent guidance, a preconscious problem had been identified, and this awareness mobilized the healthy ego of the mother to take necessary steps in her daily interactions with her child.

Another theme in the parent work was helping the D.'s to *understand the internal life of their child* as she struggled with various issues in treatment. Behavior in the child patient can often reflect intensified internal issues that are emerging in the psychotherapy. As Rita's jealousy of her younger sister became intensified, her need to overeat (and themes of food in therapy) became more prominent. Parents often have a need to act, to do something, to deal with an emerging symptom or behavior problem. An important component of parent guidance is to provide parents with a perspective that explains what their youngster is struggling with internally. Thus, the therapist explained Rita's rivalry with the younger sister who had usurped the "baby role" in the family, and the oral regression that was an attempt to deal with these feelings. The parents were able to empathize with Rita's strife, became less anxious about the immediate behavior, and allowed other forms of playful regression in the home (baby talk and play feeding) that circumvented Rita's need to overeat.

The therapist worked in similar fashion on the theme of penis envy and rivalry with the older male brother. This awareness made the parents less anxious about their daughter's preoccupation with injury.

TRANSFERENCE PARENTING

There are many parents who, either because of early disturbances in their own lives or because of acute current stresses, need further support beyond parent guidance in their work with the child therapist. In some cases, the therapist acts and functions as a nurturing parent to the troubled adult, and this "sustenance" allows the parent to provide more adequately for his/her child. We have termed this process "transference parenting." This also is a form of supportive work, and the following case illustrates this technique.

Clinical Material

Barbara was 6 years of age when she came for outpatient psychotherapy because of a history of severe enuresis. Barbara had been seen for approximately 1 year by her first therapist, Mr. B., in twice-weekly individual play therapy sessions. In addition, Mr. B. had met with both of Barbara's parents for weekly parent guidance sessions. Near the end of the first year of Barbara's treatment Mr. and Mrs. S. had decided to separate. Her parents' separation took its toll on Barbara, and she became listless and depressed. In addition, her enuresis (which had lessened to a great extent over the course of the year) became more severe once again. Around this time, Mr. B. had announced that he would be leaving the agency, and Barbara was faced with coping with two major losses (her father and her therapist) in close proximity. Mr. B. arranged for a transfer, stipulating that a male therapist was strongly indicated.

This therapist's work with Barbara quickly became divorce focused. In this case, the usual postdivorce adjustment problems were intensified by Mr. S.'s decision to stop visiting his daughter. Barbara was devastated, and her treatment was utilized to help her cope with the massive rejection and abandonment that she felt.

At the point at which he and his wife were separated, Mr. S. had stopped attending appointments with Mr. B. Several attempts to engage Mr. S. in his daughter's treatment with this therapist did not prove fruitful. Consequently, the parent work was restricted to sessions with Barbara's mother.

Given her parents' separation, her father's rejection, and the loss of her previous therapist, Barbara was quite an emotionally needy girl. Although it was evident that she would need a great deal of support from her mother, it became equally clear that Mrs. S. was terribly needy herself. When this therapist began working with Mrs. S., she was still feeling the stresses produced by the breakup of her marriage and the demands of being a single parent with little social, emotional, or financial support.

In addition to the current stresses, Mrs. S. was also struggling with intense feelings and conflicts towards her own mother, which dated back to her own childhood. She described her mother as a "dictator" who had run the household and the lives of those in it. She remembers her father as having been a passive man, "too weak" to leave a miserable marriage. Mrs. S. recalled repeated episodes of humiliation and physical abuse at the hands of her mother. She explained that she had received no affection from her parents, resulting in her own difficulty expressing affection to her own child. Recalling her own childhood, Mrs. B. claimed, "I never learned how to show love."

The clinical dilemma was to find a way to support Mrs. S. in such a way that she would better be able to lend the tremendous love and emotional support that her daughter needed from her. A pattern emerged naturally and rather quickly in the sessions with Mrs. S. that turned out to be very productive. In the first part of her sessions, Mrs. S. would voice her own concerns, worries, and the struggles that pertained by and large to her own life. Included were her difficulties at work, school (she was working full time and attending classes at the University), with finances, her relationship to her own parents, feelings about her ex-husband, and more generally, the trials and tribulations of being a single parent. Mrs. S. often began sessions in an agitated state. The therapist would listen, empathize, and offer support. This appeared to have a calming and relieving effect on her. She then was able to move on in the second part of the sessions to focus on issues having more to do with Barbara. At this point, the therapist was able to do some effective parent guidance work that included advice and education concerning child development and Barbara's emotional needs. With time, Mrs. S. became more and more able to put some of the therapist's suggestions into practice effectively as she learned to better parent her daughter. In sum, an effective two-step process had been established whereby the therapist would support and parent Mrs. S. so that she in turn could better parent and support her daughter.

Several examples help to demonstrate this type of work with parents. When the therapist began working with Mrs. S., she had been working full time and had just reenrolled at the University in order to complete her Bachelor's degree. She was quite anxious about her return to school and was able to link some of her worry to her past school failure. Approximately 10 years before, she had begun her undergraduate work in chemistry but found the program too demanding, and she had dropped out in her junior year. She was concerned that she would fail once again. The sessions not only relieved some of her anxiety about her own schoolwork, but they also enabled her to discuss Barbara's academic problems at school. (Barbara's school performance had deteriorated throughout the year following her parents' separation and her father's rejection.) Mrs. S. was prone to overidentify with her daughter's problems at school, and the therapist helped her differentiate her own problems and needs from those of her daughter. In this way power struggles between mother and daughter around homework assignments were reduced, and Mrs. S. was able to act on the therapist's suggestion that she work closely with her daughter's teacher in order to set clear and reasonable academic expectations for Barbara.

During the first few months post-separation, Mr. S. had visited with Barbara on a regular basis. When the father then stopped visiting, Mrs. S. first had to deal with her own anger and disappointment. In the therapy sessions she was able to verbalize how much she had come to expect and look forward to some free time on the weekends when visitation took place. Once her own disappointment was addressed, Mrs. S. became more able to understand and help Barbara with her missing and hurt feelings. Similarly, when Mrs. S. expressed her own ambivalent feelings as her divorce was finalized and she anticipated the first Christmas without her ex-husband, she was better able to appreciate Barbara's intense sense of loss. The therapist could then work closely with her on making sure that she kept Barbara posted on important events such as the legalization of the divorce and plans as to how the Christmas holiday would be spent.

When Mr. S. stopped visiting his daughter altogether, Mrs. S. became upset when she felt that Barbara blamed her for her father's actions. Again, once she was able to vent her own worries and feelings, she became more supportive and available to Barbara. For example, with the therapist's coaching she began to label the "big problems Barbara's father had in being a good daddy."

School, particularly around exam time, was an area that continued to provide a great deal of stress for Mrs. S. Initially, the therapist helped support her through these difficult periods and eventually to anticipate them together ahead of time. This process in itself helped make the stress more manageable. Mrs. S. also learned to appreciate that there would be times when she was more or less available to Barbara and to plan accordingly. For example, she was able to explain to Barbara that she was busier during her final exams but that once they were over, the two could do something special together.

Throughout the therapeutic work, the sessions provided "booster shots" that helped Mrs. S. to cope with the demands of everyday living, particularly the excessive demands of single parenthood. That she had come to utilize the sessions in this way became quite evident whenever a session was missed because of holiday or illness. Mrs. S. would inevitably note the long time between sessions and eagerly and enthusiastically bring the therapist up to date on the events in her own life before turning to issues more focused on Barbara.

After receiving her regular "booster shots" from the therapist, Mrs. S. was able to make good use of the advice and suggestions as to how she could be most helpful to Barbara. She became more and more understanding of Barbara's individual psychology and more sensitive to her daughter's emotional needs. Mrs. S. was particularly supportive of Barbara in helping her cope with the serious rejection she felt from her father. Mrs. S., in fact, was able to overcome her own anger, resentment, and bitterness in order to support her daughter in her desire to have a relationship with her father. Mrs. S. followed many of the therapist's suggestions to explain the divorce to Barbara, to accentuate that Barbara was not at fault or blame, and most importantly to let her daughter know that she understood how much she missed her father. Mrs. S. reported a particularly touching moment with her daughter soon after her father had rejected Barbara's Valentine heart. On a cold, wintery evening, Barbara had gone out on her front porch and started crying. When Mrs. S. went to find out what was wrong, Barbara had said, "Nobody loves me." Mrs. S. became increasingly available and adept at listening to and acknowledging her daughter's painful feelings.

In addition, Mrs. S. was supportive and helpful in Barbara's attempts to reach out and connect with her father. She helped Barbara to write letters, bought presents with her for her father at Christmas and his birthday, and helped arrange for regular visitation with many of her ex-husband's relatives, particularly the paternal grandparents.

Although it was difficult to secure information at times as to the whereabouts and goings on of Mr. S., Mrs. S. did her best to find out what she could and to pass on the information to Barbara. Mrs. S. was also helpful in anticipating potential disappointments for Barbara, especially around her birthday and major holidays.

Throughout a good portion of the 2½ years of working together Mrs. S. appeared to depend heavily on the therapist in these sessions in order to relieve some of her own anxieties and stress and in turn to work on her parenting of Barbara. During the last 6 months of the treatment, she began to show some signs of growing independence from the therapist. Some of the positive steps she took with Barbara were now initiated on her own and no longer necessarily directly followed discussions in the sessions. For example, one day in a session with Barbara, the therapist interpreted her worry that her father might have to go to jail for not paying child support. Barbara responded by saying "I'm not worried because my mom told me she would tell me as soon as she knew, even if it was bad news."

When termination was discussed with Mrs. S., she seemed to feel rather pleased at the progress that Barbara had made. We agreed that Barbara had done significant work in dealing with her father's rejection while still maintaining hope that her father would become more available in the future. Barbara's school performance had improved significantly, and she became involved in numerous age-appropriate activities such as cheerleading, learning the recorder, and earning a part in a school play. Her depressive affect had lifted, and obvious gains in self-confidence and self-esteem had been made. Despite periodic enuretic episodes Mrs. S. felt confident that it was time for her daughter's treatment to terminate.

The doubts that surfaced during the termination phase were doubts that Mrs. S. had about herself. On several occasions she voiced the following concern, "Who will I have to vent to after we stop meeting?" The therapist also had his own reservations about Mrs. S.'s ability to maintain her positive parenting practices without support. However, the therapist did appreciate and was able to point out to her the growing independence that she had developed more recently. Mrs. S. and the therapist were able to note together her increased initiative with Barbara as well as Barbara's greater ease in sharing her worries more directly with her mother. Once again, the opportunity to discuss these issues together seemed to provide the support that allowed Mrs. S. to leave treatment with a fair degree of confidence to carry on on her own. In fact, during the last session, she was able to talk about her plan to turn more to her own adult friends in order to secure the support she would need.

Discussion

It was clear that because of the impact of the divorce on Mrs. S., she became less able to function as a parent. She had many reality stresses (income, education, adult relationships) as well as the internal stresses of severe loss, which led to feelings of fatigue and depression. The therapist took on the role of a nurturer and, within the relationship, provided a form of sustenance through interest, availability, and support. Therefore, we use the term "transference parenting" to describe this process. As with parent guidance, this is a supportive form of psychotherapy in which insight and understanding do not have a major role. The critical aspect is the parenting relationship that is experienced in the transference between the child's parent and the therapist.

BIBLIOGRAPHY

Arnold, E. (1978). *Helping Parents Help Their Children*. New York: Brunner Mazel.

Mishne, I. (1983). *Clinical Work with Children*. New York: Free Press.

Sandler, J., Kennedy, H., & Tyson, R. (1980). *The Technique of Child Psychoanalysis*. Cambridge, MA: Harvard University Press.

Weisberger, E. (1980). Concepts in ego psychology as applied to work with parents. In: J. M. Mishne (Ed.), *Psychotherapy and Training in Clinical Social Work*. New York: Gardner Press.

11

*Treatment of the Parent–Child Relationship**

There are certainly situations in which the parent work needs to go beyond the technique of parent guidance. We are aware that in the advice–informational approach we do not deal with unconscious conflicts or unconscious unions between parents and child that often are a fundamental source of the difficulty. Do we then focus on the individual psychopathology of the parents and develop simultaneous treatments? It is also clear that a total treatment effort is often not absolutely necessary to help parents understand how their internal lives can impinge on their parenting role.

A number of authors have articulated a need for a variety of "in-between" techniques (between advice–guidance and total treatment) that would deal with some of the unconscious aspects of the parent-child relationship. Ackerman (1958), for example, noted that we should have a "hierarchy of levels of contact, categories of psychotherapeutic process differentiated in accordance with the depth of influence to be exerted on the personality of the parents" (p. 73). However, although he describes the "first level" as guidance or reeducation, and the reorganization of unconscious function as the "deepest level," he says very little about the in-between grades. In

*Reprinted, with changes, from "Treatment of Parent-Child Relationship," by M. Chethik, *Journal of the American Academy of Child Psychiatry*, Summer 1976, Vol. 15, No. 3, pp. 453-463. Copyright 1976 by Yale University Press. Reprinted by permission.

fact, surprisingly, there are only a small number of papers that are relevant to or deal at all with these "in-between" areas of work (Levy, 1973; Cutter and Hallowitz, 1962; Slavson, 1952; Frailberg, 1954).

The purpose of this chapter is to articulate one mode of treatment in this middle range of work with parents, which this therapist has chosen to call "treatment of the parent–child relationship." It is a process of ego clarification and *limited insight therapy* through which the unconscious meanings of a child for the parents can become evident. Despite the fact that interpretations and uncovering interventions are used, this process contains important boundaries that limit the transference and control transference regressions. In the course of the chapter, a number of case vignettes are presented, and a discussion of the principles that shape this technique follows.

The type of therapeutic management of parents described herein was a customary approach in the child psychiatric clinics of the 1950s and early 1960s. Caseworkers and the occasional psychiatrist working with a parent had evolved an exploratory technique that was focused on the parent–child relationship but involved the various developmental and psychological factors within the parent that impinged on his relations with his child. The techniques were derived from the psychoanalytic orientation of the staff members, and, differing in several ways from psychoanalytic psychotherapy of the adult for his own emotional problems, they often brought about change in other areas of the parent's life beyond his capacities for parenting. Case studies reported during those years in which the work of each member of the team was described frequently suggest such approaches with the parent.

The last decade of mental health orientation has brought an emphasis on a more reality-centered approach to parents or on family therapy if exploratory management was considered necessary. In many of the older child psychiatric facilities, what we refer to as "treatment of the parent–child relationship" undoubtedly continues, and staff members have adapted it to their private work. However, the more contemporary literature on child mental health does not provide examples of such work, nor is there much identification in the literature that casework or child psychiatric practitioners value it today.

The rationale of the approach is readily illustrated with the child case that reaches an impasse after a period of work, and we become aware that the momentum of treatment has stimulated some intense anxieties within a parent. When the parents are helped to understand and gain some perspective on what they are reliving through the child, the treatment process then proceeds again. We do not immediately refer the parent for direct personal psychotherapy, and it is common practice to work these temporary impasses through. Typically, some modified interpretation is necessary, some sector psychotherapy is accomplished, and some unconscious fantasy is illuminated. Why do we lack a body of literature on a common and often needed practice? I can only conclude that this kind of work is unfortunately considered low status and second-class psychotherapy: this form of treatment is not considered the "essential work," while the glamor lies in the articulation of the direct work with the child. I consider this pejorative aura and stigma particularly unfortunate because much skill, sensitivity, and subtle technique are often required to help a parent (as a parent) in a significant and fundamental way. And we are also fully aware that treatment with the child very often prospers or flounders depending on the work with the parent.

CLINICAL MATERIAL

Mark* and Mother

Mark was 6 years of age when he came to treatment because of a history of many behavior difficulties, particularly impulsive rage and outbursts that were fully described in Chapter 1. Mark displayed a diffuse aggressiveness, a striking out that often appeared unprovoked. During treatment, his accompanying fantasies showed that Mark feared sadistic attack, and his aggression warded off imagined danger. Further, he often provoked because he longed to be physically controlled so that he could gratify intense passive aims.

It was clear from the history that a longstanding fighting relationship existed between mother and son. In the weekly meetings with the mother, Mrs. L. was extremely cooperative and consciously and quickly (on advice) established more effective limits in the home, which helped to begin to control Mark's acting out. When we came to understand that some of Mark's chaos sprang from intense excite-

*Youngster discussed in Chapter 1.

ments, Mrs. L. (on the home front) established privacy in the bathroom and curtailed Mark's visits to her bedroom when she dressed.
She utilized parent guidance well.

After several months of treatment, a daredevil theme became
prominent in Mark's behavior. In the office, he climbed extensively;
it was as if he were challenged by an obstacle and sought to master it.
For instance, it became important for him to determine if he could
climb to the high windowsill and sit there. But the danger was never
mastered. Then he waited to see if he could move across the windowsill; and when that was accomplished, he attempted to do it in a
standing position, and on and on. Slowly, it became more evident
that Mark's mother played an important part in this counterphobic
method of handling danger.

In a session with the therapist, the mother related that Mark, a
nonswimmer, had wandered off to the neighborhood pool. The
family had been terribly worried for a number of hours, but as she
related the frightening event, a characteristic smile of pure pleasure
illuminated her face. Mark was fantastically resourceful: he had
found the pool himself seven blocks from home; he had persuaded
the guard that he could enter despite the rules that he needed a
parent and that he was well under 48 inches, the minimum height of
admission. (In his therapy at this point, Mark was preoccupied with
fears of drowning). The mother related all such events, all difficult
and narrow scrapes that Mark was involved in, as high adventures
and gave clear indications of an underlying intense pleasure. It was
clear that a good deal of Mark's frightening chance-taking was being
libidinally reinforced by Mrs. L. She was aware and accepted that
although Mark's escapades frightened her they also provided a part
of her with some pleasure. These reactions became an area of mutual
work.

Throughout the therapist's contacts with the mother, he was
impressed by the special identification she had with Mark. Whereas
Mark might be more disturbed than his two brothers, she pointed
out, he also had unique potentialities. He was brighter than they
were, he had a special tenacity the others did not have, and he was
the most attractive child. She could always get the older brother,
Henry, to do what she wanted; he would dress himself with the
clothing she had laid out for him without question. But if Mark
determined he wanted to wear something of his own choosing, she

could stand on her head and it would make no difference. As she related these incidents, her characteristic smile conveyed her obvious pleasure at the manliness that Mark displayed.

Her special tie to Mark had started early. When he had been born, she had felt that he was particularly attractive partly because he had been completely covered with hair. The family joke was that they would leave the hospital to go directly to the barbershop. In addition, when Mrs. L. was a child, her own hairiness had been a family topic for years. She had been a happy child, she felt, but had always had a rough time with her mother.

In order to maintain herself, Mrs. L. had had to fight her own mother every inch of the way. It was not that her mother was mean, she felt, but that she had always wanted to be the complete boss. Mrs. L. recalled that when she was organizing a "sweet 16" party, her mother had tried to take over all the arrangements. When Mrs. L. had reacted, her mother had continued to interfere, and Mrs. L. had moved the party to a friend's house where she could manage it completely by herself. This pattern of clear assertion had continued even during Mrs. L.'s married life. Her mother would wonder whether she was keeping the dishes in the "right" place; she had new suggestions for furniture arrangement, etc. Mrs. L., of course, would totally resist all ideas, as a result of which mother and daughter highly respected each other. This mutual esteem was in contrast to Mrs. L.'s younger sister, who acted like a child and was very dependent on her mother.

With this history, Mrs. L. could respond to the therapist's interpretations that she cherished the feisty little Mark who would never be beaten down, since it recalled and expressed her own feisty struggles with her mother. Part of her, of course, knew that Mark needed firm and authoritative limits, but another part inside of her wanted to see Mark never knuckle down or be crushed by the authorities around him. As Mrs. L. became increasingly aware that her limit setting would not choke the spirit out of Mark, she could effectively take command with less and less ambivalence. She could also with skill anticipate when Mark's "manly" defiance would promote her own subtle pleasure, and she went far in mastering any inappropriate messages she had been conveying to Mark. She also worked on new areas in which Mark's tenacity and activity could be appropriately expressed.

Matthew* and Father, Mr. M.

Matthew was a 10-year-old youngster in residential treatment who was diagnosed as a borderline psychotic child and who was fully discussed in Chapter 7. He was tall, extremely thin, and immediately alienated the staff by his overly dramatic, shrill, pseudoaffective way of relating. Most striking about Matthew was his highly developed fantasy life: Matthew played out in soliloquy, with great animation, cartoon characters who were warding off all sorts of attacks. Although it was felt that the institution had a great deal to offer Matthew, there was concern about the parents, who seemed to have totally decathected their child. The therapists believed that little progress would ultimately be made unless the gulf between Matthew and his parents could be bridged. Part of the goal in the first year of work with the M. family was to understand the nature of the impasse between father and son.

Mr. M. was a self-employed accountant, a rather charming, urbane man who had strong passive–dependent longings. He complained a great deal about his work, worked long hours, felt as though he were on a treadmill, and felt completely enervated by it. He felt he did poorly financially compared to other accountants; he feared getting into debt by buying a lot of extra equipment, yet having the equipment would make him much more efficient. But he was not a risk-taker in his business. He also felt that his secretary ran his office and made too many decisions, but he did not want to fire her: she had been with him for many years; it would be hard or impossible to replace her; and she made things run smoothly every day. After all, she knew all of his clients very well. When he came home from work, he just had enough energy to turn on the TV. He could do that for the major part of the weekend, but he worried that he was not keeping up with his professional reading. He was concerned he was falling behind professionally.

He slowly acknowledged that there was a chasm between him and his son. He felt an enormous tension when he was with Matthew, and their weekend contacts exhausted him. When the therapist helped him articulate his concerns about Matthew (What specifically made him uneasy?), he complained about Matthew's artistic flavor.

---

*Youngster discussed in Chapter 7.

He felt Matthew had a strange way of talking; he sounded high and shrill. He seemed interested in music all the time and always overdramatized a story. Why was he so often in the company of girls on campus? He was concerned about how thin Matthew looked and that he was "built" very poorly. The therapist clarified with Mr. M. that he was not only worried that Matthew was not an all-American boy, but he was really scared that Matthew was a "queer."

Mr. M. expressed intense feeling that in some way he had been at fault. This had been a major worry he had been harboring. Had he been responsible for raising this kind of child? He himself does not pursue many activities traditionally regarded as manly: he does not like woodwork; he is not a camper; and he is not too interested in cars. He noted that since he was small he had been interested in classical music. He had been a Mozart lover, and he recalled that as an adolescent, he was upset when he learned through a historical biography that Mozart was a homosexual.

A major area of preoccupation was Mr. M.'s "maternal" role toward Matthew when Matthew was young. He was the person who had been able to soothe and calm Matthew, not his wife, and Mr. M. expressed a great deal of rage at his wife for having forced him into this position. Now he realized he was frightened of the effects of his handling: had he kept Matthew on his lap too often, had he tried to compensate for his wife? He knew that he had suddenly withdrawn from Matthew a number of years ago, and he retrospectively understood that much of his uneasiness came from his fear of the boy's femininity.

As this material emerged, we could clarify Mr. M.'s anxiety. The therapist then also had the opportunity to delineate clearly Matthew's problems. Matthew did not struggle fundamentally with his sexual identity: he was concerned about having an identity at all. The therapist could discuss with Mr. M. Matthew's fears that the real world would not provide pleasure and the primitive fears Matthew had that the world would destroy him. It was because of these fears that Matthew sought the company of little girls, because he projected his fears of intense aggressive attack on the boys; and his theatrical pseudoaffect defended him against real interpersonal relationships that he feared so much.

As Mr. M. gained a sense of relief that he had not unalterably damaged his son, he relaxed with Matthew. They began to play ball together and went bowling. Matthew learned from his father how to use the family lawn mower under supervision, and he began to accompany his father to his accounting office for the first time.

Matthew and Mother, Mrs. M.

Matthew's mother hated the institution. The staff handled Matthew poorly, she said. He was dressed badly, his bureau and room were a mess, food was poorly served, and the program allowed youngsters endless free time without adequate supervision. As Mrs. M. complained and found little virtue in the treatment effort, the therapist sensed that she was attacking the institution and its staff to ward off our anticipated criticism. As she spoke of life with Matthew during the early years, it was clear that *he* had been impossible. *He* had never allowed himself to be comforted and had cried all of his waking hours—only the vibrations of a car ride calmed him momentarily. When he began to make sounds, *he* had chattered incessantly and chattered nonsense without letup. When he had begun to walk and toddle about, *he* had tolerated no limits and had embarrassed her constantly at the supermarket and on the street. He had been like a rope around her neck, an albatross. During those years, she had "hated" him, had felt imprisoned within the home, and she acknowledged that some of those feelings might even find their way into the mother–child relationship at present. Once in a rare while in therapeutic work, there was a crack in Mrs. M.'s armor. For example, as she showed Matthew's baby book, she commented gently how Matthew had resembled her physically as a child, and she caressed and patted a lock of his hair that had been saved from his first year of life. But these moments were rare.

During one session, she was vehement in her condemnation of Ed, one of the most effective child care staff members, who had developed a fine relationship with Matthew. Ed, she felt, coddled Matthew. When it was time for lunch, and Matthew isolated himself in his room, Ed spoke to him softly about leaving. Didn't they have rules in the cottage? Why was Matthew an exception? Matthew was quickly learning how to manipulate Ed, as he would the entire staff. On this occasion, and many subsequent ones, the therapist interpreted that Mrs. M. had very mixed feelings about Ed: part of her wished she could handle her son as gently and effectively as Ed. Yet it was hard for her because she was very frightened of the soft feelings within her.

For a period of time, Mrs. M. spoke of her present aversions to Matthew on his infrequent home visits. Matthew was shadowing her, and she had to get away. Why was he always in the kitchen when she was cooking? She described how she planned meticulously for every hour of the weekend. Again, it was noted that perhaps she adopted the role of "manager" because she was frightened of the role of mother. On this occasion, she began to weep. She told the therapist for the first time that she was waking up at night repeatedly: her images were of Matthew at the cottage, sad, alone, and totally cut off from the world.

This material ushered in a period of intense mourning. She had always felt she had lost her chance with her son. She described how she could never reach him, how terrible she had felt when he turned to his father every time he had fallen down and injured himself. Time and time again she saw the multiple ways he clearly showed an aversion toward her. Mrs. M. cried constantly for a period of time as soon as she crossed the threshold in the therapist's office, and it was clear that she was abreacting the lost opportunity to be a mother to her young son.

Slowly, her images of Matthew then changed and softened. He was no longer only manipulative: she knew when he was frightened and sad, and she recognized the defenses of anger and withdrawal within him. She became effectively empathic with Matthew, and her relationship to the staff became much more cooperative.

DISCUSSION

What are the criteria, principles, and particular problems that are inherent in this specific parent-child focus?

There are a number of criteria that should be considered before utilizing these techniques. In general, parents who can make effective use of this process have a level of ego intactness and psychological-mindedness that would make them accessible to limited insight therapy. In the above situations, it was felt the parents could clearly identify with the particular goals of this treatment effort. The M. family came to recognize that there was a great distance between themselves and Matthew, and Mrs. L. was concerned about the messages she had been delivering to her son Mark despite herself. There was a period in our work during which the problematic aspects of the parent-child relationship became ego-alien to these parents, and there was a conscious resolution to modify them. Therefore, these parents had the capacity for some effective self-observation. An implicit therapeutic alliance was formed: the therapist would help them understand the nature of these impasses with their children and of the role they had played.

This particular approach, although it is child-focused, provides opportunity to deal with some of the appropriate criticisms coming from the family literature. We have read a great deal about the dangers of accepting the child as the identified patient. It is often noted that parents mask their family, marital, and individual problems by making the child the conscious repository of all of the pathology. Much of the aim of this technique is indeed to deal with the interactive and mutually pathological interplays within the family. After a period of time, it was seen that Mark was not alone in the L. family with his pathology; his need to function as the fearless daredevil had been constantly libidinally reinforced by his mother. Within the M. family, Matthew could not enter the real world unless he felt there were ties to, and gratification coming from, his primary objects.

Within the scope of this technique, one can carefully evaluate the parents' need to externalize their impact on their child. There are considerable advantages in being able slowly to include the family and to clarify their roles in the child's pathology. Often, parents need the defense of the "bad" or "sick child," and with the above techniques, a therapist can titrate the amount of confrontation and clarification of parental contribution. It was clear that Mrs. L. and Mr. M. could quickly come to acknowledge that they were involved. But Mrs. M. needed to attack and criticize the agency for a long period of time until she had established a trusting relationship and felt there would be no retaliation.

We are often too quick to conclude that a parental request that asks us to remain focused on the child smacks of defensiveness and denial. The parents may be providing us with another implicit request, namely, to help them function as effective parents, as emotional educators, and teachers, and this request emerges appropriately from the impetus of the phase of parenthood in which they are. This therapist has found that many parents have seized on the opportunity of some form of parent–child work because of a healthy and appropriate guilt that they carry. They are aware internally that they have contributed to the present problem. This form of treatment speaks to their parenting need, for it provides an opportunity to clarify, undo, and reverse some of the past mishandling. There was much, for example, that Mr. M. wanted to teach Matthew, and his effort in therapy was to understand directly those aspects of himself that had made it impossible for him to relate to his son.

What problems emerge in a limited insight therapy? Often, in this process, unconscious material is elicited and can then be interpreted. Mrs. L had had no awareness that she was identified with Mark's rebelliousness and was reliving her own childhood struggles with her mother. Mr. M., although he was intensely aware of his uneasiness with his son, learned through his own therapeutic work that Matthew represented his feared and projected femininity. Mrs. M. came to understand that her rage with her son embodied her failure as a mother and woman generally and that she was simultaneously terrified of her softness.

Not only is the therapy a process of insight development, but there are obvious reconstructions. These parents have learned that their inappropriate affect responses (rage, withdrawal) to their children are not reality-based but come from earlier childhood contexts (repetition of their struggles with their parents, or internal struggles with parts of themselves). In fact, creating and reliving within a historical context was enormously helpful in removing the child as the target and source of the family pathology. Yet, this therapist has found that despite the intense process of self-observation work with memories, affects, and dream material, transference and regressions are limited and controlled. This occurs because there are constant opportunities to redefine the boundaries of the work. With all the parents, there is a constant question—how has this material (e.g., the struggle you had with your mother) influenced what goes on between you and your child now? These comments immediately address their current parenting image and move them from the angry, frightened child role they had assumed during the treatment hour.

This technique is explicitly a form of sector psychotherapy (Deutsch & Murphy, 1954–55) with delineated goals that particularly meet the developmental needs of children. We are aware that in order to minimize pathology, we need to intervene early, as close to the developmental interference as possible. Often, even effective individual personal psychotherapy of a parent comes too late, because even though he/she might make significant gains over the years, the child is beyond many of the significant developmental stages. Treatment of the parent–child relationship as a technique aims to focus immediately on the interlocking struggle between parent and child so that fixations will not become entrenched and constantly reinforced.

BIBLIOGRAPHY

Ackerman, N. (1958). *Psychodynamics of Family Life*. New York: Basic Books.

Cutter, A., & Hallowitz, D. (1962). Different approaches to treatment of the child and the parents. *American Journal of Orthopsychiatry* 22:15–159.

Deutsch, F., & Murphy, W. F. (1954–55). *The Clinical Interview*. New York: International Universities Press.

Fraiberg, S. (1954). Counseling for the parents of the very young child. *Social Casework* 35:47–57.

Kessler, J. (1966). *Psychopathology of Childhood*. Englewood Cliffs, NJ: Prentice-Hall.

Levy, D. M. (1937). Attitude therapy. *American Journal of Orthopsychiatry* 7:103–113.

Slavson, S. (1952). *Child Psychotherapy*. New York: Columbia University Press.

12

*Treatment of the Child Via the Parent**

Another form of parent work with the young child, "treatment via the parent," has been articulated primarily by the child analytic group in Cleveland (R. Furman & Katan, 1969; E. Furman, 1957). While this process incorporates many of the purposes of "parent guidance," it goes a great deal further in making use of this unique bond between parent and child. It attempts to help parents directly to *do* therapeutic work with their young child when the child has already developed internalized conflicts, and it also attempts to help parents understand some of the unconscious internal meaning their child has for them. Unfortunately, the techniques of "treatment via the parent" have had only limited discussion and usage, and this is particularly distressing because these techniques have enormous potential advantages. Fundamental is the potential of avoiding the costly process of direct psychotherapy for the child and the sense of "losing" the child to the therapist that treatment so often evokes in parents. Treatment via the parent, since it primarily involves the parent, also can maintain the parent's sense of activity and parenthood in undoing some of the psychic damage his/her child has suffered.

*Reprinted, with changes, from "Betsy: Treatment via the Mother of a Pre-Schooler," by M. Chethik, in *Psychotherapy and training in clinical social work* (pp. 135-151), edited by J. Mishne, 1980, New York: Gardner Press. Copyright Gardner Press. Reprinted by permission.

The major purpose of this chapter is to provide a clinical illustration of this form of guided treatment through the example of a child
named Betty and her mother. They were involved in a process that
lasted about 1 year. The therapist's sessions with the mother, the
mother's work with her daugher, and the impact on Betty's functioning as the treatment unfolded are described. Also reviewed are some
aspects of parent guidance and treatment of the parent–child relationship techniques that were also used in this case.

THE PATIENT: SYMPTOMS AND HISTORY

Betty was 5½ at the time of referral. She was a tall, pleasant-looking
child with large, heavily ringed eyes who generally, however, gave a
"not-all-put-together" impression. There was an awkwardness about
her that was immediately striking. She seemed somewhat untidy and
disheveled, and she had a lost, faraway, preoccupied look. Her eyes
looked inward rather than outward, and her gait was stiff and
restricted and lacked any grace.

She came from a middle-class family. Her father, Mr. M., was an
executive accountant for a large firm. Betty was the middle child in a
sibship of five. Claude, her oldest brother, was 12. The other children's ages were clustered together: at the time of referral, Lisa, her
oldest sister, was 7 years old, Doug was 4, and Donald, her youngest
brother, was just a few months old.

As we gathered material in our evaluation, it seemed clear that
Betty was in a great deal of emotional trouble. She appeared to be
profoundly depressed, inhibited, and at times disoriented. Her preoccupation seemed to interfere markedly with her cognitive development, and the parents had been concerned for several years that
Betty might be retarded. She seemed unable to remain involved in
any sustained play, and tended to drift from any house or doll play
with peers to less structured role-defined play (such as climbing)
with children younger than herself. Anything that required some
concentration (learning to dress herself) caused her intense frustration. At 5 years of age, Betty was unable to use crayons, cut with
scissors, or make any kind of distinguishable representational forms
in her drawings. All of her drawings deteriorated into messes, with
one color on top of another.

Another area of concern involved behavior problems at home. Betty was extremely messy and spilled many things; the parents felt, despite her awkwardness, that there was an intentional quality about her activity. For example, shortly after the family had acquired new carpeting, Betty tore papers on the floor, put baby powder all over the rug, and managed to break some eggs on it. In addition to this indirect form of aggression, she expressed open, continuous rage toward her brother Doug. At times she hurt him rather severely by biting him or attacking his head with her fists. In contrast to the evident behavior difficulties at home, Betty was characteristically shy and enormously fearful outside. She resisted playing outdoors, was frightened of new situations, and was afraid at times to enter the church, library, or neighborhood supermarket.

For several years there had also been periods of intermittent bed wetting, nightmares, and sudden tendencies to wander off, later to be found several blocks from home.

A major factor in Betty's history was the mother's marked depression. The mother had become enormously sad after the birth of Doug, when Betty was just over 1 year of age. She had been dominated by the thought that Doug would be her last child, and the fact that this might end her child-bearing years was intolerable to her. Her depression became increasingly acute, and she was aware that she felt more and more estranged from her family. When Betty was 3, Mrs. M. began psychotherapy, and after 6 months of treatment, it was necessary for her to be hospitalized for several months.

In describing Betty, Mrs. M. said she felt that the other children seemed to handle the family turmoil much better; Betty was always the sensitive one. She had cried more easily as an infant, fought toilet training at the age of 2, unlike the others, and had regressed markedly (with constant bed wetting, crying, and intense sleep troubles) during her mother's hospitalization.

Psychological testing (projectives and intelligence tests) indicated that Betty had at least an average IQ potential, and there were surprising strength and form in her fantasy production. We were left with many diagnostic questions. Was Betty a child who was showing a great deal of narcissistic damage because her mother had libidinally withdrawn during Betty's early developmental years? What was involved in her profound lack of general skill development? Were we dealing with a child who had a fundamentally inadequate ability to neutralize energy, or was there much secondary interference with ego functioning resulting from an excess of primitive defenses? Our recommendations were twofold: (1) to have Betty enter the therapeutic nursery school that was part of our clinic, and (2) to have a therapist begin work with the mother for further clarification. Our intent was to reassess the situation periodically to determine whether direct treatment for Betty would be necessary in the future and to try to understand how much of Betty's problems were immediately reactive to family pathology.

INITIAL PHASE OF TREATMENT: SEPARATION THEMES AND PROBLEMS OF AGGRESSION

The therapist's first meeting with Mrs. M. was during the summer prior to the start of nursery school. In this way, they had ample time to prepare Betty for this new experience. Mrs. M. was a slight, brown-eyed, attractive woman in her mid-30s. In those early summer meetings, Mrs. M.'s anxiety was striking. She appeared very frightened and did a lot of hand wringing and eye blinking. She seemed very remote, allowed little eye contact, and spoke almost inaudibly in short sentences and phrases, breathing deeply. The therapist reassuringly noted to her that in a number of ways it was often hard for mothers to come to discuss their children or openly bring out problems their children might have. However, Mrs. M.'s overt anxiety was maintained for quite a period of time.

There was a passive, resigned, fatalistic acceptance by the mother of the nursery school plan. This arrangement had been recommended for Betty by many (her own therapist, her pediatrician, and this therapist), so she assumed it was a good idea. When she spoke about Betty, her problems and troubles faded into the past, and she emphasized how well Betty was doing that summer. She had more friends; she was uncomplainingly going off to Bible school with Lisa, her sister, and she was well liked by her teachers. The therapist felt that she was minimizing Betty's difficulties in a plea to him to conceive of her as an acceptable mother. The therapist reiterated that from time to time parents sometimes worried when they began this kind of therapy that they would be criticized, found wanting, and blamed for their child's problems.

There was also a helpless, fragile quality about Mrs. M. during those early contacts. She only slowly introduced the problem of Betty's attacks on Doug. As we discussed this, it became apparent that the mother had been an overwhelmed witness and bystander to severe onslaughts and would allow Betty to express fully her aggression. As she spoke, Mrs. M. began to talk about intervening forcefully and physically stopping the battles (which idea the therapist strongly and firmly supported), but it was evident at this point that the mother could actually do very little. Similarly, although the therapist attempted to help the mother anticipate with Betty her fears (such as those involving separation), the mother was totally unable to address herself to her child's needs.

It became clearer that Mrs. M. was preoccupied with herself, and she responded quickly to the therapist's comments about her self-absorption. Having recently given birth, she was very fearful that her acute depression might recur. Yes, she was watching herself carefully for the early warning signs, and for the present acknowledged that it was hard for her to attend to Betty and her problems.

When Betty finally started nursery school in the fall there were extensive separation problems. Betty was totally frozen and inert, and her mother seemed at least as lost and frightened.

In her session, Mrs. M. denied Betty's tears. Betty "loved" her new school, although any specific discussion with Betty that she quoted involved fears of other children and concerns about injury. Mrs. M. also "loved" Betty's teacher, Sandy, and proclaimed how wonderful and helpful she was. The underlying feeling, however, was that Sandy was a much more adequate, thoughtful, maternal figure than she. In this period, she reported an upsetting incident that had happened at home. The children were discussing a neighbor who was raising three children who were not her own, since the natural mother was chronically ill. In the midst of the discussion, Betty suddenly turned to her mother and asked, "Are you going away again, Mommy?" As she described this, Mrs. M. looked distressed. The therapist commented that this seemed like a rather natural question to expect from Betty as she started school, but this observation was very upsetting to Mrs. M. For the first time, she brought forth some real affect as she described how guilty she felt about Betty. For a long period of time during her depression, she had only gone through the motions of being a mother to both Betty and Doug. She had walked like a robot, had been in a continual daze, and had been unable to think about her children. She was not even sure that she had always taken adequate physical care of them. It was clear that her present separation from Betty was evoking feelings of the earlier traumatic separation. After some time, the therapist noted that she was very much afraid that she had really hurt Betty emotionally and that this made it very hard for her to look at Betty's problems. For example, at present there were understandable separation problems, and some of the observations and impressions of the school personnel about Betty's frozen behavior were described. The therapist noted that now things were different because while these were indeed problems, she was seeking help with them. The school could be helpful, talking here could help, and she herself could be enormously helpful to her daughter. The staff then began to observe in our school that the mother seemed less lost and was more comforting to Betty in the morning when she was brought to the classroom.

During the initial phase of work, the therapist begins to use an important technique of parent guidance. *He identifies difficulties in the mother's life that seem to be impairing her ability to parent and are also impeding her child's entry into the therapeutic experience (nursery school).* The mother's early depression and subsequent guilt had produced many difficulties in her ability to handle and communicate with her child. Clarification of these dynamics brought some relief to the mother.

For the annual fall Halloween party at the school, Mrs. M. had forgotten to get a costume for Betty. The following day she had found an old Mighty Mouse costume that Betty had used the previous year, and Betty began carrying it with her all the time. She became inseparable from the costume and kept it with her at school, at home, out of doors, and at night. This obviously distressed Mrs. M., who was aware that she was finding ways of getting the costume away from Betty; she was frequently misplacing or washing it. The therapist began to discuss why Betty clung to the costume. He noted how lonely and sad the girl had felt at school and that the costume was like having a little piece of Mommy with her when she was away. Mrs. M. recalled Betty's earlier attachments to a blanket and some soft nylon fabrics. Although the mother increasingly recognized the separation anxieties, she described them with fear. Betty now manifested much more clinging behavior at home: she sometimes sucked her thumb, and she always wanted to know what part of the house her mother was in, particularly at night. The therapist noted that Betty was showing much more clearly how frightened she was about school and leaving her mother and that she now had the opportunity to help her put those feelings into words.

When her mother directly pointed out Betty's worries to Betty, the two began to talk. The mother reported that Betty was really terrified of school and had all sorts of irrational fears. The teacher, Sandy, Betty noted, was always angry with her and said, "She locks you in the closet if you are bad." She had many questions about what they did to Stephanie (an acting-out pupil) when they took her out of the class. She always, every day, missed her mommy very much, but she was afraid to cry. Sandy would not like her if she did not listen at school, as had happened when she had not held onto the handlebars of the teeter-totter. Mrs. M. became aware that when these fears were expressed, they had less reality for Betty, and she also found that she could alert the school staff to some of Betty's particular worries.

Once the talking started between mother and daughter, it was hard to contain Betty. She said she hated school because Doug stayed home with Mommy. From now on, when she came home, she would sit in her mommy's lap all the time. When she was at school, she thought Doug and Mommy played cards all day, and she just hated Doug because he stole all her things from her room when she was away. It was clear after these discussions that Betty felt much better and was less out of control.

Simultaneously, the mother remembered the impact of her hospitalization on the children. The Halloween incident helped her to recall the Halloween weekend during her hospital stay. She had promised the children she would visit them but had not been able to do so. She had felt terrible about disappointing them, but she also recalled guiltily that she had absolutely dreaded the visits with the children. She could not stand to face them when she had to leave. On her trial weekends, subsequently, she had always disappeared rather than say good-bye in the morning because her children had looked so terribly lost.

As the mother's and Betty's separation anxiety abated, Betty "thawed out" at school and invested increasingly in the activities around her. She began to do more craft work at home: she colored with Doug, wanted her pictures hung up all over the house, and was having Lisa (her sister) teach her letters and numbers. She began constantly to practice writing the Letter "B," and her mother was quite proud of the change.

The decrease in the mother's guilt allowed her to view her daughter more objectively and to acknowledge the separation symptoms. With encouragement from the therapist, the mother put these affects into words, and this opened an ongoing dialogue between the two. The "good-enough" mother can often naturally deal with the verbalized fears of the young child, helping them with reality testing.

In the fall the mother became ill with an upper respiratory infection that lasted, off and on, for several weeks. When she was not sick enough to go to bed, she often stayed on a sofa, and the father increasingly took Betty to school. Betty was evidently upset. She reinstituted holding onto her costume, and her involvement in school learning tapered off. Then suddenly, for a solid week, when Betty returned from school she would break into a deep and intense sobbing that was hard for the mother to bear. Betty also began a game with her mother: she would lie down on the sofa and play that they were sick together.

The mother quickly came to understand that Betty's crying was an old crying that she had never expressed before, and her mother's present fatigue recalled the old sickness for her. Betty, unlike the others, the mother reported, could not talk about the long hospitalization and seemed to have no memories of it. At the same time, Mrs. M. was also frightened about entering into this area with Betty. She felt she could not fully reassure Betty because she did not know if all of her own personal difficulties were over. In her next session with the therapist, she was very excited because she felt she had discovered an effective vehicle for slowly involving Betty in this dreaded area. She talked freely with Lisa, who responded with many questions, while Betty silently listened to all the discussions. The older daughter asked the mother why she had to go away, and the mother sensitively explained to the children for the first time the nature of her problems. When she (the mother) had been very young, her own mother and father had traveled a good deal, for long periods of time, and had left her with people who could not adequately take care of her. These experiences made for strong, sad feelings inside of her, which she had never been able to understand and which caused her a lot of trouble as a grownup. Now she was getting help with those feelings through talking with a special doctor. (One could not help but note the parallels and close identification between mother and daughter). Betty remained very attentive to these discussions.

Within the next few days Betty herself wanted to know all about the various doctors the mother saw. The baby doctor, the family doctor, and the talking doctor were distinguished. Betty wanted to meet the talking doctor, and the mother made arrangements to have Betty come to Hill Hospital (the place where she had been hospitalized) and also to briefly meet the therapist. Betty recalled the old waiting room, the elevator, and her favorite nurse, with whom she played ring-around-the-rosie when she visted her mother.

It was clear as we worked together that the mother's hospitalization had had a traumatic impact on Betty that could only slowly be undone as the mother herself reintegrated the old events.

Within the aegis of parent guidance, the therapist helped the mother understand *her child's specific symptoms and behaviors and their internal meaning*. The current separation fears were limited to the mother's early (and traumatic) separation at age 2. Mrs. M. utilized this knowledge sensitively in helping her daughter to understand her difficult emotional reactions and to link them to the past events that had never been integrated by Betty.

However, the above process went considerably beyond parent guidance. Normally, drawing some meaning about a child's behavior with the parent (e.g., Betty's intense crying as an "old" crying) allows a parent to gain some perspective and not overreact to the disturbing behavior. In this case, the therapist helped the mother use this awareness to do some treatment work. Betty's current separation anxiety was linked to the mother's other traumatic hospitalization. The mother slowly recontacted these past events with her daughter, helped explain her past illness, and allowed her daughter to bring and reintegrate some other memories of the past (the waiting room, the "ring-around-the-rosie" nurse, etc.).

PHASE II: PENIS ENVY AND THE PROBLEM OF SEXUAL IDENTIFICATION

After 6 months of treatment, the Mighty Mouse costume, which earlier had been a transitional object important to Betty, developed other meanings. The mother described that now the Mighty Mouse mask was most important because in that way Betty could pretend she was a boy. The mother displayed concern about Betty's open sexual preference. Betty was intensely disappointed with her Christmas presents. She had wanted the hockey sticks that Doug and Claude got and had had a tantrum when they were put in the boys' room. The word "weiner," Betty's and Doug's expression for Doug's penis, was constantly used in the house. On inquiry, however, it seemed Betty used no words for her own body except the word "toilet," which generally referred to Betty's genitals. Doug and Betty at times played an exciting game when Doug asked to sit on her toilet.

Mother described Betty's new habit of rubbing herself, particularly while she was watching TV. It made her mother very uneasy, and the therapist discussed methods of having Betty become more private with her masturbation. Bathroom policy had been to bathe Doug and Betty together, but since it was becoming evident that Doug delighted in showing himself off, Mrs. M. began to take appropriate educational steps. Privacy around toileting and bathing was enforced, and Mrs. M. was able to distinguish sexual, exciting play from fighting between Doug and Betty and could limit both better.

In early January, Betty's sexual anxiety emerged more clearly. She was angry with all boys. Now Claude, the older brother, as well as Doug were targets. She also began breaking her girl dolls. She cut off their clothing, drowned them, and cut their hair. Finally, she made an attempt to cut her own long hair (she cut out a big "V" in front) and explained that she wanted her hair as short as Doug's. Mrs. M., after setting some rules for Betty, began to point out to her that Betty seemed to feel it was terrible to be a girl. For several days there were triadic discussions among Lisa, Betty, and their mother about sexual differences. Lisa was very curious, and she, Betty, and their mother named the parts of the body, discussed their functions, and noted how these differences were there from birth. Although Betty was relatively passive during these talks and interrupted by saying, "I'm scared, Mommy," she seemed to be relieved, and her mother was enormously pleased with her own efforts.

After a short, smooth period at home, the earlier messing patterns recurred, along with increased body exhibiting. Betty was always picking up her own skirts, and when her mother wondered with Betty if she was not again showing some of her earlier boy-girl worries, Betty began to argue that she indeed did have a "weiner." For several days she had many different theories: nobody could see it yet, it was up inside, it could come out and go in, and, when she was very young, she had had one. She insisted that little Jennifer (a newborn cousin) had one, and they would check together when she came to visit. Mrs. M. handled this material rather sensitively, pointing out that while Betty had a strong wish to be a boy, she was really a whole girl who had everything a girl should. Betty reacted with some rather significant changes. For the first time she wanted to help her mother in the kitchen. She began to set the table and was in charge of tearing up lettuce for salad, she helped clear the dishes, and it was her special job to serve desserts. Simultaneously, however, the ambivalence continued. Sudden outbreaks occurred against the boys, and at times Betty would secretly put on Doug's pajamas at night.

At the semester break in January, it was decided to promote Betty from a half to a full day at nursery school. The change was very enhancing for Betty. She had been waiting a long time for this, she said, and it meant that she was a bigger girl. Now, like Lisa, she went to school for a full day. The mother reported that Betty felt much closer to school. She became a regular chatterbox at home, describing each school activity fully and with pleasure. She had to remember everything she did on the weekends so she could tell Sandy (the teacher) all about it when she returned.

Betty continued throughout the year to show her ambivalence about her femininity. In early April, the class visited a regular kindergarten room, a preparatory gesture in anticipation of the next year. Betty reacted with what appeared at first to be regressive behavior. She had taken some of Donald's (the youngest brother's) rubber pants to bed with her and wore them one night. In discussing this with her mother, however, Betty made a point of stressing that she had taken a boy's rubber pants. She definitely did not like the girl's kind, with frills on them. In another discussion, Betty brought out her concern about Stephanie, a black child at school. She did not like her color, and she wished everyone were the same. She also, one day, told her mother that Batman was now her favorite TV program, and that she could do everything that Batman could do (such as jump down four steps). She said that she wished there were such a thing as a Lady Batman. The male wishes persisted and needed continued working through.

Betty also increasingly teased her mother. What had begun as a game in which her mother would find her, and which involved

separation themes, now seemed to express directly much more
anger. With much empathy, and evoking all of the recent incidents,
Mrs. M. had a number of discussions with Betty about her continued
wish to be a boy. The mother summarized: Betty felt that everyone
should be the same—black and white, boys and girls. Maybe, the
mother suggested, Betty was very angry with her at times, because as
her mommy she had not made her a little boy like Donald when she
was born. As their talks continued, Betty's aggression toward Doug
increased (she openly bit him), along with her verbalization that she
hated all boys. Mrs. M. discussed the meaning of the biting. Since
Betty often showed acute remorse about hurting Doug after such an
attack, she spoke to Betty about helping her to stop. There was an
angry part inside of Betty that wanted to bite Doug. This was the
part that was angry with boys because they had weiners, and like
many girls, Betty sometimes wanted to bite off the weiner; but this
really would not help her become a boy. This seemed to be an
important interpretation for Betty, because much of the aggression
abated after this period.

A new seductiveness emerged instead. It was directed toward
Claude, the older adolescent brother. She often touched him or
playfully invited him to wrestle. She was very interested in Claude's
bed and loved to watch TV and bounce up and down on it. As she
seemed more comfortable with the idea of being a girl and becoming
a woman, Betty found it acceptable to experience the sexuality of the
oedipal period.

As nursery school advanced and preparations for kindergarten
were discussed, Betty began to directly express to her mother her
worries about school. Who would go with her to class, where would
school be held, and so forth. She also talked of her worry about
having a baby. She decided she did not want to have a baby. She did
not want to go to a hospital, since the doctors hurt you there; she did
not think babies could really come out of a baby hole. Look at how big
Donald was, and how little her hole was. The mother again discussed
the process of childbirth, and also reassured Betty that growing up
and going to kindergarten did not mean that she would be a woman
and have a baby right away.

In this section, there is a mixture of parent guidance and direct
treatment by the mother. With advice from the therapist, the mother
took steps to deal with her daughter's budding sexuality. Mrs. M.

enforced modesty around toileting and bathing, diluted the sexual play between Doug and Betty, and provided natural sexual information for her daughter. However, a good deal of Betty's conflicts about penis envy and her femininity remained internalized conflicts. Mrs. M. did a significant amount of uncovering work with her daughter about her strong wishes to be a boy, her sense of defectiveness, and her rage toward Doug (biting wishes) and toward her mother for not making her a boy. This was done under the supervision of the therapist. It also highlights the special life-space opportunities a parent has to work with problems as they emerge in daily living.

TERMINATION: THE MUTUAL IDENTIFICATION OF MOTHER AND DAUGHTER

Throughout the treatment, the therapist was aware of a strong overidentification between Betty and her mother. It seemed clear that Mrs. M. relived some of her own terrors of childhood by reexperiencing them through Betty. And Betty on her part kept her mother closer to her when she herself became like her mother—ill, depressed, and frozen. Through the treatment process, as Betty found gratification through learning and activity, the therapeutic staff increasingly saw less of the depressed mother in Betty. In the latter part of the therapeutic work, there were increasing opportunities to help the mother become more aware of her need specifically to overidentify with her daughter, and, narcissistically, to endow her with her own feelings.

On one occasion, Mrs. M. reported that Betty had awakened several times one night with an anxiety dream that concerned a fat man sitting on her. Her mother was very upset and had a rather strange reaction. She noted that when she was a child, she herself had been attacked by a fat man. How could Betty know that? This was an opportunity to help the mother separate her reactions from her daughter's; the therapist was quite puzzled and wondered why Mrs. M. would connect Betty's dream with her own experience. He underlined the naturalness and commonness of this kind of fantasy in a little girl (recent excitement and aggression with her daddy seemed like natural sources for the dream content). Perhaps there were times, he noted, when Mrs. M. gave Betty credit for feelings that actually came solely from her own past. There were a number of occasions on which the therapist could gently point out this puzzling process, which Mrs. M. increasingly came to understand. She spoke directly about her concerns about Betty. She, indeed, had always had a fear that Betty would turn out exactly like her, and she wondered if that was not really her underlying reason for the referral of Betty to us. The more she heard Betty talk directly about herself and express her own thoughts, the more reassured she felt.

In the spring, as we neared the end of the nursery school year, Mrs. M. was "not with it." She seemed pale, preoccupied, and brought in few observations about her daughter. It was like a repetition of the earliest period of therapeutic work. When the therapist noted her current lack of involvement, she commented that she was not feeling well physically because she had "female trouble." It later emerged that she was trying a new contraceptive device and had reacted by excessive bleeding. I was aware, however, that Mrs. M. had attempted to cope with earlier depressions by becoming pregnant and that her physical complaints often heralded emotional crises.

For several weeks, it was clear that she was becoming acutely despondent. She could cope less with Betty's teasing or with exciting play between Betty and Doug. She appeared helpless under the force of her internal difficulties; with the therapist, she was apologetic and distraught about neglecting her children. She discussed her temporary need for additional help at home, and she had a family maid live in for a period of time. The therapist also met conjointly with her husband during this period.

Mrs. M.'s therapist was on vacation, and she acted out her distress. She took excessive tranquilizers so that she was often groggy. She wandered away from home for several hours one evening without informing anyone of her whereabouts, and on another occasion, she shattered a window by throwing a cup through it. Mrs. M. kept her appointments with this therapist, however, indicating that she was determined to try to stay out of the hospital. She noted repeatedly that she was beset by horrible childhood memories and anxieties. The therapist must add, however, that she used her time with him appropriately. She made no attempt to share these memories, however, and it was as if both were waiting for her therapist to return. She could describe what was happening to Betty at home, but she made it clear that she could not talk with the children at that time. This therapist felt his presence to be a stabilizing factor during this turmoil and that it served as a temporary and indirect link to her own therapist. The crisis passed shortly after the return of Mrs. M.'s psychiatrist.

Although this was a very difficult period for the entire family, Betty experienced little regression. The waif-like, lost, wandering child did not reappear at the nursery school. During this period she appropriately intensified relationships with teachers and peers. She formed a strong and exclusive attachment to a girlfriend that barred outsiders, and she sought to have this peer, Judy, all to herself. This was clearly an active step to cope with loss through constructive means, in contrast to the aimlessness and overwhelmed inhibition noted earlier.

The mother quickly became active and reinvolved in her work. For example, when Betty came in to check on her mother's whereabouts, they could talk together about her fears stimulated by recent events that the mother would go away again. Betty began to use the word "upsetness" in referring to her mother's mood and depression. The mother could acknowledge that there might be times when she would get her "upsetness" again. Betty wanted to know why the "upsetness" came again, and they reworked some of the childhood events they had earlier discussed. As Betty used the word "upsetness," it more clearly became a distinct phenomenon linked solely with her mother.

As Betty's therapy neared termination, the staff were pleased with her progress. She showed much less ambivalent behavior toward her parents and much more control with her brothers. She functioned adequately in all the preprimer readiness tests that were part of the nursery school curriculum. Few of her inhibitions were shown. Her ability to play with peers appropriately and to enter new situations markedly improved. She was involved with and accepted by children of her own age, and she was able to sustain continuous and structured games.

Much of the focus, in this period of work, was on the mutual depression that both child and mother fostered. The mother projected her own background, events, and reactions onto her daughter, and Betty internally represented to the mother a negative, fragile sense of self. There were opportunities to interpret this misidentification, and the therapist engaged in the process of "treatment of the parent–child relationship." In the work around the "fat man" dream, Mrs. M. became aware how readily she imputed her own ideas onto her daughter. The growing insight that part of Mrs. M. had a need to see herself in her daughter helped her to separate more fully. This tie and need for fusion with her daughter was an unconscious need of Mrs. M., and it was through the intervention with the mother that it became both conscious, ego-alien, and "worked through." Later it became evident, though the mother can become acutely agitated and depressed, that Betty can now see this as a separate "upsetness" and not identify with the ill mother.

DISCUSSION

At the start of treatment, there was enormous concern about Betty's personality functioning. The severe separation problems and the sense of disorientation were noted. Her primitive aggressive expression had early anal and oral forms (biting, hitting, messing). The greatest concern, however, was the generalized ego arrest. Speech was not used for effective communication, Betty's synthetic functioning was poor, and she was unable to orient herself to new surroundings. She not only showed a marked lack of general skills but could not invest and involve herself in the activities around her. She generally tended to restrict herself, seemed phobic of the world, and used regression prominently in the face of stress. Observations indicated that her defenses were not adequate for most situations, and her states of anxiety seemed to paralyze her ego.

Therefore, there was concern that there was a major problem of early ego arrest, and the possibility of the development of an atypical or borderline personality structure. History could confirm this hypothesis, since one could speculate an early libidinal decathexis of Betty by her mother with the onset of the mother's depression. There seemed to be evidence that Betty had little primary self-investment and self-regard and a poor ability to neutralize instinctual energy.

However, as the work with the mother and Betty began, considerable strides were made within the first few months. After Mrs. M. began to discuss her extreme guilt about the impact of her depression on Betty, it became clear that we were dealing with a different kind of problem. Betty's general lack of progress was *centered on a strong identification with her depressed mother*, and this process was reinforced markedly by the mother. The mother was terrified that this child represented the depressed part of herself, and she reacted to Betty with guilt by giving in to her demands and primitive needs. Betty used this identification process for two purposes: to keep her mother close to herself by becoming like her, and to ward off fears of the environment around her by inwardly living a constant mother–child union in fantasy. Much of Betty's pathology, therefore, was based on secondary interference of ego functions as a result of this pathological identification.

Within the process of treatment with the mother, as the therapist specifically identified the feelings that Betty had (for instance, toward nursery school or her mother), her mother experienced a good deal of relief. The therapist was constantly pointing out that Betty had a whole raft of *her own feelings and thoughts*, and her mother was reassured that Betty was not a carbon copy of herself. This allowed her increasingly to differentiate Betty, and we saw a growing shift from narcissistic investment to more wholesome object relatedness. The mother developed a searching attitude about Betty, made realistic observations and reports, and had independent insights about her child's functioning. She improved in her ability to empathize and communicate with her.

Mrs. M. was then much more able to become an adequate *emotional* educator for Betty, as she had been with the other children. She actively interfered with her daughter's primitive, aggressive outbursts and slowly helped her to express her anger through verbalization. This process went on not only in relation to Betty's relationship with her brothers but also directly with her child's aggression toward the mother herself. There is little question that this enormously helped the daughter, who was terrified of the flooding of her aggressive impulses. Mrs. M. also became able to help Betty reconstruct the difficult realities of the past—her mother's traumatic hospitalization and the meaning of her illness. In addition, for the first time she could express open pleasure and pride in the tentative and growing cognitive achievements that Betty was able to accomplish, and this stimulated further sublimatory activity.

With the growing rapport between mother and daughter, Betty quickly moved into phallic and oedipal problems that were phase-adequate for her age. Her masturbatory and excitement problems unfolded, and her mother was able skillfully to help her work through some of her penis envy and fears of femininity.

At the close of treatment, though there were many evident gains, we were left with some doubts. Betty retained some tendency to turn aggression against herself, and this showed in her motor awkwardness and her tendency to sustain minor injuries. Despite her attempts to make herself pretty and draw positive attention to herself, she maintained an inner lack of self-assurance. Of greatest concern, however, was the mother's ability to continue to see Betty in terms of adequate positive object cathexis rather than to include her child in her concept of what was "wrong" with herself. We wondered: did the mother's effective work depend on her relationships with her parent therapist and the nursery school teachers? According to subsequent reports, Betty was able to go through her kindergarten year quite well, and little regression was seen during that year.

As was noted in the introduction, the process of "treatment via the mother" particularly capitalizes on the close unconscious communication between mother and young child. In this case, this form of treatment and "treatment of the parent–child relationship" seemed particularly appropriate since much of the central cause of the problem rested on the unconscious bond and identifications between mother and daughter. Once the mother became somewhat free to observe her daughter, her intimate symbolic understanding of Betty was particularly useful in the treatment process. Mrs. M. often understood the developing conflicts before the therapist could infer them, and the therapist frequently functioned as someone who affirmed and corroborated her intuitive impressions. A major additional advantage of this process was also the timing of interventions. Mrs. M. was often able to discuss and interpret material with her daughter as situations developed in the "life-space" of their lives. Her interventions could be particularly effective because they came quickly after affective encounters (fighting with her brothers, separations, and the like).

It was interesting to note that despite the evident psychopathology of the mother, Mrs. M. had enough healthy ego to enlist in the process of helping her daughter. Mrs. M. was often severely depressed, had a history of hospitalization, and yet managed to mobilize energy to help her child sensitively through developmental crises. The process of "treatment via the mother" can often capitalize on the healthy, adaptive energy devoted to parenting, despite conflicts in other areas of the parent's life.

The author also feels that this particular form of treatment helps to develop transference boundaries between therapist and mother which permit maximizing work. Though Mrs. M. was evidently tempted at times to become a primary patient, the reality task that had been defined together (and repeatedly reaffirmed) served to limit transference regressions. In the process of the work together, the therapist made relatively few comments about her relationship within the transference except as it dealt with her role as a mother (e.g., the therapist as critical and condemning). Although this limitation caused temporary frustrations for Mrs. M., it served constantly to clarify the limits of the mutual task and facilitated help for Betty during her critical developmental years.

BIBLIOGRAPHY

Furman, E. (1957). Treatment of under fives by way of parents. *Psychoanalytic Study of the Child* 12:250–262.

Furman, R., & Katan, A. (1969). *The Therapeutic Nursery School*. New York: International Universities Press.

Katan, A. (1959). The nursery school as a diagnostic help to the child guidance clinic. *Psychoanalytic Study of the Child* 16:250–264.

Katan, A. (1961). Some thoughts about the role of verbalization in early childhood. *Psychoanalytic Study of the Child* 16:184–188.

Nagera, H. (1963). The developmental profile: Notes on some practical considerations regarding its use. *Psychoanalytic Study of the Child* 18:511–540.

Index